ANNAPOLIS

By W. D. Puleston

THE ENSIGN (SECOND FROM LEFT) HAS CROSSED THE GANGWAY TO THE
QUARTERDECK

ANNAPOLIS

Gangway to the Quarterdeck

BY

CAPTAIN W. D. PULESTON
United States Navy

D. APPLETON-CENTURY COMPANY
Incorporated

New York   London

1942

TO MY SISTERS

Sallie and Cornelia D. Puleston

☆ INTRODUCTION ☆

WHEN the eyes of the entire nation are centered on its fighting services, the publication of a book recording the history of the Naval Academy is particularly timely. For the Naval Academy is the veritable cradle of the Navy, and has been so for nearly one hundred years. The author, a Naval Academy graduate, Class of 1902, reveals a deep affection for his Alma Mater and a genuine devotion to the naval service.

In his early chapters he describes the methods employed in training and educating midshipmen before the Naval Academy was founded in 1845. He shows how opposition to a naval school ashore was gradually overcome and how the achievements of its graduates in both war and peace endeared the Academy to the country. Some of the Academy's outstanding graduates who have distinguished themselves in the service and in civil life have been singled out for special mention, but the author considers the unknown sons of the Academy to be her greatest glory.

Captain Puleston performs a distinct service to the Navy by correcting an impression which has long been prevalent and which has been fostered by responsible writers. That is the idea that ranking officers in our early Navy opposed the education of its junior officers. The leading officers of the old Navy, including such redoubtable characters as John Paul Jones, Thomas Truxtun, and Edward Preble, vigorously urged the adoption of some regular system of education for its young officers. They differed only as to the means to be employed. The proponents of a naval school ashore won out. Captain Puleston explains how this was accomplished and how the Naval Academy, from small beginnings, developed into the modern institution of the present day.

JOHN R. BEARDALL
Rear Admiral, United States Navy
Superintendent, United States Naval Academy

THE FIRST American midshipmen were trained in the colonial navies, aboard wooden sailing ships under a régime evolved from the colonial merchant service and the Regulations of the Royal Navy. The midshipmen of to-day are trained at a well-organized and well-administered Naval Academy which has become the basic school for commissioned officers of the regular Navy and the Naval Reserve Corps. The purpose of this book is to trace the development of and describe the Naval Academy of to-day, and to reveal how the Naval Academy—founded, dominated, and strictly controlled by the Old Navy—became the cradle of the Modern Navy.

The largest single deposit of information on the Naval Academy is in the back numbers of the *United States Naval Institute Proceedings;* its 90th Anniversary number of October, 1935, in particular, contains valuable essays on the history of the Academy. In the Library at the Academy, source material has been assembled, and it can be conveniently verified by reference to the official records in the Superintendent's office. The history of the Naval Academy by E. C. Marshall, published in 1862, gives the best account of the early practice cruises and of the Academy at Newport during the Civil War. *A Historical Sketch,* by Professor James R. Soley, 1876, presents an outline of the development of the Academy, with a full account of the Academy under Admiral Rodgers. Park Benjamin's history, published in 1900, is entertaining, but some of his inferences are questionable. James Fenimore Cooper's *History of the Navy*, published in 1839, and G. W. Allen's histories of our early naval wars give the clearest accounts of our early midshipmen. Chaplain E. C. Wines describes them in the 1830's. Mahan and Dewey give accounts of them in the 1850's. Park Benjamin, of the class of 1867, describes midshipmen of the Civil War from personal knowledge. The author was a student at the Academy from 1898 to 1902, and instructor there from 1909 to 1911. It was comparatively easy to follow the methods of training midshipmen from 1795 to the present day. And it is the progressive development in the training of midshipmen that supplies continuity to a study of the Naval Academy.

In the records of the Navy Department, the orders for Chaplain Thompson established the date of origin of the naval school at the Washington Navy Yard, probably the first naval school ashore, and a report of Commodore John Rodgers showed that the Board of Commissioners favored a naval academy ashore as early as 1816, and had very definite ideas of how it should be organized and administered.

In the Department archives, Miss Craven; in the Superintendent's office, Lieutenant C. H. Smith; in the Naval Museum, the Curator, Captain H. A. Baldridge, retired; and in the Academy Library, Associate Professor Charles W. Mixer, Librarian, were very helpful. President Kenneth Sills of Bowdoin College, who has served on the Board of Visitors several times, and Commander Felix Johnson, Secretary of the Academic Board, read the manuscript and made useful suggestions. Mr. Louis H. Bolander, Assistant Librarian, who has done much research in Academy history, assembled the source material at the Library, acted as a guide throughout the preparation of the manuscript, and read it chapter by chapter as it progressed.

The author is indebted to the editor of the *Trident*, Midshipman J. C. Hill, II; to Midshipman James D. Schnepp, editor of *Reef Points;* to Midshipman E. E. Kintner and Midshipman C. W. Adams, Jr., editors-in-chief of the *Log*, for information on the Academy of to-day and for permission to use material and illustrations from their publications.

Special acknowledgement is made to Dr. C. S. Alden, recently retired as Head of the Department of English, History, and Government; to Dr. O. C. Paullin; to Professor Charles Lee Lewis, biographer of Buchanan and Farragut, whose articles in the *Naval Institute Proceedings* were very helpful; and to the Institute for its permission to use the material. "Captain" W. H. Stayton, 1881, furnished valuable data on graduates who had entered civil life.

Rear Admiral Wilson Brown, who was Superintendent when this work was undertaken; his successor, Rear Admiral Russell Willson; and Rear Admiral John R. Beardall, the present Superintendent, gave aid and encouragement to the author.

W. D. PULESTON

CONTENTS

☆

xiii

☆ ILLUSTRATIONS ☆

xv

ANNAPOLIS

Genealogy of the Naval Academy

DURING the summer months of any non-emergency year, groups of alert-looking young Americans, hailing from every state in the Union, converge upon the Main Gate of the Naval Academy at Annapolis. Following literally in the footsteps of their predecessors, they proceed down Maryland Avenue between two small brick guard-houses which shelter a squad of uniformed guards known to midshipmen as Jimmylegs. There is more than a suggestion of a military barracks in the thick brick walls and bronze gates; sensitive youngsters get a distinct impression of prison walls, which, fortunately, is soon dispelled. The majority are sufficiently awed as the bronze gates click behind them, but they are all over the first and most difficult hurdle: they have passed the entrance examination and have planted both feet on the lowest rung of the naval ladder. They know that the climb to the top will be long and arduous, but they are not terrified by the prospect.

There is no immediate suggestion of the Navy in the low, solid-looking buildings on either side of Maryland Avenue. The neat brick sidewalks and the concrete roads that lead off the avenue between attractive lawns resemble those in any well-kept government station. Not until the Severn River breaks into view is there a real suggestion of the Navy, which is quickly reinforced by the handsome figurehead of the Macedonian at the foot of Stribling Row. A closer investigation of adjacent monuments will confirm

the impression, and a glimpse of Dewey Basin crowded
with small craft will convince the arriving plebes that they
are at last in the Naval Academy.

On the tip of this peninsula, formed by the mouth of
the Severn and the Chesapeake, Uncle Sam has invested
over forty million dollars in grounds, buildings, and equipment to exercise, shelter, and instruct his midshipmen.
These brick and granite structures merge so naturally with
the flat tide-water land that they have an unearned air of
age. Only the modest little guard-houses go back fifty years;
the remainder were built after the Spanish-American War.
Even for our young country, these buildings are new. The
Academy itself has not celebrated its centenary; compared
with its venerable neighbor, St. John's College, it is a mere
stripling.

The Academy may be a child, but its midshipmen date
back to the colonial era. They appeared first in the colonial navies maintained by Massachusetts, Virginia, Rhode
Island, and Connecticut. A few entered the Royal Navy.
Midshipmen appeared spontaneously in the Continental
Navy and the states' navies to fight for our independence.
They reappeared immediately on the threat of war in
1793-94. Midshipmen behaved so well during our first four
wars, responded so readily to their meager education—the
severe but unsystematic training given them at sea—that
some of our finest officers considered the quarter-deck of
an American man-of-war the only proper school for midshipmen.

Advocates of training and educating midshipmen afloat
could offer many excellent reasons for their convictions.
The most convincing evidence they advanced was the
records of the lieutenants and captains that the system of
training at sea provided during the Barbary Wars and the
War of 1812. A system that produced officers like David

Porter, Stephen Decatur, Jr., Richard Somers, Oliver H. Perry, and Thomas Macdonough could not be lightly discarded. The opponents of a school ashore delayed the establishment of the Academy until 1845. For approximately one-third of its life, including its golden age, the Navy got along without a naval academy. During that time, midshipmen were trained and educated at sea and at naval schools in navy yards, in a most haphazard fashion. The Navy protected itself from uneducated lieutenants by very severe examinations; midshipmen who were not well grounded in seamanship and navigation, and later in gunnery, could not pass the examinations.

Although not always examined in gunnery, midshipmen were trained assiduously at every type of gun—32- 24- 18- 12- and 6-pounders, boat and ship howitzers, and the carronades. The gunnery results during the War of 1812 proved that they were well taught. In addition, they served in the "powder-division," which supplied the ammunition, and were in command of the sharpshooters and grenade-throwers, the sea-going grenadiers, who manned the fighting tops. Midshipmen were trained by oral instruction and example, as opportunity and helpful seniors provided; those who could not, by their own initiative, fill in the gaps and become all-round officers were dropped.

The advocates of a school ashore for midshipmen did not contemplate a college, and that term has never been applied to the Navy's school. They advocated a school where midshipmen and instructors would be congregated and would pursue certain subjects essential to the training of naval officers. The opponents and advocates both kept a weather eye on the Academy after it was founded to make sure that it was not turned into a college and that it stuck to its task of preparing young Americans to be junior officers of the Navy.

In a restricted sense, the Naval Academy is less than a hundred years old; in a real sense, the United States Naval Academy goes back to colonial times when midshipmen were brought up at sea by their senior officers. And to understand the present-day Academy, it is necessary to recall the colonial atmosphere and to review the methods of training midshipmen in the early naval wars. This retrospect may suggest a sketchy history of our early Navy. It is really family history, which might have been recorded in a Navy Family Bible. It is the genealogy of American midshipmen.

As the plebes of each new class proceed up Stribling Row to Bancroft Hall and through its almost endless corridors to their rooms, they will encounter the first suggestion of an American man-of-war, a sense of order. When they enter their plainly furnished rooms, they will be impressed with the feeling that every piece of furniture is in its exact place. When they obtain their outfit of clothes, they will be given a plan of stowage, and every article from a handkerchief to working clothes has its proper place in the locker. A visitor on a modern man-of-war, inspecting the lockers of the crew, will see the same neat arrangement of a sailor-man's clothes. To the initiated, the Academy to-day will furnish abundant proof that it evolved from early American squadrons and is still a sea-going institution with only one foot ashore. The entering plebe, who naturally is striving to understand his new home, should not be content with learning about the present-day Academy; he must know something of his naval forebears, something of colonial midshipmen, of the midshipmen of the Revolution, and of that brilliant group of midshipmen who appeared as if by magic in our early naval wars. He will hold his head a little higher and fight harder when he gets acquainted with his professional progenitors.

Colonial Midshipmen

☆

COLONIAL midshipmen were a natural product of their environment. Colonial towns and villages were all located on the seacoast, along the shores of bays and the banks of navigable rivers; small sailing craft and coasting vessels furnished the only means of transportation and, with the fishing fleets and early whaling vessels, offered adventurous youths numerous sea-going berths. Colonial lads could pull an oar and sail a boat soon after learning to walk. These striplings of the sea were often mates in their teens, and the more successful were captains in their early twenties.

In a few instances, sons of the older colonial families were entered as midshipmen in the Royal Navy, but no documentary evidence can be found in the naval records in London to support the oft-told tale that George Washington intended to join the Royal Navy as a midshipman. Officers and men of the colonial merchant ships frequently served in British merchant vessels, and during the wars with France and Spain the colonial merchant marine usually furnished and manned the storeships and transports of the Royal Navy.

Soon after Virginia and Massachusetts were settled they found it necessary to organize colonial navies just as they did colonial militias. Ships of the Massachusetts Navy escorted the New England Militia to Cape Breton Island when Louisburg was captured in 1745. Connecticut organized a navy to fight the Dutch in New York for control of Long Island Sound. Rhode Island, New York, Pennsylvania, Maryland, and South Carolina maintained armed ships to protect their sea-borne trade from pirates and enemy privateers. During the wars with France and Spain the colonies fitted out privateers and letter-of-marque ships to attack enemy commerce.[1] The officers, midshipmen, and men of these colonial navies and private ships of war came from the colonial merchant marine, which enjoyed many, but not all, of the privileges of the merchant marine of England, and they adopted, with few changes, the organization, regulations, and customs of the Royal Navy to their smaller ships.

In the colonial period the officer personnel of the Royal Navy and of the British merchant marine had much in common. When hostilities threatened, officers from merchant ships were commissioned in the Navy; when peace was obtained, the Admiralty discharged most of them, and they returned to the merchant service. The organization of British men-of-war and merchant ships was similar: the captain was comparable to the master, the first lieutenant to the first mate, and midshipmen to the fourth mates and cabin-boys. Men-of-war were larger, and they mounted more and heavier guns, but the rigging was practically the same, and intelligent merchant officers were competent to sail a man-of-war and quickly learned enough gunnery to command a battery. In a British man-of-war there was usually a sailing master, certified by Trinity House, who piloted, navigated, and sailed the ship. The master was under orders of the captain, who fought the ship, with the first lieutenant in general charge as his assistant. The sec-

---

[1] Privateers cruised solely for the purpose of attacking enemy ships. Letter-of-marque ships were armed merchantmen primarily designed to carry cargo but authorized to capture enemy ships.

ond, third, and fourth lieutenants were in charge of the batteries in different parts of the ship, and of the supply of ammunition to the guns.

Midshipmen assisted the lieutenants in their duties, supervised the execution of the orders of the sailing master, and attended the captain and first lieutenant to carry important messages to their subordinates. Midshipmen were stationed aloft to supervise the dispositions of the rigging, spars, and sails that were ordered by the sailing master, and to command the sharpshooters whose particular targets were the captains and officers of enemy ships. The brief and general references to midshipmen in the regulations of the Royal and United States navies may convey the erroneous impression that midshipmen were not considered important. General terms were employed because the duties of midshipmen were too numerous and varied to enumerate. They assisted all the senior officers and carried out all the duties not specifically assigned other officers, their tasks taking them from the main truck to the orlop deck. At no time in their history have American midshipmen been neglected, and many times they have felt they were getting too much attention from their seniors.

As soon as General Washington took command of the Army in front of Boston, he created his own navy under Captain John Manley, which captured valuable military stores and reinforcements consigned to the British Army. Washington's navy was soon demobilized, Captain Manley entering the Continental Navy. Under the leadership of John Adams and Robert Morris, in November and December, 1775, the Continental Congress authorized thirteen frigates and provided their personnel. They obtained most of the "Rules for Regulation of the Navy of the United States" by substituting Congressional authority for royal proclamation in existing British regulations. At Benedict

Arnold's suggestion, General Washington recommended the creation of a naval squadron on Lake Champlain, which, although defeated, delayed the British advance from Canada in 1776. When the advance was resumed a year later, the Continental Army forced Burgoyne to surrender. This was the greatest single contribution of the Continental Navy to American independence.

During the Revolution, eleven of the thirteen independent states established their own navies. As the war progressed, a reinforced British squadron operating in American waters destroyed the Continental Navy and the states' navies in succession. It was not the Continental Navy, however, nor the states' navies, nor American privateers, but the French fleet in coöperation with Washington's Continental Army and Lafayette's contingent which finally gained our independence.

Although they were overcome by the superior British fleet, the gallant conduct, audacious seamanship, and indomitable spirit displayed by the best of our sea-going officers bequeathed a rich legacy to the next naval generation. Midshipmen served in the Continental Navy, the states' navies, and aboard the privateers. Midshipman Fanning of the *Bonhomme Richard* probably made the greatest individual contribution: a hand grenade which came from his fighting top, thrown from the yard-arm of the *Richard*, passed through a hatch on the *Serapis* and caused the explosion on her lower deck that made her capture possible. Midshipman Mayrant earned the praise of John Paul Jones. Midshipman Samuel Barron of the Virginia Navy captured a small British ship in the Chesapeake with a little gunboat. Midshipman Alexander Moore of the Virginia Navy commanded a brig-of-war and distinguished himself in the Caribbean. Christopher R. Perry, father of Oliver Hazard Perry and Matthew C. Perry and founder of a naval dynasty, served first as a midshipman on a privateer and later on the *Trumbull*, continental frigate, under Captain James Nicholson. Oddly enough, the Nicholson family is the only one, with the exception of the Truxtuns and their collaterals, the Cravens and the Tingeys, that can compete with the Perrys and their collaterals, the Rodgers, in their contribution of distinguished members to the Navy.[2] Midshipman Edward Preble served first on a privateer, then on the 26-gun Massachusetts frigate *Protector*, which, after several successful engagements, was captured by H.M.S. *Roebuck* of 44 guns and the *Medea* of 26 guns. Preble was exchanged after his capture and served as a lieutenant in the Massachusetts ship *Winthrop*.

The Navy Regulations of Great Britain and the United States recommended midshipmen to the special care of the captains. John Paul Jones required two of his midshipmen to be on the quarter-deck at all times. The remainder were distributed between the waist (the part of the ship between the quarter-deck and the forecastle) and the forecastle. They were to be ready to "lay aloft" at any time. Midshipmen were punished severely during the Revolution. It is recorded in the log of the *Ariel* that John Paul Jones put

[2] Three brothers, James, Samuel, and John Nicholson, were all captains in the Continental Navy. Samuel had four sons in the Navy; John had three. In three generations of Nicholsons there were fifteen naval officers, two of whom became commodores. A third died just as he was due for that rank. Captain Christopher Perry's five sons all entered the Navy: Oliver Hazard, Raymond Henry, Matthew Calbreath, and James Alexander as midshipmen; Nathaniel Hazard as a purser. A daughter of Christopher Perry, Jane Tweedy, married Surgeon William Butler of the Navy. Among her fourteen children was General Matthew Calbreath Butler, a distinguished Confederate officer. Another daughter, Anna Maria, married George Washington Rodgers. In the next generation, Sarah, daughter of Commodore Matthew C. Perry, married the son of Commodore John Rodgers. The Rodgers and Perrys can be considered one naval clan. Similarly the Truxtuns, the Tingeys, and the Cravens have intermarried, the last flag officer of that clan being Vice-Admiral Thomas Tingey Craven, lately retired.

Midshipman Potter in irons and kicked the afterwards distinguished Midshipman Fanning. Conditions in the Revolutionary ships, with their undisciplined officers, demanded the methods of the merchant marine, which most of them accepted as a matter of course.

John Paul Jones was soon convinced that special instruction was necessary for officers of the American Navy. In his plan for the Navy submitted to the President of the Continental Congress in April, 1777, he recommended that candidates for a commission serve as "Midshipmen or Master's Mate" before they were examined for promotion to lieutenant. Jones also recommended an academy at each of three dockyards "under proper Masters, whose duty it should be to Instruct the Officers of the Fleet when in Port in the Principles and Applications of the Mathematics, Drawing, Fencing and other Manly Arts and Accomplishments." American midshipmen had borne themselves well during the War of Independence, and the leading officer of the infant Navy had the vision to recommend a comprehensive course of instruction for them.

CHAPTER 3

The First Midshipmen of the United States Navy

AMERICANS lost their privilege of trading with the British West Indies when they gained their independence. Undaunted, they continued to trade with the French and Spanish West Indies and sought new markets in the Mediterranean, the Pacific, and the East Indies. Between 1785 and 1798 the United States did not possess a single naval vessel to protect this growing and venturesome merchant marine, whose captains stoutly defended their ships and cargoes against pirates and privateers with their own small guns. Many captains and officers had served in the Continental Navy, in the states' navies, or in privateers during the Revolutionary War and were equal to fighting their batteries. Outstanding among them was Captain Thomas Truxtun, Revolutionary privateersman, who sailed the first Philadelphia ship, the *Canton*, to China in 1786.

War between France and England began in 1793, increasing American foreign trade and its risk of capture by belligerent men-of-war. The restraint usually exercised over the Barbary Corsairs by the Portuguese Navy was removed about the same time, and the capture of eleven United States merchant ships trading in the Mediterranean by these Moslem pirates moved a reluctant Congress to appropriate for six frigates—the afterwards celebrated *Con-*

stitution, Constellation, United States, and *Congress,* the
ill-fated *President,* and the proverbially unfortunate *Chesapeake.* Midshipmen had proved themselves essential during
the Revolutionary War, and Congress authorized eight
midshipmen for each frigate in our first national Navy;
since its foundation midshipmen have formed an integral
part of the officer personnel and have contributed their
full share to the development of the United States Navy.
The pay of midshipmen varied at that time from $13 to
$19 a month, plus one ration.[1] The boatswain got $20; the
ship's cook received $18. Eight to sixteen midshipmen were
allowed to a heavy frigate like the *Constitution;* two to a
sloop-of-war.

These six frigates had a profound influence upon the
strategy and tactics of the United States Navy and the
military character of the personnel. Joshua Humphreys,
their designer, had sound ideas on naval warfare: he proposed to construct frigates "superior to any European
frigate," which would never be "obliged to go into action
but on their own terms" except in a calm.

To handle these frigates with their lighter spars and
rigging and longer and heavier hulls required a high degree of seamanship among the officers, and strictly disciplined, alert crews. Orders must be executed smartly, but
these lively frigates demanded more than blind obedience
to orders from their midshipmen, who were stationed in
all parts of the ship from the berth deck to the fighting top,
from the forecastle to the quarter-deck. Midshipmen did
not have senior officers at their elbows to tell them what

[1] A term in general use in all military services, meaning the amount
of food issued daily to a soldier, sailor, or marine. A ration consists of
a certain amount of meat, bread, and vegetables. Its money value was
frequently commuted to officers who purchased their own food. To-day
a ration has a value of thirty to sixty cents, depending upon the cost of
provisions.

to do in an emergency, and they were often required to make important decisions. As soon as they learned their way about the ship they were expected to exercise their own judgment and were given the necessary authority to enforce their·orders. These smart frigates set the tone of our young Navy, and in the naval atmosphere that they created our first American midshipmen were reared. Joshua Humphreys created the necessity for smart officers, for they alone could handle his frigates.

There was little sentiment in Congress or the nation for a Navy. Before the frigates were completed, the Government negotiated a humiliating treaty with the Dey of Algeria and halted their construction. President Washington urged their completion, but it was not until French privateers, encouraged by our national supineness, captured United States merchant ships in United States waters that Congress, in 1797, provided funds to finish three of the frigates. Lack of suitable spars, guns, and naval stores further delayed their construction until the spring of 1798, and our new Navy began the war against France with the converted East Indiaman *Ganges*, commanded by Captain Richard Dale. The British and French guns, round shot, and powder were distinctly superior to American. But the American frigates were finally finished, and then the infant United States Navy began its new career with "the most powerful and the most useful ships" of their class.

Americans along the Atlantic coast were in favor of the war with France. The Navy was the popular branch of the armed forces, and commercial and shipping interests advanced funds to the Government to finance the cost of men-of-war. Seaport towns contributed money and ships, Essex, Massachusetts presenting the famous frigate *Essex*. Naval officers and privateersmen of the Revolution hastened to volunteer their services, and many entered their sons as midshipmen. Younger officers of the merchant service were commissioned lieutenants. Merchant sailors heartily approved fighting the French, and entire crews for the frigates were shipped in the larger seaports within a few hours.[2] Among the hastily assembled crews a few cowards appeared. Those who flinched were summarily handled. Third Lieutenant Andrew Sterrett of the *Constellation*, during her fight with *l'Insurgente*, was obliged to "put an end to a coward" with his sword. He wrote an intimate friend: "We would put a man to death for looking pale on this ship." Prompt action was necessary, for one or two cowards fleeing from their guns might create a panic among brave but only partly disciplined crews.

Benjamin F. Stoddert, appointed by President Adams as Secretary of the newly established Navy Department, recreated the Navy while carrying on a war. Secretary Stoddert was convinced that while its character was being formed the Navy "ought to be commanded by men who will be unhappy if they do not receive and merit praise, who have talents and activity as well as spirit." And he proved his theory by ordering such officers as Captain Thomas Truxtun, lately trading to China, to command the *Constellation*; Captain John Barry to the *United States*; Captain Samuel Nicholson, commander of the *Trumbull* in her fight with the *Isis* in the Revolution, to the *Constitution*; Captain Stephen Decatur, Sr., to the *Delaware*; Captain Christopher R. Perry, who took his son Oliver H. Perry as a midshipman, to the *General Greene*. Other distinguished captains included Samuel and James Barron, Alexander Murray, Moses Brown, and Richard Dale; John Rodgers, who began as first lieutenant with Captain Truxtun but was soon promoted to captain; and Captain

[2] James Fenimore Cooper, *History of the Navy*, Vol. I, pp. 270-277.

FOUR EARLY AMERICAN NAVAL COMMANDERS

ABOVE: John Paul Jones (from a painting by Cecilia Beaux); Thomas Truxtun. BELOW: Oliver Hazard Perry; David Porter. (Jones, courtesy U. S. Naval Academy Library. Truxtun, Perry, Porter, courtesy U. S. Naval Institute and U. S. Naval Academy Museum.)

Thomas Tingey, brother-in-law of Captain Truxtun, who in 1771 had been an officer in the Royal Navy. Tingey settled in the colonies prior to the Revolution, and may have served in the Continental Navy.

The Secretary could not be as careful in choosing his lieutenants, but among them were Charles Stewart, Isaac Hull, Andrew Sterrett, and Isaac Chauncey. Richard Somers, Stephen Decatur, Jr., David Porter, and James R. Caldwell entered as midshipmen but were soon made lieutenants. The revenue cutters were taken over by the Navy, among them the *Pickering*, carrying fourteen guns, commanded by Lieutenant-Commander Edward Preble, who, next to Thomas Truxtun, was destined to exert most influence upon the character of the American midshipmen.

Secretary Stoddert entered his son Benjamin as a midshipman; Truxtun and Perry did likewise.[3]

Both Captain Truxtun and John Rodgers, his first lieutenant on the *Constellation*, were severe disciplinarians, and the habits acquired in the merchant service sometimes led them to depend upon their physical strength to maintain discipline. David Porter, afterwards captain of the *Essex*, came near resigning as a midshipman on the *Constellation*, but later became devoted to Truxtun and Rodgers.

Commodore Truxtun was not a mere martinet. In a

[3] Among other midshipmen of our new Navy were two Decaturs, Stephen, Jr., and James; three Biddles, Clement, James, and Edward; three Nicholsons, W. R., John B., and James; two Macdonoughs, James and Thomas; William H. Allen, James Lawrence, Stephen Cassin, John Trippe, John Downes, Edward Trenchard, John Dorsey, Henry Wadsworth, States Rutledge, Robert T. Spence, James Jarvis, Johnston Blakely, Lewis Warrington, James Renshaw, Daniel T. Patterson, William and Thomas Burrows, Robert Henley, Robert Tilghman, Joseph Israel, George Spotswood, Edward O'Brien, L. Warfield, Timothy Pickering, Ralph Izard, James and Thomas Rodgers. Captains and lieutenants showed their confidence in the future Navy by eagerly entering their sons, nephews, and cousins as midshipmen.

memorial addressed to his midshipmen and circulated among many others, he admonished them to remember that "rigid discipline and good order are very different from tyranny, the one highly necessary and the other abominable and disgraceful to the character of an officer." As midshipmen commanded enlisted men at an age when they might be tempted to abuse their authority, such advice was excellent.

Truxtun specifically urged midshipmen to: "Learn to rig and unrig [a ship], to hand, reef and steer, and to navigate a ship scientifically, and to perform every act of duty, belonging to the highest and lowest order of seamen and sea officers. Make yourselves acquainted with the construction of all sorts of vessels and the general principles of mechanics."

Whatever knowledge is necessary to an admiral, a captain, a lieutenant, or a master, is, in a high degree, Truxtun considered, essential to a midshipman. He recommended astronomy, geometry, and mechanics "as the materials which form the skilful pilot and the superior mariner. The theory of navigation is derived from the two former, and the movements of the ship upon the latter. The action of the wind upon the sails, and the resistance of the water at the stem naturally dictate an inquiry into the property of solids and fluids; and the state of a ship floating upon the water requires the study of hydrostatics and the influence of gravity. These branches will enlarge the midshipman's views on the operations of naval war, as directed by the effect of powder; and the knowledge of projectiles.

He charged midshipmen "to pay the closest attention to Naval Tactics, which you can never know properly until you know mathematics; consequently until then fighting in a line of battle and maneuvers will always appear a confused business." Before there was a 74-gun ship of the line in the United States Navy, Thomas Truxtun exhorted his brood of midshipmen to prepare themselves to fight in a line of battle.

"Learn to be seamen of the first order. Each of you calculate and prepare yourselves to be Admirals and to command the American fleet." This advice was given before the rank of admiral existed and when our little fleet consisted of about thirty frigates and smaller craft. But Truxtun and a few others of his generation had already visioned the future growth of our Navy and the greatness of our country.

In conclusion, Commodore Truxtun exhorted the ambitious midshipman, "while the dunces who are his officers or messmates, are rattling the dice, roaring bad verse, hissing on the flute, or scraping discord from the fiddle, to direct his attention to more noble studies which would sweeten the hour of relaxation." He should allow "no example from Fools" to influence his conduct, or seduce him from that laudable ambition which his honor and advantage are equally concerned to pursue.

Thomas Truxtun gave our new Navy a fine start with the capture of the French frigate *l'Insurgente*, and followed it up with the night action with *la Vengeance*. He showed American midshipmen in his own person how to fight, repeating the example set for them by such captains as John Paul Jones, John Barry, Lambert Wickes, and Samuel Nicholson. Truxtun had a fine sense of honor, a fiery temper, and was quick to take offense. In 1802 he resigned command of the squadron fitting out for the Mediterranean because the Department would not allow him a flag-captain. The Navy Department construed his action as resigning from the Navy, while Captain Truxtun intended only to resign command of the squadron. Thus Truxtun passed from the service, but not before he had left an indelible impress upon it and particularly upon the officers and midshipmen.[4]

Altogether, between 350 and 400 midshipmen served during the war with France, of whom only 159 were retained in the Peace Establishment of 1801. In this drastic weeding-out process the Department followed the idea of Captain Thomas Truxtun, to encourage the meritorious and to rid the service of the unworthy. Thomas Truxtun inaugurated the custom of removing idle or vicious midshipmen from the Navy. This was continued by the Department in 1806 and has persisted to the present day.[5]

[4] Captain Truxtun was a mathematician and navigator as well as a sailor. In August, 1794, he published a treatise on latitude and longitude and the variation of the compass, to which he added a chart of the globe tracing the routes used by him in different ships to the Cape of Good Hope, Batavia, and Canton, China, on which he encountered the most favorable winds.

In the appendix Captain Truxtun gave his views on the proper organization of our Navy. He believed that the British Navy was the first maritime power on the globe in naval tactics, discipline, and the general management of ships of war; they afforded a proper example for the United States to imitate in its infancy. The customs and manners of the United States sea service were similar to the British; therefore he was convinced that by a steady attention to their naval system we should very soon have our ships of war and marine affairs in good order, and our internal government aboard the different ships in the United States Navy similar to each other.

[5] Many of the midshipmen who entered between 1794 and 1800 met the highest standard. Among them were James C. Jarvis, who went overboard with the mainmast of the *Constellation* rather than leave his post, and David Porter, whose seamanship and sound judgment saved the foremast of the same ship. Stephen Decatur, Jr., and Richard Somers, who were brought up by Captain Barry on the frigate *United States* one rung below the fourth lieutenant, Charles Stewart, soon became lieutenants. James Lawrence was thought by Mahan to be "one of the most gallant personalities in the annals of the American Navy." Midshipmen Thomas Macdonough and Oliver Hazard Perry, whose victories on Lake Champlain and Lake Erie preserved our northern frontier in the War of 1812, both entered the Navy during the war with France. Midshipman Henry Wadsworth entered on the *Congress* from Maine. Midshipman Benjamin Carpender of New Jersey died in service in January, 1800. Edward, Clement, and James Biddle joined from Penn-

It was not customary in Europe to provide half pay for midshipmen when they were unemployed, but Secretary Stoddert realized that they were the future commanders of our Navy, and at the close of the war with France he recommended that midshipmen as well as commissioned officers be allowed half pay, for they "are among the most promising young men of our country, possess all the materials to make officers equal to any in the world." To obtain half pay, unemployed midshipmen were required to spend at least four months each year "in acquiring a better knowledge of [their] profession, if not in foreign service, at least in the merchant ships of [their] own country."

The training of midshipmen begun under Commodore Truxtun in the Caribbean was carried on in the Mediterranean mainly by Commodores Preble and John Rodgers during the Barbary Wars, assisted by Stephen Decatur, Andrew Sterrett, Richard Somers, James Lawrence, Charles Stewart, Isaac Hull, and others. The senior officers learned to fight by fighting and instructed their midshipmen while they were learning themselves.

Instruction was not systematic or progressive. Before some of the midshipmen learned seamanship or navigation, they were given command of squads of sharpshooters, also armed with hand grenades, in the fighting tops; they acted as seconds in command of a gun battery; they went on cutting-out expeditions in armed boats. Practice made them expert in hand-to-hand fighting with pistols, pikes, sabers,

sylvania; Edward died at sea soon after entering. John Trippe, from Maryland, who later showed the Tripolitans a trick or two in hand-to-hand fighting, joined the brig *Experiment.* Lewis Warrington, from Virginia, joined the *Chesapeake.* Edward Trenchard was on the *New York.* John Downes was on the *Constitution.* From Maine to Georgia, American lads eagerly offered themselves as midshipmen in the hope of earning their commissions as lieutenants in the United States Navy.

and tomahawks; they were exercised in boarding enemy ships and in resisting hostile boarders.

Lieutenant-Commander Sterrett in the *Enterprise* showed how, by skilful seamanship, a superior tactical position could be taken and held and an enemy ship disabled without loss. Decatur, Lawrence, Porter, and Somers demonstrated the method of fighting and boarding enemy gunboats. Preble showed how land fortifications could be temporarily subdued by bombardment, and in the attack on Tripoli forts and gunboats on August 3, 1803, gave midshipmen their first lesson in squadron tactics. The *Constitution* with her battery of 24-pounders kept down the fire of the shore batteries; the brigs supported the gunboats, who pursued and boarded the enemy gunboats. No lesson from a textbook on naval tactics could equal the one Preble gave his midshipmen that afternoon off Tripoli. They were fighting immediately under his eye, and he quickly noted any unusually gallant action. That afternoon, lieutenants and midshipmen proved themselves definitely superior in hand-to-hand fighting with the Tripolitan pirates. Midshipman Thomas Macdonough was present during most of the fighting in the Mediterranean. Midshipman Oliver H. Perry was present for some. The War of 1812 proved that they had been attentive scholars.

Americans were not always successful. The attempt of the fire-ship *Intrepid* was a complete failure, costing the lives of Lieutenant-Commander Richard Somers and Midshipmen Henry Wadsworth and Joseph Israel. Midshipman Israel, who was designated to carry the last-minute instructions to Somers, pleaded so eloquently to be allowed to remain that Commodore Preble permitted him to go as a supernumerary in recognition of his ardent spirit. The war in the Mediterranean was full of hard knocks, and

American midshipmen were taught to persevere in any undertaking, even if their first efforts failed.

When the *Philadelphia* was captured and her officers and men imprisoned, Captain Bainbridge ransomed the professional books and organized a school for midshipmen under the direction of his executive officer, Lieutenant David Porter. While their more fortunate colleagues were learning to fight by fighting, Midshipmen Bernard Henry, James Gibbon, B. F. Reed, James Renshaw, Wallace Wormley, Robert Gamble, James Biddle, R. R. Jones, D. T. Patterson, Simon Smith, and William Cutbrush studied the theory of navigation, seamanship, and ordnance. Their minds wandered from their books when the *Constitution* bombarded the forts or a gunboat fight took place beneath their prison windows, but the positive interest taken by senior officers of our infant Navy in the training and education of midshipmen is strikingly revealed in the care Preble took with their training afloat, and Bainbridge with their education behind prison walls.

Lieutenants and midshipmen alike responded to the leadership of Commodore Preble and later of Commodore John Rodgers. Captains and officers had an opportunity to compare the frigates and brigs-of-war with the British and found them superior. A spirit of emulation and professional pride arose spontaneously in the squadron. Each day in the Mediterranean Squadron added to the knowledge, skill, and spirit of the midshipmen, who, like their captains and commodore, were ready to challenge comparison with any vessels of war afloat.

Dueling was a universal custom among the military and naval professions when our Navy was founded. It was accepted as part of the code of officers, and American midshipmen adopted the custom as they did others associated with their profession. Preble boasted that there were no "duels" between American officers during his short command, but there were duels between British and American officers. And Stephen Decatur probably saved the life of Midshipman Joe Bainbridge by acting as his second in an affair with an experienced British duelist. There were numerous duels between American midshipmen before and after Preble's régime. Some duels between midshipmen occurred for trivial, a few for unworthy, reasons; most of them arose because at that time an officer was not only required to be brave, but was further required to prove his bravery on any and all occasions when it was questioned. In the first few years of our Navy, dueling among midshipmen was firmly established, and it persisted for the first half century of its history.

Our midshipmen contributed their share to the successful conclusion of the wars with France and the Barbary pirates. During these two wars, the Navy established high standards for its officers, and particularly for its midshipmen, for the captains realized that the future of the Navy lay in the hands of the entering midshipmen.

James Fenimore Cooper, who served a brief period in the Navy and who knew many of the officers personally, followed its development with a friendly but not uncritical eye, and was jealous of its honor; he wrote: "Perhaps no service, either in the way of ships or officers, ever had so large a proportion of what was excellent in it, and so small a proportion of that which was defective, as the Navy of the United States, the day peace was signed with Tripoli. A stern discipline, a high moral tone, rare models in seamanship, active warfare, and a spirit of emulation ... had conspired to produce this end." [6] Cooper may be dismissed as a biased witness; Admiral Nelson, commanding the British Mediterranean Squadron, thought the recapture and

[6] James Fenimore Cooper, *History of the Navy*, Vol. II, pp. 85-86.

burning of the *Philadelphia* the most daring act of the age. His Holiness, the Pope, said that the United States had done more for Christendom against the Moslems than all of Europe together.

Early Education of Midshipmen

☆

JOHN PAUL JONES had recommended an academy for junior officers of the Navy in 1777. Alexander Hamilton proposed an "academy for military and naval instruction" in 1798. Secretary of War McHenry recommended a slightly modified plan in 1800, which was revived but not acted upon by President Jefferson in 1808. While the discussion of an academy continued, the Navy Department, on its own initiative, provided school-masters for midshipmen and fixed their pay at thirty dollars a month and two rations. Before there was a military academy at West Point, thirty naval students, mainly midshipmen, were regularly attending school on the frigate *Boston*, where they were taught navigation and other naval sciences. On ships without school-masters, chaplains were required by Navy Regulations to instruct the junior officers.[1]

After the Barbary Wars many men-of-war were laid up and there were few berths for the midshipmen. Those entering, and many already in, were advised to make voyages to the West Indies, East Indies, or Europe in merchant ships in order to become proficient in seamanship, and no midshipman received half pay unless he spent at least four months of the year at sea. While they were serving in the merchant service, midshipmen were forbidden to wear their

[1] Oscar C. Paullin, "Beginnings of United States Naval Academy," *United States Naval Institute Proceedings* (February, 1924).

naval uniform or to draw any advance pay from the government.

The actions and correspondence of Honorable Robert A. Smith, who succeeded Secretary Stoddert, proved his interest in the midshipmen. During the reduction to the Peace Establishment in 1801, he rid the Navy of the less deserving, and after the reduction was effected no appointment was made without a preliminary investigation of the candidate's qualifications. To each appointee the Secretary forwarded a copy of the Navy Regulations, a Mariner's Dictionary, and a copy of the midshipman's uniform. The young gentleman was then given a furlough without pay, with orders to report to the Secretary when he was ready to be examined in navigation. If he passed and a vacancy existed on a man-of-war, the midshipman was ordered to fill it.

As early as 1803, when the Barbary War was at its height and when Major Jonathan Williams was struggling to establish a military academy at West Point, Secretary Smith ordered Robert Thompson, Chaplain, United States Navy, to establish a school in mathematics and navigation at the Washington Navy Yard and offered its facilities to any midshipman or other officer who wanted to attend. Chaplain Thompson continued on this duty until 1810, gradually extending the system until it embraced New York, Philadelphia, and Norfolk Navy Yards, thus carrying out the recommendation of John Paul Jones. The chaplain's task was no sinecure: his orders in 1807 were "to attend at your rooms of instruction from sunrise to sunset, and to ten o'clock at night as Captain Gordon shall tell you the service will most conveniently admit." By 1810 the system was well established, the chaplain spending three months on the *Constitution*, then in succession for a similar period of time on the *President*, the *United States*, and the *Essex*, to "instruct young officers in the theory of navigation and lunars." [2]

In 1811 Chaplain Thompson was succeeded by Chaplain Andrew Hunter, who had served as chaplain in the Continental Army, and as professor of mathematics at Princeton. By 1813 Chaplain Hunter had instructed more than one hundred midshipmen, averaging fifty per annum at one school. He enlarged the course until it included arithmetic, geometry, trigonometry, logarithms, astronomy, navigation, geography and the use of globes, English, a short course of history and chronology, together with parts of natural philosophy, particularly mechanics, hydraulics, and some selections of chemistry and electricity. All these subjects could not be absorbed by the midshipmen during their short stay, but the interest of some was stirred and they studied these subjects at a more convenient season.

The Navy has always possessed a few studious officers whose intellectual curiosity has kept them abreast of current knowledge. But most midshipmen, including many ardent spirits who later distinguished themselves in their chosen profession, desired to learn only enough to pass their examinations and become proficient naval officers. Their lack of interest in learning for learning's sake excited the direst forebodings in the pious pedagogue, who said that his pupils wanted only "a kind of mechanical knowledge" and who hoped that Divine Providence would direct the helm when they were in command, otherwise "the ship and crew will go to ruin." Professors and even officer instructors have entertained these same apprehensions of each succeeding generation of midshipmen, and yet almost all the incorrigible youngsters who never were enamored of books have managed to absorb enough theoretical knowledge to become efficient junior officers of the Navy.

[2] The method of determining longitude was known as "lunars."

Chaplain Hunter's young gentlemen were more interested in practical methods of navigation than in nautical astronomy, and fortunately they could keep their ships afloat if they were thoroughly acquainted with the practical formulas and could use the logarithm tables.

The Peace Establishment of 1806 provided for 153 midshipmen, but so many ships were decommissioned that there were not enough berths for them on Navy ships. Secretary Smith insisted that those not employed in the Navy should obtain berths in the merchant marine, and he facilitated their instruction in mathematics and navigation. Their instruction was neither systematic nor comprehensive and their training in the merchant marine was not the equivalent of that in the Navy, but an ambitious midshipman could obtain an adequate knowledge of mathematics and navigation in naval schools as early as 1803 and could become a competent sailor-man aboard the smartly handled American merchant ships. Serving in merchant ships, attending schools, doing odd jobs ashore, the midshipmen spent the humiliating days between the *Chesapeake-Leopard* encounter and the War of 1812. They felt the mortifications more keenly than their seniors and got greater satisfaction from Captain Rodgers' avenging of the *Chesapeake* by firing into the *Little Belt*.

Many American midshipmen distinguished themselves during the War of 1812. The great majority behaved with credit, some were barely respectable, and a few proved unworthy. The deserving were promoted rapidly.[3] David G. Farragut, the midshipman of 1812 whom the nation and the Navy honors most, was denied his fully earned

[3] Three Shubricks, John T., Edward, and Willam; two Perrys, Raymond and Matthew C.; Silas Stringham, W. A. C. Farragut, William H. Allen, David Conner, John D. Sloat, John Y. Yarnall, Stephen Champlain, Catesby Jones, and John H. Aulick were among those who earned their commissions as lieutenants.

promotion because his foster-father, Captain David Porter, thought he was too young to be made a lieutenant, although he had commanded one of Porter's prizes at twelve, which made him the youngest commanding officer on record. The youth of Midshipmen Isaacs and Ogden, messmates of Farragut, likewise delayed their commissions.

Many other midshipmen of 1812 carried on in a manner that would have delighted John Paul Jones. Midshipman Sigourney commanded a three-gun schooner that was attacked by armed boats; although he was severely wounded, he would not go below but went on encouraging his men to fight, until he was killed. Midshipman Yorick Baker led the boarders from the *Wasp* to the deck of the *Frolic*. In the tops of the *Wasp*, Midshipmen Henry Langdon and Frank Toscan, mortally wounded, stuck to their posts and directed the musketry fire that broke up the gallant effort of Captain Manners to retrieve his defeat by boarding. Other midshipmen performed more unpleasant tasks with equal determination. When their gun crews on the *Chesapeake* flinched from their guns, Midshipmen Ballard and Cox drove them back with their swords. Midshipman Berry in the *Chesapeake's* mizzentop fought single-handed against three Royal Marines who tried to throw him overboard.

Midshipman Gregory was detected in an attempt to explode a torpedo against the British ship *St. Lawrence* in the North River. Rowing away in his small boat, he threw overboard an English lieutenant he had captured, and while the pursuing British boats stopped to recover the lieutenant, Midshipman Gregory made good his escape. Midshipman Isaac Mayo saw much hard fighting: he was on the sloops-of-war *Wasp, Argus,* and *Hornet* and served also on the *Ohio, Dolphin,* and *Franklin.* He was in the actions between the *Hornet* and *Peacock* and the *Hornet* and *Penguin,* was aboard when the *Hornet* was chased by the 74-gun *Ramilles*, and again when it was chased and almost cut to pieces by the 74-gun *Cornwallis*. He was promoted lieutenant in February, 1815, and remained a lieutenant for seventeen years, as did his contemporaries during the long peace that followed the war. Thomas A. Conover, appointed midshipman in January, 1812, served on the *Essex;* later, as an acting lieutenant, he distinguished himself in the Battle of Lake Champlain, in command of the galley *Borer*. Acting Lieutenant Breese displayed conspicuous courage in command of the *Netley* during this same engagement, and Midshipman Hiram Paulding was on the *Ticonderoga* under Lieutenant-Commander Cassin. The behavior of the officers and crew of the *Ticonderoga* excited the admiration of all beholders; when her battery fired, the nearest vessels thought she was afire, for a solid blaze came from the muzzles of her guns.

The most unusual duty performed by midshipmen during the War of 1812 fell to Midshipmen Feltus and Clapp, who were put ashore on the Island of Nooaheevah in the Marquesas, in a fort erected to protect three of Captain Porter's prizes. The fort was commanded by Lieutenant John M. Gamble of the Marine Corps, with a garrison of twenty-one volunteers from the crew. As soon as the *Essex* sailed, the natives attacked. Some of the crew mutinied and fired upon their officers. Midshipman Feltus and three men were killed. When the *Essex* did not return, Lieutenant Gamble sailed for the Sandwich Islands, with a crew of eight men and Midshipman Clapp, only to fall in with the British sloop *Cherub* and be taken prisoner on arrival.

The United States Navy was scarcely fourteen years old when it began the War of 1812. Its captains were in their late twenties and early thirties. Half its lieutenants had had less than six years naval service. Some of its youthful midshipmen had served as mates in merchant ships, but many others came directly from their homes to the quarter-deck, often on a father's, brother's, or uncle's ship. The senior midshipmen had served in the Barbary Wars. Henry Adams declared that Americans developed "in the course of twenty years a surprising degree of skill in naval affairs." Cooper attributed American successes to their aptitude for the sea. Unquestionably it was the experience gained in the French and Barbary wars that enabled the United States Navy to offer the resistance it did to the largest navy in the world. A British historian gave very strong testimony to the deadliness of American gunners; William James asserted that "the slaughtered crews and the shattered hulks" of the British ships taken proved the British did not lack their old fighting qualities. Their American opponents would ungrudgingly confirm this statement. Henry Adams added that there was nothing to indicate that Nelson's ships, frigates, or sloops fought any better than the *Macedonian* and *Java*, the *Avon* and *Reindeer*.

Two important facts concerning the War of 1812 should be remembered. First, not our frigates, nor our sloops-of-war, nor our privateersmen, certainly not our land militia, but the hard-fighting squadrons of Perry and Macdonough preserved the United States from serious British invasion. Those hardy frontiersmen who scorned a Navy and boasted of their riflemen would have been driven into the Ohio River except for Perry's squadron on Lake Erie. The second fact is more important: the United States lost the War of 1812, and was saved from the consequences of the defeat only by the action of Czar Alexander, who informed Castlereagh at Vienna that he took the American view of impressment and the right of visit and search. This hint was immediately communicated to the British Cabinet, who had received a report from Wellington that control of Lake Champlain would be essential to an advance along the Hudson. The victory of Macdonough gave that control to the American forces. Confronted with another hard campaign to secure their gains and the possible hostility of their ally Russia, the British cabinet decided for peace. They gave up their claims to United States territory, although they controlled Maine east of the Penobscot River and held Martha's Vineyard and Nantucket Island. They did not abandon their asserted claim to impress seamen or abate any of the belligerent rights they had enforced on the high seas. The administration of Madison hastened to accept the terms.[4]

[4] Mahan, *War of 1812*.

The Navy without a Naval Academy

T HE victory of Captain Isaac Hull in the *Constitution* over the *Guerrière* aroused the enthusiasm of American people for their Navy; Congress responded with generous appropriations. In January, 1813, the construction of four 74-gun ships of the line was authorized, and a school-master was provided for each, at a salary of $25 per month. Three years later additional ships and school-masters were provided. During the winter of 1814-15, at Sacketts Harbor, Commodore Chauncey organized a naval school under Chaplain Cheever Felch, who taught mathematics to one hundred officers and as many ship's boys. Felch was placed in charge of the naval school at Boston Navy Yard the following year. In the autumn of 1814 the Secretary of the Navy requested the views of Captains Bainbridge, Decatur, Hull, Morris, Perry, Porter, Stewart, Tingey, Evans, Shaw, and Warrington on measures to improve the Navy. Captain Tingey, already familiar with the naval schools conducted at the Washington Navy Yard, and Captain Evans recommended the establishment of a naval school ashore.

Captain Charles Stewart vigorously opposed a school ashore. Distinguished in three wars, Stewart had a lofty conception of duty and of the future of our Navy, but he was sincerely convinced that "The best school for the instruction of youth in the [naval] profession is the deck of a ship. . . . The pride of command, the sensitiveness of rank,

and the high bearing so essential to a gallant officer must
necessarily become impaired by employment on shore. . . .
Only an active and devoted career in his own service and
on his own element [the sea] can constitute the accomplished seaman and skilled commander." [1] The remaining
captains expressed no opinion. Captains Bainbridge and
Porter conducted classes for their midshipmen in Tripoli
prison; Captain Bainbridge sponsored the first practice
cruise for midshipmen on the *Prometheus* in 1817; Captain Porter recommended an academy ashore in 1816; and
Captain Warrington subsequently supported the school at
Annapolis. The silence of other captains did not necessarily
imply opposition to a naval school, only their preoccupation with measures immediately necessary to the prosecu-
tion of the war.

In November, 1814, Congress established a Board of
Navy Commissioners to administer the Navy. Commodores John Rodgers, Isaac Hull, and David Porter, members of the first board, continued the Department's efforts
to secure a uniform system of interior organization in naval
ships and shore establishments. In this task they drew upon
their own experience but did not hesitate to adopt features
of British and French naval administration suited to the
customs of American seamen and needed in the American
Navy.

Late in 1814 Secretary Jones recommended the establishment of a naval academy to instruct officers in mathematics,
experimental philosophy (physics), gunnery, naval archi-
tecture, and the art of mechanical drawing. The Board of
Commissioners, at the request of Congress, submitted a
well-considered plan for a naval academy ashore, emphasiz-
ing the fact that the time was opportune because the advent
of peace would relieve a number of young officers of their

[1] Captains' Letters, Navy Department.

active duties and permit them to acquire the scientific attainments hitherto denied them. Aware that some older officers in the Navy had been scantily educated, the Board recommended that the facilities of the proposed school be available to any officer who wished to attend.

The suggested course included writing, arithmetic, gunnery, fortifications, drawing, navigation, mathematics useful to the profession, French, and sword exercise. No scholar would remain at the school less than two years unless his services were required at sea, and none could remain longer than three years or after he was nineteen years of age. In effect, the maximum age of entrance was fixed at sixteen; there was no minimum age limit. Scholars were encouraged to enter at an early age. The provision for sword exercise obviously anticipated young scholars; it read: "When a scholar is of sufficient age and strength he shall be taught the sword exercise." Commodore Rodgers, who signed this report, had gone to sea at thirteen, was first mate before he was eighteen and in command of an ocean-going ship before he was twenty.

The routine and discipline recommended smacked of a man-of-war. The scholars would rise with the sun in winter and summer, at the beat of a drum, breakfast at 8 A.M., dine at noon, and sup at 8 P.M. At five o'clock in summer and four in the winter they were to be dismissed for exercise, but were not allowed out of the grounds after nine o'clock in the summer and eight in the winter. The usual punishment for minor offenses was extra duty or confinement, both naval punishments; for more heinous offenses they would be expelled, and any one expelled would be forever precluded from becoming an officer in the Navy.

When scholars were sufficiently grounded in the rudiments of their profession, two days in each week were assigned to practical work—in fitting and rigging ship; in the economy of store-houses, sail lofts, and similar establishments which might be connected with their profession. The Commissioners also anticipated stationing a ship in ordinary of a small rate near the academy to permit the students to rig and unrig her, and providing two guns with furniture and ammunition, that students might occasionally practise gunnery.

This academy would be the sole source of officers for the United States Navy. "When there shall be a call for the employment of an additional number of Midshipmen, the selection is to be made from those [scholars] who are best qualified." To ascertain the "qualifications," the Headmaster semi-annually would furnish the Commissioners with the name, conduct, character, and peculiar genius of each scholar, and would particularly state whether the scholars revealed "an aptitude or an aversion to the sea service." The Master was enjoined to treat every "scholar with equal attention, and never on any occasion to make any distinction, but what was due to merit and capacity."

The Master was clothed with ample authority, but the Commissioners constituted themselves a Board of Visitors to inspect the school, to be present at the examinations, and to note the progress of the scholars. They specifically reserved the right to fix the policy and make interior changes in the school. The Board prepared to keep a close watch on the school, which they designed to be the cradle of the Navy.

Commodore Rodgers remained at the head of the Board of Commissioners for the next ten years. In 1826, when commanding in the Mediterranean, he was still interested in a naval academy. In 1831, again President of the Board, he recommended an academy at Annapolis, where regular instruction in modern languages, mathematics, surveying, navigation, drawing, and fencing should be given; a small ship-rigged vessel, armed with several cannon, would be stationed at the school to train the youngsters in seamanship and gunnery.[2] From 1815 until his death in 1838, Commodore Rodgers, Commodore Truxtun's first lieutenant on the *Constellation,* was the most influential officer in the Navy. During all this time he was in favor of a naval academy ashore, and, except for Commodore Charles Stewart, he had the support of the leading officers of the Navy and of practically every Secretary of the Navy.

During the decade following the war of 1812, the Navy gradually cast off the last rough and ready methods of discipline it had inherited from the merchant service, in favor of the more severe but regular naval discipline.

During the Revolutionary War, John Paul Jones recorded in the log of the *Ariel* that he had kicked Midshipman Fanning; such action excited no comment, for it was customary. In 1817, Captain Oliver H. Perry was court-martialed and given a private reprimand for "giving a blow" to a captain of Marine. Another captain had been acquitted of a charge of striking a midshipman the previous year. Ward-room officers and midshipmen memorialized Congress, stating that American officers had actually been struck by their commanding officers. Congress wisely ignored the memorial. The action of the naval court-martial in awarding a private reprimand to the hero of Lake Erie reminded other captains that, while the authority of a commanding officer can not be questioned, his punishments are limited to those prescribed by the regulations, and he can be held accountable for abuse of his authority. This transition to naval discipline improved the status and fixed the position of midshipmen in the naval hierarchy.

As early as 1817, the *Niles Register* recorded: "Efficiency of the Mediterranean Squadron is universally admitted ...

[2] Oscar C. Paullin, *Commodore John Rodgers,* p. 391.

it is everywhere treated with respect . . . and is the best
school in the world for the acquirement of nautical knowledge." Although required to stand frequent watches, drill
morning and afternoon, study navigation, ordnance, and
seamanship, and keep a "note-book," midshipmen generally managed to have a jolly time. In 1816, Midshipman
James A. Perry, younger brother of Captain Oliver Perry
of the *Java*, wrote of his midshipmen mess-mates: "We
are happy as the day is long . . . there is a-plenty of girls,
but the devil of it is we can't speak their language." For
himself, Midshipman Perry determined to learn the French
language.

Congress increased the number of school-masters and
chaplains in a genuine effort to improve the educational
facilities of the Navy; and in spite of its many other tasks,
the Board of Commissioners in 1817 fitted out the brig
Prometheus as a midshipmen's practice ship, under Captain
Wadsworth, to cruise along the New England coast. The
midshipmen performed the duties of seamen, holystoning
the decks, steering, making and furling sail. In addition,
they served as junior officers, handled the brig under sails,
navigated, and made a marine (running) survey of the
harbor of Portsmouth. This first practice cruise of American midshipmen embraced the essential features of all future practice cruises under sail.

The Regulations of 1818 prescribed the duties of midshipmen in general terms and recommended them again to
the "fostering care" of their captains. The Board fixed a
higher standard for promotion to lieutenant, which automatically compelled greater exertions by midshipmen who
aspired to a commission. They were examined in arithmetic, geometry, trigonometry, navigation, and astronomical
calculations; further, they must have served at sea for two
years and be acquainted with the rigging and stowing of a

ship and the management of artillery at sea before being promoted. In compensation, practically all vacancies among lieutenants were reserved for midshipmen, which did them little good, as few vacancies occurred.

In 1818 there were four hundred midshipmen, a greater number than during the war with France. Special legislation provided for the promotion of seventy Midshipmen in 1825, most of whom had served during the War of 1812; they then stagnated in the lieutenants' list. In 1827, of 374 midshipmen, nineteen for whom there were no vacancies had passed for promotion. To improve this condition, Congress gave them, after three years at sea or five in the Navy, a new title, "passed midshipmen," and increased their pay from $20 to $25 per month, with an additional daily ration. In 1835 the pay of all midshipmen was again increased. In 1836 there were 199 passed midshipmen and 251 midshipmen. By 1840 some passed midshipmen had been in the Navy sixteen years. In 1841 the largest number of midshipmen, 219, ever appointed in one year, was warranted on account of the war scare with Great Britain; 186 of them were still in the service in 1845, and 136 graduated from the naval school in 1847-50. In August, 1842, there were 490 midshipmen in service, which led Congress to limit the number by law; only a dozen were appointed in 1842 and none in 1843 or 1844.

Piecemeal legislation could not improve the lot of midshipmen when there was no means of removing senior officers except by death, court-martial, or resignation. The only remedy was a steady flow of promotion. It is not surprising that Congress hesitated to establish a naval academy to educate midshipmen to become lieutenants when there were no vacancies in the lieutenant's grade for passed midshipmen already qualified for promotion.

The Mediterranean Squadron was the favorite station of

young American officers, and it was nearly always the "smart" squadron. Chaplain E. C. Wines served in it during 1829, 1830, and 1831, mainly on the *Constellation,* Captain A. S. Wadsworth commanding, and he has left an excellent account of the station.[3] The ships were famed for their cleanliness and excellent organization, which Wines said resulted from the indefatigable training of their crews to a thorough practical knowledge of their duties and the ready obedience paid by inferior officers and men to the orders of their superiors. American naval officers with scarcely an exception were good seamen; native enterprise and sagacity were their usual characteristics. They were not finished mathematicians or acquainted with languages, but there were libraries on every ship and many officers were fond of reading. The library on the *North Carolina* was purchased with voluntary subscriptions from the officers. They maintained a military discipline of a very high order, and American ships surpassed those of other nations, including Great Britain.

This description of the officers of the Mediterranean Squadron was written by an educated clergyman serving temporarily in the Navy, where he saw the officers under actual service conditions. The traits he noted had been developed by actual service at sea on their own men-of-war before there was a naval academy. Officers realized that they were the product of a sea-going environment. They were self-reliant and resourceful, and had measured themselves, their frigates, sloops-of-war, and gunboats against their British cousins, reputed masters of the sea, and were not ashamed of the record. They bore themselves proudly. Many of them feared the effect of sending midshipmen to shore school during their formative years. When the school was eventually established, these same apprehensions caused

[3] *Two Years and a Half in The American Navy* (1832).

the officers to keep the Academy under naval control so that it could be made a proper cradle for sea-going officers.

The midshipmen of the 1830's had few comforts: their mess was allowed one servant; wood for cooking their meals was always scarce; twice a week they had butter and fresh bread; only their active exercise and the vigor of their digestive apparatus prevented them from ruining their health. They were deprived of grog-money in 1842. Their pay was small. Many of them were improvident and not a few were ruined at the monte tables at Mahon. One of the reasons midshipmen were given so little shore leave was their perpetual poverty. Few of them had a complete civilian wardrobe, and before going ashore a midshipman usually borrowed raiment from his messmates; it was not difficult to obtain clothes, for never were more than half of them allowed ashore at one time. The youth, high spirits, and natural gaiety of midshipmen enabled most of them to endure and enjoy their hardships afloat. Those who could not stand sea-going resigned. Midshipmen continued to be improvident and to share their shore-going clothes, at least until 1904. They usually owned a complete set of uniforms, but one particularly reckless midshipman, who subsequently became a distinguished aviator, was reduced to his full dress trousers. He met the situation by removing the gold stripe for daily wear and pinning it on for Sunday inspections.

Chaplain Wines gave a detailed description of the highly trained crews, who handled the sails and guns more smartly than the British, their nearest competitors. The men were an odd assortment—generous with a sort of grumbling contentment with their lot, susceptible to kindness. Their chief characteristics were a mixture of credulity and skepticism, with a superstitious dread of imaginary and a contempt of real dangers, an imperturbable effrontery in lying, an insatiable thirst for strong drink, and shocking profanity. If one of the crew of the *Constellation*, chosen at random from Davy Jones' locker, were questioned, he would unblushingly admit that the Sky Pilot of 1830 had made a shrewd estimate of his character. The good chaplain believed that, though debased, sailors still had some generous traits in their characters; he was convinced they could be reformed, and he labored earnestly with his shipmates on the *Constellation*. He recommended that the use of the "colt," a small whip made of three-inch rope, unlaid, with three knotted tails, should be limited to the captain and first lieutenant, and the "cat," a short wooden stick covered with baize, with nine tails of tough knotted cord about two feet long, be authorized only by a court-martial. At that time, the captain could award a punishment of twelve lashes of the cat, and officers could authorize the use of the colt by a petty officer to hasten the movements of laggards. On some ships it was customary to give a couple of lashes with the colt to the last man aloft before an evolution and the last to reach the deck after completion. Chaplain Wines was ahead of his time; the cat was abolished in 1850, and until other means of enforcing discipline had been developed, there was a noticeable falling off in the behavior of the old-timers who dreaded nothing but the cat.

Captain Wadsworth encouraged his men to commute their rum ration, and two-thirds of the crew did. On the *John Adams* it is reported that not a man of the ship drew grog, and that throughout the entire squadron two-thirds of the crew were "stop grogs." Commodore Truxtun asserted that a "drunkard ought never to be employed." Commodore John Rodgers was a teetotaler and refused a ship to a distinguished captain because he was intemperate. Commander Buchanan and many others did not tolerate intem-

perance. But there were "broadside officers," as they styled
themselves, who drank freely. Mahan states on second-
hand authority that in 1832, in this very Mediterranean
Squadron, a sloop-of-war was put under two reefed topsails on Christmas Eve in a two-knot breeze and the whole
ship's company, officers and men, celebrated the entire
night. This same sloop later stood into the harbor of Malta
under all sail, royal and studding, and made a flying moor.
Within fifteen minutes the sloop was moored, sails furled,
and yards squared. The Navy differed in its drinking
habits, but drinking was not allowed to prevent smartness.

Between 1815 and 1850, the Navy was a mixture of
"license and smartness," and so were its midshipmen. But
through the darkest days of the naval stagnation, Mahan,
who knew some of the leading characters when he was a
midshipman and was familiar with the era by oral tradition and study of the records, asserted that "the high sense
of duty and of professional integrity" was never wanting
in the United States Navy.[4]

Chaplain Wines wished to establish a naval school ashore
similar to West Point; he said that the existing system produced good sailors but not thorough navigators. Schools
afloat were subject to interruptions and irregularities; other
duties took precedence. Arrival in port was always fatal
to school, for midshipmen not on duty were trying to get
ashore and those on duty could not attend. Wines testified
that there was no lack of talent or enterprise among the
midshipmen but that it was difficult to "train the mind to
systematic thinking and philosophical reasoning on board
ship." Most midshipmen did not aspire to "philosophical

[4] This fact should be emphasized. Park Benjamin's *History of The
Naval Academy*, Chapter VI, leaves the impression that the Navy had
been developed by a set of drunken tyrants who bullied one generation
of midshipmen, who in their turn grew up to be dissipated martinets
and abused the next generation of midshipmen.

reasoning" and would have accepted Mahan's statement that "the object of a naval education is to make a naval officer."

Captain M. C. Perry, commanding the *Brandywine* in 1832, not only directed the studies of his midshipmen, but advised them what books to read and gave them hints on how to live as gentlemen on small salaries. In every way he sought to elevate the ideals of his officers. All captains were not as interested in the development of their midshipmen as Perry and Wadsworth, but many of them were, and at no time has the Navy been without a group of leaders to set the tone of the service.

Chaplain George Jones corroborates the testimony of Chaplain Wines in his description of the school on the *Constitution:* "In a short time study was all the go through the steerage, extending itself into the wardroom. The cobwebs were soon brushed from their brains, and a more diligent, and I may add successful set of pupils will nowhere be found, than in a few weeks were those of our ship. Thus it continued through the summer." The course included Bowditch, algebra, and geometry. Jones stated emphatically that he "did not know what older officers thought but the rest cry for a naval school and resent the preference shown the Army in West Point." Perhaps some of his pupils yearned for more education, but the chances are the majority wanted the exact amount necessary to make them proficient lieutenants. They bitterly complained of the moderate restrictions of the naval school at Philadelphia when they got it.

Chaplain Jones took extraordinary interest in the establishment of a naval school ashore. When the school at the Naval Asylum started, he recommended the expansion of the course to include mathematics, gunnery, seamanship, natural philosophy (physics), belles-lettres, languages, and drawing. He noted that the Secretary had authority to establish a school ashore by assembling in one place the professors scattered throughout the Navy and ordering midshipmen not employed at sea to attend. He convinced Commodore Lewis Warrington, one of the Commissioners, and Secretary Upshur that the Department possessed the necessary authority, but the Secretary, although in favor of the school, refused to exercise this authority without the express approbation of Congress.

In the spring of 1836, fifty-five officers of the *Constitution* memorialized Congress to establish a naval academy; officers of the *Vandalia* supported their recommendation. Neither group specifically recommended a school ashore, and Lieutenant Maury, an outspoken advocate of a school, recommended that it be established aboard a 74-gun ship of the line, on which the duties of the school would take precedence over all others. Midshipmen would be assembled aboard the school ship, and every officer aboard would take part in the instruction as follows:

The captain, ex officio president and tactical officer.

The chaplain, instructor in languages.

The purser, instructor in small sword and single stick exercise.

The surgeon, teacher of chemistry and natural history.

The lieutenants, instructors in mathematics, astronomy, navigation, natural philosophy (physics), gunnery, pyrotechnics (a branch of ordnance), etc.

Maury was convinced that four years aboard a school ship would qualify midshipmen for their ordinary duties and indoctrinate them in the leading sciences. Maury, a natural student, suggested that a naval officer's education include cultural subjects, but he wanted midshipmen taught aboard ship—moored to the dock, to be sure, but afloat. Three months each year this ship would go to sea on a practice cruise. Lieutenant L. M. Powell's conception of a school was the same as Maury's, but he thought a small sloop-of-war would serve instead of a ship of the line. The essential idea of Maury and Powell was that the education and training of midshipmen should take place at sea and be paramount to any other duties. By a curious coincidence, as American opinion was veering toward a school afloat or ashore, the British abandoned their naval academy at Portsmouth as a failure and resorted to the system of sea-going instructors and schools at navy yards, which the American Navy was about to discard.

As late as 1842, Commodore Stewart reiterated his objections to a school ashore. Some congressional opposition arose from the same high motives as those of Commodore Stewart. Senator Woodbury asserted in debate that "the deck of a ship was the best schoolhouse or academy. The naval officer should be a sailor; an informed, intelligent, moral and intellectual sailor, but still a sailor—a son of the ocean,—dedicated for life to all its arduous duties." Other senators opposed on the ground of expense. Senator Smith of Connecticut declared that an academy would stimulate one class of individuals at the expense of others. Senator Allen was typical of a group who opposed the establishment of a naval academy because it would "degenerate like West Point" into a nursery for wealthy young men who obtained their education at the public expense. It required the Mexican War and General W. S. Scott's public testimony to the value of West Point graduates to silence a formidable group in Congress which was determined to abolish West Point. This same group had resolved to prevent the establishment of a naval school, and it is entirely possible that Secretary Bancroft's infant school would have been snuffed out, except for the Mexican War.

The mutiny on the *Somers* in 1842, led by Midshipman

Spencer, a son of the Secretary of War, is sometimes credited with hastening the establishment of the naval academy on the assumption that it revealed a deplorable morale among midshipmen and created a demand for a naval school ashore. This theory will not bear analysis. The naval school at Philadelphia had attracted the favorable attention of the Navy and the Navy Department before the mutiny occurred.

The Navy knew that Midshipman Spencer had served only one year and was in no way representative of the corps of midshipmen. During his short service, he had been recommended to be dropped, but through his father's influence had been retained. When he attempted to incite a mutiny his plot was frustrated, and after a court-martial, he and two other conspirators were run up to the yard-arm by the crew he had attempted to seduce, which then "cheered ship." The prompt and decisive manner in which the attempted mutiny was suppressed revealed the inherent discipline of the Navy, but the conduct of Spencer affords no evidence of the morale existing among other midshipmen and certainly had no effect on the establishment of a naval school.

The introduction of the screw propeller on the gunboat *Princeton* by Captain Stockton in 1843 vitiated many of the arguments against educating midshipmen ashore. The paddles of paddle-wheel steamers were extremely vulnerable to gun-fire, and the unwieldy wheels required so much space that there was little room for guns. Conservative officers could reasonably argue that paddle-wheel steamers would never displace sailing ships on the high seas. And they never did. But no such argument could be brought against the screw-propelled man-of-war, whose propeller and shaft were compact, well submerged, and protected, whose unencumbered decks provided more room for guns than sail-

ing ships did. Plainly steam was the motive power of the
future, and midshipmen could only study steam ashore, for
there were practically no steam-propelled men-of-war on
which midshipmen could be instructed afloat.

CHAPTER 6

Evolution of the Naval Academy

IN 1838 Secretary Paulding reported to Congress that its liberal provisions for teachers and professors aboard ships and at navy yards were not satisfying the educational needs of the young officers of the Navy, and cautiously suggested a naval academy ashore. Six months later Commodore Biddle, commanding the Naval Asylum at Philadelphia and President of the Board of Examiners, recommended to the Secretary that a naval school be established at the Asylum where midshipmen preparing for examinations could be quartered in the building, more effectively controlled, and more efficiently instructed in classrooms at scheduled hours, undisturbed by the activities of a ship or navy yard. The commodore proposed to begin with a single professor to teach the midshipmen mathematics and navigation, but he contemplated the eventual abandonment of all other schools and the concentration of sufficient instructors in one school to provide a comprehensive curriculum.

In November, 1839, Secretary Paulding ordered Professor McClure and fifteen midshipmen to the Naval Asylum. Rooms were provided free, but meals cost the midshipmen $20 per month, which left the young gentlemen less than $10 per month for incidental expenses and such amusement as Philadelphia offered. Night life in a city cost money even then; the middies had little, and the stories of their escapades have probably grown with telling. There were a few duels: hotspurs of that era could not settle disputes with anything less deadly than a sword or a pistol. The routine prescribed by the commodore included recitations from 9 A.M. to 2 P.M. Curfew was at 9 P.M., when all lights were extinguished. Accustomed to overnight liberty in all parts of the world, midshipmen did not understand why they should suddenly be treated as children, and dubbed the school "Biddle's Nursery."

ᵀThe midshipmen grumbled, but they knew that the commodore was President of the Board before which they must soon appear for promotion. Final examination was a dread ordeal and no midshipman in his senses would jeopardize his future by neglecting recitations of which records were furnished the commodore by Professor McClure. They snatched all the amusement they could afford, but the majority kept within bounds. Consequently, the first session was a success, which encouraged the Secretary and the commodore to enlarge the school. In 1842 Professor William Chauvenet, brilliant, young, and enthusiastic, succeeded Professor McClure and, encouraged by Commodore Biddle and his successor, Commodore Samuel Barron, expanded the school along the lines anticipated by Biddle. In 1843 the course was extended to nine months. Additional professors were obtained, and the curriculum was improved. With the success of this innovation, Professor Chauvenet and Commodore Barron proposed, and Secretary Henshaw approved, a two-year course embracing algebra, geometry, plane and spherical trigonometry, nautical astronomy and surveying, mechanics and the steam engine, drawing, gunnery, and naval tactics. During their time at the naval school, midshipmen would cruise in the summer on ships detailed solely for training. Secretary Henshaw placed the plan in operation early in 1844, but his successor, Secretary Mason, abandoned it the following September, stating that midshipmen could not be spared two years from their duties at sea. Secretary Mason increased the number of professors at the school, and in April, 1845, the staff included Lieutenant J. H. Ward, instructor in ordnance and steam; Professor William Chauvenet, instructor in mathematics and moving spirit of the institution; Julius Meire, modern languages; J. H. Belcher, international law; H. H. Lockwood, pyrotechnics; Assistant Engineer W. F. Mercier, assistant to Ward.

On March 11, 1845, George Bancroft, a well-known scholar and founder of Round Hill School at Northampton, Massachusetts, succeeded Mason as Secretary of the Navy. His actions immediately after he became Secretary indicate that he was aware of the previous failures and was determined to establish a naval school ashore. In April, Passed Midshipman Marcy, son of the Secretary of War, was ordered to the staff of the school. On May 1st the Secretary requested Professors Chauvenet, Lockwood, Belcher, and Meire to report upon the nature of their duties, the number of hours daily engaged, and the number of students, and to make suggestions for improvements. These reports enabled Bancroft to understand the internal problems of the naval school.

Some opposition to the school resulted from rivalries for its location in particular places. The Military Academy was in the north, and in Congress there had developed a feeling that the Naval Academy should be located in a southern state. The Maryland legislature had previously petitioned Congress to establish the Academy at Annapolis. By June 1st Bancroft had decided upon Annapolis, and a week later, probably with the assistance of Passed Midshipman Marcy, he obtained the transfer of Fort Severn from Secretary of War Marcy to the Navy.

GEORGE BANCROFT

As Secretary of the Navy in 1845, he took the lead in founding the Naval Academy.

Bancroft now had a suitable site promised and a clear idea of what the school should be. The action of Secretary Henshaw constituted a precedent for the concentration of midshipmen and professors at one school for a period up to two years, and in the official files was a memorandum from Chaplain George Jones to Secretary Upshur citing the necessary legal authority. Bancroft, as Secretary, could have established a school forthwith, but he was too sagacious to risk offending the Navy and Congress by precipitate action.

The day he obtained Fort Severn he formally solicited the advice and assistance of the Board of Examiners at the Naval Asylum in "maturing a more efficient system of instructions for the young naval officers." Bancroft's persuasive letter is *prima facie* evidence that he was familiar with the objections urged against a naval school ashore. He met the charge that practice in naval gunnery could not be given young officers ashore by stating that Fort Severn had been recommended as a suitable site especially because "a vessel could be stationed [there] to serve as a school in gunnery." That statement was also an argument for the site he had chosen. Beyond stating that the course of instruction was too short, Bancroft made no criticism of it, offered no plan for the proposed school, only asked: "Might it not be well to have permanent instruction, and to send all midshipmen *on shore* [author's italics] to school?" If only midshipmen ashore were sent to school, the training of midshipmen actually at sea would not be interrupted; this met the stock objection of officers who insisted that midshipmen could be properly trained and instructed only at sea. Of four hundred fifty midshipmen in 1834, approximately one hundred were on shore. The annual average did not vary much; there were enough midshipmen habitually ashore to justify a school. Bancroft asked the Board, "What plan of studies is most advisable?" and appealed to its members to help him.

After consulting with Lieutenant Ward, Professor Chauvenet, and Professor Lockwood, the Board recommended that the Secretary:

1. Establish a new grade, naval cadets, junior to midshipmen. The primary classes at the naval school would be composed of naval cadets, and future appointments of midshipmen would be limited to those naval cadets who had successfully completed the course at the naval school.

2. Appoint naval cadets to the naval school in the same manner as military cadets were appointed to the Military Academy at West Point.

3. Assign to the naval school one captain in command, one commander as executive officer, three lieutenants, one surgeon, one assistant surgeon, one chaplain, and an officer's guard of marines whose commanding officer would give instruction in infantry tactics and the sword exercise.

4. Establish a board of instruction with one professor and one assistant professor of the English language who would also instruct in constitutional and international law, one professor and one assistant professor of mathematics who would also instruct in marine surveying, one professor of the French language, one professor of natural philosophy and chemistry, one instructor in drawing and mapping.

The Board contemplated transferring Ward, Lockwood, and Chauvenet, who had conducted the naval school at Philadelphia, to the new school. They added the commander and three lieutenants to supervise the drills and practical instruction, which they were convinced should reinforce the theoretical instruction in the classrooms. The Board further recommended that a practice frigate and a small steamer be attached to the school for instruction in naval gunnery, tactics, and the operation of the steam engine.

During the first two years at the school, naval cadets would take the course given during the corresponding period to military cadets at West Point, except calculus. The subjects thus recommended for the naval school included algebra, plane, solid, and descriptive geometry, spherical projections and warped surfaces, shades, shadows, and perspectives, French, English, grammar, geography, and history. Naval cadets who successfully completed the course would be given warrants as midshipmen and ordered to sea; those who failed would be dropped. Only graduates from the naval school could "find their way into the Navy." After two years at school, midshipmen would spend their third, fourth, and fifth years constantly at sea in men-of-war. They would then serve a year on a practice ship "to pursue a course of practical studies" before taking their examination for lieutenant. Even after six years' preparation, midshipmen would not be commissioned unless they were required in the Navy.

The Board recommended that naval cadets be not less than thirteen or more than sixteen when appointed, reported that there was ample accommodation at Fort Severn for officers, instructors, and cadets, and reminded the Secretary that the Government possessed "all the necessary means for commencing at once a naval school, which may be enlarged and perfected at some future time." Obviously the Board regarded their proposal as only the first step in creating a proper school for the Navy.

Pushing steadily ahead after securing the endorsement of the Board of Examiners, the Secretary convened a younger board composed of Commanders McKean, Dupont, and Buchanan to recommend the location and personnel of the school, cautioning them to keep within the means at the disposal of the Department. The second board could find no authority for the preliminary school recommended by the first board and did not believe that the existing five-year probationary period should be extended. Accordingly, it recommended only one year's preliminary instruction for acting midshipmen. The Board recommended Annapolis as the site for the school and nominated Lieutenant Ward and Professors Chauvenet and Lockwood as professors. On August 7th Secretary Bancroft appointed Commander Buchanan Superintendent and directed him to prepare a plan of operation for the new school.

The Secretary bestowed upon the Superintendent "all the powers for discipline conferred by the laws of the United States," and assured him that the Department "will recommend no one for promotion who is unworthy of it from idleness or ill conduct, or continuing ignorance, and who can not bear the test of a rigid examination." He directed the first Superintendent of the Naval School to "begin with the principle that a warrant in the Navy, far from being an excuse for licentious freedom, is to be held a pledge for subordination, industry and regularity, for sobriety and assiduous attention to duty. . . . The President [Polk] expects such supervision and arrangement as shall make of them [midshipmen] an exemplary body of which the country may be proud." [1]

The Secretary left to the new Superintendent the preparation of a plan for the school at Annapolis, with a promise, faithfully kept, to sustain the Superintendent in his every "effort to improve the character of the younger branch of the service." Within a week Buchanan forwarded his plan, which, with slight modifications, was approved August 28, 1845, and became the first charter of the naval

[1] Superintendents' Office, United States Naval Academy.

school. Bancroft confided the new school to the younger element of the Navy by ordering that "no officer of higher rank than of Commander shall be ordered on duty at the Naval School," except that two captains at least shall serve on the annual board of examiners. Bancroft directed that professors and instructors be selected as far as practicable from officers of the Navy, which continued the responsibility, voluntarily assumed by the first generation of naval officers, of training their successors.

Commander Buchanan was forty-five years old when he became Superintendent. The son of a Baltimore physician, reared in a cultured home, he entered the Navy in January, 1815. His first midshipman cruise was in the crack Mediterranean Squadron on the frigate *Java*, Oliver H. Perry commanding. During thirty years' service, Commander Buchanan had cruised in every ocean, on every type of ship, and had earned the reputation of being a strict disciplinarian, an educated, efficient officer. He attributed all breaches of naval discipline to overindulgence in alcohol. His avowed antipathy toward drunkards was one of the reasons Bancroft made him Superintendent. Buchanan had sailed with Oliver and Matthew Perry, Decatur, Bainbridge, and David Porter when they were in the prime of life; he was familiar with the latest developments in gunnery and had been executive officer of the first steam frigate, *Mississippi;* he understood and loved the navy of masts and spars, and sympathized with the changes necessary for the steam navy. Finally, he was a frugal administrator of government funds, which enabled him to establish a naval school without additional appropriations.

Three of the heads of departments, Lieutenant James H. Ward, Professor William Chauvenet, and Professor Henry H. Lockwood, had served happily together in Philadelphia and were animated by the single purpose of establishing a proper system of education for junior officers of the Navy. They coöperated cordially throughout their service at Annapolis, and spared the Superintendent any internal bickering.

Lieutenant Ward, born in 1806, graduated from the Military Academy at Norwich, Vermont, before he was seventeen, served as a midshipman on the *Constitution* in the Mediterranean Squadron, spent one year at Trinity College, Hartford, in postgraduate work, and during almost fifteen years at sea continued his studies of naval tactics, gunnery, naval history, and scientific subjects. He believed that his generation needed to educate themselves in those subjects if they wished to preserve "the glorious reputation" built by the officers of the War of 1812. He undertook his duties as Executive Officer (subsequently designated Commandant of Midshipmen), as well as instructor in ordnance and steam, with enthusiasm.

Professor Chauvenet, only twenty-five years old, had been largely responsible for the success and the enlargement of the school at Philadelphia, had proposed the extension of the one-year course to two, and in 1849 was instrumental in getting the course at the naval school enlarged from two to four years. He remained at Annapolis until 1859 and did much to establish the high standard of the mathematics and navigation departments.

Professor H. H. Lockwood, graduated from West Point in 1836, served in the Second Seminole War in Florida, subsequently resigned from the Army, and later entered the Navy as a professor. His military experience led to his selection as Naval Adjutant of the landing party from the frigate *United States* which captured Monterey, California, prematurely in 1842. Two years later he was assistant to Professor Chauvenet at Philadelphia and was selected to accompany him to Annapolis. Lockwood was a soldier as

FOUR MEMBERS OF THE FIRST ACADEMIC BOARD, 1845-46

ABOVE: Lieutenant James Harmon Ward, executive and instructor in gunnery and steam; Professor William Chauvenet, instructor in mathematics and navigation. BELOW: Professor Henry Hayes Lockwood, instructor in natural philosophy; Chaplain George Jones, instructor in English.

well as a teacher, always ready to drill a battalion of unwilling midshipmen in infantry or field artillery.

Chaplain George Jones had been a stanch advocate of a naval school ashore. In October he became head of the Department of English Studies, including history and geography. Professor Arsène N. Girault reported in October as head of the Department of Foreign Languages. His "energy, zeal and talent for teaching French" soon gained him the respect of the Superintendent and his colleagues on the Academic Board.

Commander Buchanan took possession of Fort Severn on August 15, 1845, and began alterations in the buildings to accommodate the midshipmen, officers, and instructors. In addition to Fort Severn, which stood at the east point of the rectangular enclosure of about nine acres, the Navy obtained nine buildings, and a Gate House opening on Scott Street, which ran parallel to and just outside of the south wall. The south wall began at Chesapeake Bay and continued a short distance beyond the Gate House, where it met the west wall which ran in a northerly direction until it reached the Severn. Nearest the fort stood a small brick bakehouse, which was converted into quarters for midshipmen and was subsequently christened Brandywine Cottage by a group of youngsters who had sailed around Cape Horn in the *Brandywine* prior to arriving at Annapolis. Next stood an Army hospital, also made into midshipman quarters; from the conviviality of its occupants it earned the name of "Rowdy Row." Beyond the hospital was the barracks for married enlisted men, which was made another midshipman dormitory, dubbed "Apollo Row" after the statuesque figures of some of the first occupants who strutted in its doorways. Next in line and abreast of the Commandant's House was the two-story barracks for unmarried soldiers. Two rooms on the lower floor were converted into the midshipmen's messroom and kitchen; two corresponding rooms on the second floor were converted into recitation rooms. The need for midshipman quarters was acute, and a small structure of two rooms and a hall on the west wall, known as the Abbey, and another on the south wall near the bay, known as the Gas House, were also utilized.

The officers fared better. The Superintendent inherited the Commandant's quarters, and the first four members of the Academic Board fitted exactly into four sets of subalterns' quarters adjacent to the Superintendent's house. When Chaplain Jones reported, he was assigned the renovated quartermaster's office, built into the south wall. In retrospect, to retired admirals writing memoirs in modern houses with numerous bathrooms, the midshipmen's quarters were "bare and uncomfortable," very cold and bleak in winter. Actually, their quarters were comparable to the average frame buildings of the time and place. Three to eight midshipmen were assigned to a room, depending upon its size, but their quarters were spacious compared with those they enjoyed in the cockpit of a sloop-of-war or the steerage of a ship of the line. A contemporary account in the *Nautical Magazine* states: "The Midshipmen are made very comfortable in frame buildings ... put in good repair" for their accommodation.[2]

The Department faced two problems at its new school—the completion of the education of midshipmen who had entered in 1840, 1841, and 1842 (none entered in 1843 or 1844), and the provision of increased facilities for those entering in the future. Midshipmen who had entered in 1840 were practically all ordered to the school to prepare

---

[2] E. C. Marshall's history of the Academy, written in 1862, corroborates the *Nautical Magazine*. Park Benjamin's history, written about 1900, and memoirs of rear admirals give a contrary impression.

for their final examinations due in 1846. Those who had entered in 1841 or 1842 and who were not needed at sea were also ordered to Annapolis, but were subject to recall when their services were needed. Acting midshipmen entering in 1845 were given a preliminary examination for physical defects that might disqualify them for the arduous duties of sea life, and a mental examination in reading, writing, arithmetic, and geography. They were also required to present evidence that they were of good moral character and also between the ages of thirteen and sixteen years. Those qualifying to enter the school remained on probation for one year. If their conduct was satisfactory, they were sent to sea for three years. At the end of six months at sea those whose conduct met the approbation of their captains were warranted midshipmen. At the end of three years at sea they were ordered back to the naval school for one year to prepare for their examination for lieutenant.

The essential difference between the two schools at Philadelphia and Annapolis was that the latter had a provision requiring candidates for a naval commission to spend their first year of training at school ashore. As the plan was executed, the practical difference was the closer supervision of the students at Annapolis, which arose from concentration of all midshipmen within the walls of Fort Severn, and, in addition, the strict disciplinary methods of Commander Buchanan. The senior midshipmen of the 1840 date gave little trouble; they were too busy preparing for their final examination. The acting midshipmen were too young and overawed to make trouble, but the intermediate dates, whose promotion was distant, looked upon the school as an abridgment of their usual shore-going privileges and resented the new system. Commander Buchanan secured the coöperation of most of the senior midshipmen and did not hesitate to take effectual steps to control the unruly.

There were only two classes at the school, Senior and Junior. All midshipmen of the 1840 date were in the Senior class; all acting midshipmen of the 1845 date were in the Junior Class. Midshipmen of the 1841 and 1842 dates were assigned to the Senior or Junior classes, according to their previous education; sometimes the Intermediates were assigned to subjects with both classes. It was the intermediate dates which caused the complications, for they were ordered to the school only when not needed at sea and were liable to be detached at any moment when their services were required. The ages of the students ranged from thirteen, among the acting midshipmen, to around twenty-eight, among the Seniors. The Senior Class averaged forty-five members and was divided into two sections for recitations; the Junior Class rarely exceeded a dozen and recited in one section. Recitations began at 8 A.M. and lasted until noon. Midshipmen were allowed from noon to 1:30 for dinner and recreation. Afternoon recitations continued from 1:30 to 4:30 P.M. Recreation and supper were from 4:30 to 6, and study from 6 to 10 P.M.

The Senior Class had daily recitations in mathematics, natural philosophy, and modern languages, three recitations a week in history and composition, two recitations a week in ordnance, gunnery, and steam, and one a week in chemistry. Mathematics included navigation, algebra, plane and spherical geometry, nautical astronomy, and descriptive geometry—sixteen hours a week according to present-day college measurements, with four hours home work per night. In addition, midshipmen were exercised with the sextant and other astronomical instruments at any favorable hour, provided such exercise did not interfere with recitations or preparations for recitations in other branches.

The Junior Class had daily recitations in mathematics, including arithmetic, elements of geometry and algebra, and elementary navigation. With the exception of Saturday, there were daily classes in English, which included geography, history, grammar, and composition, and in the modern languages. They were taught the use of the quadrant. Both classes attended lectures in natural philosophy, ordnance, and chemistry, and were drilled in fencing and infantry when the indefatigable Professor Lockwood introduced those exercises.

Commander Buchanan formally opened the school on Friday, October 10th, with a brief address outlining the purpose and requesting the aid of the senior midshipmen in maintaining the dignity and discipline of the institution. Those familiar with the Naval Academy to-day will have difficulty in imagining the naval school in 1845-46. There was no suggestion of militarism; midshipmen were not in uniform and did not march to recitations. A bell rang, and students reported within five minutes or were marked tardy. There were between fifty and sixty midshipmen, divided in two classes and three sections, taught by four to six instructors. There were no athletics, organized or unorganized; midshipmen could spend their recreation periods in the town of Annapolis by writing their names in books and reporting their return to the officer in charge. The midshipman officer of the day was stationed at the Gate House and was given one watchman to patrol the grounds, extinguish the lights and fires at 10:30 P.M., and maintain order by occasionally walking through the yard to prevent any improprieties. The institution was governed by the regulations of the Navy and by special orders issued by the Superintendent. Officers were required to observe toward each other a polite, respectful deportment, and midshipmen were enjoined to conduct themselves with the propriety and decorum of gentlemen. More than one officer who entered the naval school in its earliest days has testified that midshipmen were treated as gentlemen and were expected to behave as such. That custom, begun in the early days of the Navy, crystallized into a law, and to-day an officer can be court-martialed for conduct unbecoming a gentleman.

The schedule of study and recitations was heavy for midshipmen unaccustomed to regular study hours, and heavier for the professors who prepared the courses, examined and classified incoming students, taught, lectured, examined, and graded their pupils. Only devoted professors, determined to establish a naval school, could have established that variegated curriculum, especially fitted to the needs of naval officers. Commander Buchanan supervised the alterations and construction of buildings which continued throughout his tenure. He maintained friendly but not intimate relations with his staff, and gave special attention to the conduct of the midshipmen.

Commander Buchanan fixed the tone of the school and established the same discipline there as he had helped to maintain upon the United States Ship *Delaware*. Annapolis was a small town, he was an active officer, and his letter book shows that he knew what his midshipmen were doing. He was determined to suppress overindulgence in liquor when two rations of grog, given each day to the men, was regularly exceeded by many officers. Buchanan recommended that a certain midshipman, whose marks were highly creditable, be dropped because his occasional intemperance would prevent his becoming an "ornament to the service."

He dropped another midshipman whose studies were creditable but who was hot-tempered and insubordinate; he wrote that another "has not the capacity to acquire a

COMMANDER FRANKLIN BUCHANAN, FIRST SUPERINTENDENT OF
THE NAVAL ACADEMY

knowledge of the branches taught at the school, and the time devoted to him is thrown away." The reasons for these three dismissals outline Buchanan's policy: he would not tolerate midshipmen who were insubordinate, who could not control their tempers and their appetites, or who did not have the mental ability to become naval officers. He formally denied false accounts of the behavior of midshipmen made by a Baltimore clergyman and, knowing the severity of the examination in seamanship, he recommended that midshipmen be given a two months' refresher cruise before their examination for promotion. He regarded himself as the guardian of their good name and interests.

The appointment of Acting Midshipman Cyrus H. Oakley of New York was revoked October 13th. In the official language, he was "returned to his friends"; in the vernacular of Annapolis, he was a "bilger," the first of a long line of disappointed youths who could not meet the Navy's requirements. John Adams, J. R. Hamilton, Frank B. McKean, Ralph Chandler, and Thomas Truxtun Houston passed highly creditable examinations and were the first acting midshipmen to enter the naval school. The first three graduates were Houston, Chandler, and Hamilton, in the order named, in 1851-52. Houston died a lieutenant on the *Iroquois* in 1860; Chandler died in 1889, after becoming a rear admiral; and Hamilton resigned to enter the Confederate Navy in December, 1860, and died in his native state, South Carolina, in 1907.

Commander Buchanan made his first quarterly report January 30, 1846. Eighty-seven midshipmen had been ordered to the school. Their generally correct conduct indicated their appreciation of the new school, and their gentlemanly bearing had been favorably commented upon by strangers, but several were so far behind in their studies that they had little hope of passing their examinations.

Buchanan stated that the midshipmen were comfortably accommodated in their converted quarters, the hospital was completed and well supplied with medicine, and target practice would commence as soon as work on the batteries was completed. He requested from two to three hundred dollars for text-books for the instructors and reminded the Secretary of the advantages of having a lightly equipped sloop-of-war stationed at the school "to afford the midshipmen healthful and useful exercise in their *leisure hours* [author's italics] in performing the practical duties of seamen; in rigging and unrigging ships, sending up and down yards, etc., all of which it is very important and they should understand practically."

When Congress convened in December, 1845, Secretary Bancroft explained exactly what had been done: "Congress . . . had permitted the Department . . . to employ professors and instructors at an annual cost of $28,000.00." Migratory teachers had proved inadequate aboard ships which were not suitable places for schools. It was decided to improve the time midshipmen were ashore by collecting them in one school for instruction; this same institution could give "some preliminary instruction" to midshipmen recently appointed "before their first cruise." He then reported that a school had been organized on a "frugal plan" at Fort Severn, where Commander Buchanan had successfully adapted "simple and moderate means to a great and noble purpose." The Secretary did not need additional appropriations; he improved the method of instruction by a wiser application of money already appropriated. His straightforward report averted all congressional opposition, and the following year Congress formally approved his action by altering the phraseology of the appropriation bill to cover "repairs, improvements and instructions at Fort Severn, Annapolis, Maryland."

The war with Mexico began about six months after the
school opened. Naturally the Superintendent and midshipmen desired to go to sea. Secretary Bancroft considered
the successful establishment of the school so important that
he refused Commander Buchanan's request, explaining,
"Were it not for the important business you are now on,
you would be one of the first sent." By March, 1847, Secretary Mason, who had succeeded Bancroft, felt that
Buchanan's services could be spared and ordered him to sea
in time to participate in the capture of Tuxpan and To-
basco, Mexico.

Secretary Bancroft also dealt wisely with the midshipmen; he advanced the examinations of the 1840 date and
of the acting midshipmen from November to July, 1846,
and ordered the successful candidates to sea at once, which
gave them all an opportunity for active service. In October,
1846, he assembled at the school about one-third of the
1841 date, who were graduated in July, 1847, and were
sent to sea again, while the war was still in progress. The
second group of 1841, which reported in October, 1847,
had already seen active war service. All midshipmen of the
1840, 1841, and 1842 dates were given an opportunity to
serve at sea during the war without interrupting their
courses at Annapolis. Midshipmen grumbled about being
kept ashore at all during wartime, but the Department was
very considerate of them and established the precedent followed in all subsequent wars of graduating midshipmen
early and maintaining the Naval Academy to prepare
others. This scheme added to the burden of an already
overworked staff, but its faithful members did not com-
plain.

About fifty-six midshipmen were at Annapolis in
1846-47. They raised a fund for the first monument erected
in the grounds, in honor of the midshipmen lost during the

Mexican War; this is now known as the Mexican monument. Midshipmen of the Mexican War were in their late twenties, only a few years younger than many of the captains of 1812, and they displayed the spirit and enterprise of their predecessors. All midshipmen volunteered for duty with the naval battery which breached the walls of Vera Cruz; it was the most exposed position. They cast lots for the privilege. Among the winners assigned the coveted post was Midshipman T. B. Shubrick, who was killed at his post.[3] It required ten days to land this battery and only four days to make the first and largest breach in the forts attacked and to silence every Mexican gun within range. Those continuous drills at the batteries during thirty years of peace kept American gunners efficient. Three midshipmen were drowned—Clemson and Hynson when the brig *Somers* was lost, and, when a boat from the *Mississippi* capsized, Wingate Pillsbury, who was assisting a sailor to a more secure position on the overturned boat.

The landing operations up the rivers of Tuxpan and Panuco appealed to the genius of midshipmen. Foxhall Parker landed a 32-pound gun from the *Potomac* by running a boat ashore and cutting the bottom out of it. Midshipman Young, acting as a mounted courier liaison officer between the Army and Navy, inadvertently led a charge when his calvary horse answered the bugle call. His messmates in the steerage asserted that Young led all the Army officers.

To avoid congressional and naval opposition, Secretary

[3] Midshipman Shubrick came from a distinguished naval family. John Templar Shubrick, the eldest of four brothers who served in the Navy, entered in 1806, was on the *Constitution* when she escaped the British squadron and when she took the *Guerrière* and the *Java;* was first lieutenant on the *Hornet* and on the *President* with Decatur. All the Shubricks served with credit and most with distinction. They were related to the Draytons and Haynes.

Bancroft had accepted practically impossible conditions for the naval school. His real preoccupation was his unfinished history of the United States, and after serving as Secretary zealously and intelligently for eighteen months, he sailed for England, leaving his successor, Secretary Mason, struggling with the almost insuperable difficulties arising from the irregular admission, attendance, and graduation at the naval school, which differed little from the one at Philadelphia except in the stricter discipline enforced by Buchanan. In justice to some who preceded Secretary Bancroft and to those who came after him and completed his unfinished work, definite limitations should be placed on any claim of George Bancroft to be considered the sole founder of the Naval Academy.

It was a physical impossibility to classify some of the incoming students without creating special classes for individuals. Commander George P. Upshur, who succeeded Commander Buchanan, did not enforce the strict discipline of his predecessor but, assisted by a devoted staff, he held the school together, meeting each situation as best he could until 1849, fearing that proposals for changes might create opposition sufficient to destroy the school. By that time friends of the school felt strong enough to initiate changes, step by step. The course was extended from one year to two years, as originally recommended by the Board of Examiners in 1845. Then came three years at sea, to be followed by two more years at school prior to final examinations for lieutenant. This change provided four years of instruction, which was the goal of Professor Chauvenet and others. Examinations for extrance were held in October, insuring simultaneous entrance of students. The naval school was placed directly under the Chief of Bureau of Ordnance and Hydrography. Its name was changed to Naval Academy in 1850. The Superintendent continued in immediate command, with a Commandant of Midshipmen to act as executive officer and instructor in naval tactics and practical seamanship. An acting midshipman was required to spend two years at the Academy and six months at sea before being warranted a midshipman. A uniform was designed for acting midshipmen, and all midshipmen were required to wear uniforms in the Academy. A sloop-of-war was promised to the Academy to cruise the midshipmen and practise them at great guns during the summer.

This plan was scarcely agreed upon before the advocates of the Academy felt strong enough to make another change. The Academic Board recommended that the four-year course at the Naval Academy be consecutive with a practice cruise each summer. Graduates would become passed midshipmen and would spend two years continuously at sea, returning to the Academy for examinations for lieutenant. In October the Board of Examiners concurred, and Secretary Graham approved the change on November 15, 1851.

While the Academy was crystallizing into its present form, the method of appointing midshipmen was radically altered. Until 1845 most midshipmen had been appointed from the Middle Atlantic States, usually on the recommendation of some relative or friend in the Navy or with influence in the Navy Department. These naval clans proved distinct assets in the early days of the Navy, but they introduced nepotism, and the preponderance of officers from the central seaboard would in time have created a sectional Navy. In 1845 Congress provided that thereafter all midshipmen should be appointed in proportion to the members of the House of Representatives, and that each appointee must be an actual resident of the state from which he is appointed. In 1852 it further provided that midshipmen could be appointed only on recommendations of their Congressmen. The method of appointment has made the officer personnel representative of the nation, and the Navy a national institution. Every Congressional District, every large city, and many towns in the country have representatives among the officers of the Navy.

Midshipmen Practice Cruises

COMMODORE BAINBRIDGE, who sponsored the first practice cruises in 1817, probably obtained the idea from the French Navy. Subsequently, Commodore Rodgers, Lieutenants Maury and Powell, Chaplain George Jones, Professor Chauvenet, and others included a practice cruise as an essential feature of their plans for educating midshipmen ashore. West Point cadets encamped each summer to gain experience in the field; the analogy between a summer camp for military cadets and a practice cruise for midshipmen was obvious. An Army officer was on the 1849 board which recommended changes in the naval school; he may have repeated the suggestion, but the idea of a practice cruise for midshipmen did not originate in the Army.

Lieutenant, soon after Commander, Thomas Tingey Craven, by common consent one of the finest sailor-men in the Navy, commanded the first practice cruise and seven of the nine succeeding ones. Commander Craven began with a short cruise inside Chesapeake Bay on the steamer *John Hancock*, and later in the same summer he embarked the midshipmen for a cruise on the ship-rigged sloop-of-war *Preble* along the coast of New England. The summer of 1852 he extended the cruise in the *Preble* to the Azores, Madeira, and the Canaries, returning via St. Thomas, West Indies. In 1853 in the *Preble* he included a visit to Coruña, Spain. It quickly became apparent that the division of a midshipman's year's work into eight months at school and three to four months at sea on ships whose paramount duty was training midshipmen made it possible to educate midshipmen more systematically ashore and simultaneously to train them at sea. The officers of the Naval Academy were confident that they had found the solution to the baffling problem of preparing young Americans to be junior officers. They extended the summer cruises to include one European port except in 1855 and 1856, when Lieutenant Green cruised along the New England coast. Commander Craven returned to the academy and commanded the practice ships of 1857, 1858, 1859, and 1860. More than any other officer, he developed the organization, routine, drills, and exercises of midshipmen practice cruises which persist to the present day.

The organization of midshipmen in gun crews facilitated the transition from shore to ship. For a cruise, midshipmen were divided into six gun crews: gun crews one to four manned the four batteries; the fifth, the powder division, supplied the ammunition to the guns; the sixth, the master's (later the navigator's) division, furnished the quartermasters, helmsmen, battle lookouts, and special details. Accustomed to working and drilling ashore in gun crews, there was no confusion when midshipmen with their sea-bags embarked on the training ships. Arriving aboard, each midshipman was given a ship's number in the watch, quarter, and station bill [1] which assigned him to the first or third section of the starboard watch, or the second or fourth section of the port watch. The same num-

---

[1] A large diagram of the ship's organization on which, after each number, appear the name, the rating, the duties, the mess table, and the hammock hooks of every sailor aboard. Copies of the watch, quarter, and station bill are hung on bulletin boards in various parts of the ship, so that every man can familiarize himself with his duties and his place to eat and sleep.

ber fixed his station at all evolutions under sail and his battle station at boarding an enemy ship or resisting hostile boarders; it designated the bilge pump he manned to free the ship from water if she were hulled during battle or stranded on a reef; it determined the fire pump he manned or the hose he led out if the ship took fire. The same magic number located his locker, in which he could just squeeze his clothes and toilet articles; the mess table at which he ate, and his seat at the table; the pair of hooks on which he swung his hammock, and the netting in which he stowed his hammock—after he had learned to take seven taut turns at equal distances and had tucked the clews in neatly.

Before they reached the Atlantic, all midshipmen were exercised at their battle stations and the emergency drills— fire, collision, and abandon ship. Midshipmen were shown the ladders and the routes they must use going to and returning from the scene of an imaginary fire or collision; their duties in fighting the flames and getting the collision mat over the side; the equipment they supplied and the boat they manned if it were necessary to abandon ship. After every drill each midshipman returned the equipment he had supplied, secured the gear he had cast loose, and fell in with his own gun crew in its part of the ship.

Midshipmen were divided equally between the port and starboard watch. The starboard watch was subdivided into the first and third sections, the port into the second and fourth. Between 8 A.M. and 8 P.M. an entire watch was on deck, available for duty. During the forenoon and afternoon watches midshipmen were four hours on and four off duty. All three night watches lasted four hours, but only a section—one-quarter of the midshipmen—was on watch at one time. Thus a midshipman was on deck six hours in day watches, and four hours three nights out of four; the fourth he enjoyed an "all night" in his hammock. When on watch, midshipmen answered all special calls such as trimming the windsails, wooding or coaling the galley, and laying up the gear, but their primary duty was to be ready to man all gear in bracing the yards, in making, furling, or reefing sails, or any evolution such as tacking, wearing, or working ship.

Besides their day and night watches, midshipmen were given daily drills. In the forenoon, the watch on deck spent an hour and a half aloft, reefing, furling, and unbending sails, sending up and down yards, and making and taking in sail. After these sail drills, from 10:30 to 11:30 A.M. and again from 1 to 3 P.M., the watch on deck was employed in knotting, splicing, strapping blocks, and fitting rigging. The watch below studied navigation from 2 to 2:30, and both watches were exercised at the batteries at 4 P.M. Each midshipman was practised in steering, heaving the lead, and calculating the ship's speed by "heaving the log." There was little leisure, but there were no shore distractions. Midshipmen were naturally active, and usually thrived on the strenuous régime. Occasionally there was an outbreak of some juvenile disease like measles, and on one cruise, through laundry sent to washerwomen in Madeira, the midshipmen caught the Portuguese "itch" and scratched themselves across the Atlantic. They never suffered from insomnia, and would fall asleep the instant they swung themselves into their hammocks.

The training of midshipmen was the paramount duty of a practice ship. Heavy weather altered but did not interfere with the daily routine of exercises; during gales, midshipmen reefed topsails under the prevailing conditions; if topsails were torn, midshipmen shifted topsails. They took great pride in becoming competent seamen, and first-class men vied with each other for the honor of passing the weather earing when the topsails were reefed.[2] As long as they cruised in sailing ships midshipmen worked alongside seamen on the yards, in the tops, and tending and manning the gear on deck. Later, when they made practice cruises on steamers, they heaved coal with the coal passers, cleaned fires with the firemen, and, when they had learned to start and stop a pump and to watch the water gage and the safety valve, they were allowed to tend water in the boiler. In the engine-rooms they learned to feel a rapidly revolving crank pin without losing a finger, to check the temperature of the thrust bearings, to regulate the feed pumps, and to watch the pressure gages. As they gained experience, they were allowed to work the throttle valves slowly back and forth to warm up the engines. There was no idleness in port; midshipmen not on leave were exercised at boats under oars and sails, carrying out anchors, and performing other drills not feasible at sea.

Some midshipmen learned sooner than others, but within a few weeks they all found their sea legs, developed an astonishing immunity to seasickness, and could go on the double to any part of the ship. They learned that there was a place for everything aboard ship, and that lack of space made it necessary that each thing be kept in its place. The unvarying naval routine, the repeated drills and exercises, the tidiness and orderliness of the ship itself, the homely but sage advice of veteran seamen and petty officers, the friendly counsel of warrant officers, and the more formal precepts and examples of commissioned officers insensibly molded the habits of midshipmen, most of whom acquired that sixth sense of order which is the foundation of a man-of-war's man.

Under supervision of officers, midshipmen of the senior

[2] A difficult and dangerous operation, executed on the end of the yard-arm.

class performed all the duties of lieutenants. Groups of them were assigned in rotation to the navigator to do a "day's work" in navigation, fixing the ship's position at 8 A.M., noon, and 8 P.M. daily. In approaching Cape Henry in 1858, the First Class located the *Plymouth's* position accurately; the lighthouse was sighted dead ahead. Captain Craven reported, "I have never known a more perfect landfall." First Classmen, under the watchful eye of the captain or first lieutenant, were allowed to tack, wear, or boxhaul ship. It was a great moment in the life of a midshipman when he first tacked ship, and if he brought her around smartly enough to earn a gruff, "Well done, Mr. Gish!" from his captain, Midshipman Joe Gish was elated. First Classmen, under the supervision of the regular officer of the deck, were habitually in charge of the watch, and carried out the ship's routine.

Man overboard drill was a regular evolution. With the *Plymouth* sailing at eight knots, the life-buoy was let go, the life-boat lowered, the buoy recovered, the boat brought alongside and hoisted, and the *Plymouth* away and standing on her course under sail in seven minutes and twenty seconds from the time of the first alarm.

The practice cruises continued substantially as developed by Captain Craven until 1909, when sailing ships made their last appearance. Usually the First and Third Classmen cruised together on a sailing ship, the Second on a steamer, and the entering Fourth Class did "knotting and splicing" and held boat drill at Annapolis until the scholastic year began on October 1st.

The practice cruises soon proved that midshipmen acquired more valuable sea training in a three months' cruise especially organized for their development than during a year at sea on a regular man-of-war. The effect on the midshipmen was transmitted to the Naval Academy; midshipmen acquired the habits and customs of a man-of-war's man. None was so salty as a Third Classman after his first cruise; he rolled when he walked, his nautical vocabulary was wonderful and freely displayed for the benefit of admiring girls back home, and if he had managed to have a boatswain's-mate tattoo his forearm with a mermaid or a dolphin, he was truly a deep-sea sailor. Their exaggerated mannerisms, resulting from their first cruise, arose from their honest pride in becoming seafaring gentlemen and their determination never again to be landlubbers. This professional pride helped the officers preserve the naval spirit at the Academy. Midshipmen habitually took more interest in professional subjects and were inspired to become first class sailor-men. The cruise accustomed the young American to the habits of a seaman: to feel at home aboard ship; to stow himself and his belongings in a small compass; to sleep soundly in a hammock, unconscious of the normal ship noises; to live at close quarters with the same shipmates day after day and eat canned vegetables, kippered herring, and corned beef without becoming dyspeptic and querulous; to use the proper gangway ladder; to refrain from whistling and boisterous behavior; to conform naturally to the etiquette of a man-of-war. These habits were acquired unconsciously, and they constituted the essential difference between a college-bred landlubber and a promising young midshipman.

There was no practice cruise in 1861, but cruises were made in 1862, 1863, and 1864. During the war, practice ships were sometimes sent in search of Confederate raiders. The *Macedonian*, on her return from Europe in 1863, disguised herself as a Spanish merchantman in the hope of luring the C.S.S. *Alabama* within reach of her guns. After the return to Annapolis in 1865, the *Macedonian*, *Savannah*, and *Dale*, full-rigged ships, the steamers *Winnepec* and *Marblehead*, the ferry boat *Wyandank*, and the monitors *Tonawanda* and *Amphitrite* were used as practice ships. The *Constitution* was a school ship and the *Santee* was the gunnery ship, and for a time the *Dale*, *Marion*, *Savannah*, and *Macedonian* were added to the list of station ships. The famous *Constellation* made her first midshipman cruise in 1871, and until 1893 this stately frigate, whose war record was excelled only by the *Constitution*, made every cruise, sometimes in company with other ships, more often alone. It was altogether fitting that "Tom" Truxtun's flagship should have been employed for so many years to carry out his idea that midshipmen must qualify themselves for commanding seamen by themselves becoming competent seamen.

The *Bancroft*, named for Secretary Bancroft, was constructed especially for cruising midshipmen. She mounted different types of guns, with various gun-mounts and assorted breech-blocks; her engine-room and fire-rooms carried as many different kinds of pumps, auxiliary machines, and boilers as her enthusiastic sponsors could crowd into her hull. They forgot the midshipmen, who could scarcely find room aboard. Much had been expected of her, but she was a failure. After cruising midshipmen in 1894, 1895, and 1896, she was transferred to the Caribbean for gunboat duty.

The successor of the *Constellation*, the *Monongahela*, had a first-class war record. In the Battle of Mobile Bay she was the first to ram the Confederate ram *Tennessee*, turning the tables on her opponent; not content with this, she returned and repeated her feat. After the war her engines were removed and she was given full sail power, but, designed for steam, she was always a dull sailer. Competent officers alleged that she had never been tacked without gaining sternboard. During the summer cruise of 1899 Captain Charles T. Hutchins, 1866, commanded. In a gale off the entrance to the English Channel the midshipmen reefed topsails, and then, taking advantage of the strong breezes in the rear of the gale, Hutchins sailed into Plymouth to an anchor in a manner entirely worthy of "Tom" Craven of the *Preble*. Five days' leave and a pound for every day was granted the midshipmen, who embarked on a special train for London and saw much of the big city in those five days. London Tower was the favorite place, with Westminster Abbey and the British Museum close seconds. Madame Tussaud's wax-works were not forgotten, nor were the theaters and music halls overlooked. How those five pounds stretched was marvelous.

On the night of the Fourth of July all hands turned up at Edna May's "Belle of New York," and when she made a pun about the *Monongahela*, they cheered wildly. A few lucky souls were invited to her dressing-room between the acts, and one red-cheeked Third Classman claimed that in honor of the Fourth, Edna gave him a kiss. He was the envy of the ship's company during the return voyage. After leaving Madeira, the *Monongahela* lost ten precious days becalmed. Determined to regain them, Captain Hutchins directed that all sail be carried at all times. During a squall an officer of the deck took in the royals and topgallant-sails, and the captain ordered them reset, saying that he had spare yards and sail. Every day lost at sea came off September leave. The midshipmen made a hero of Captain Hutchins.

The *Monongahela* was succeeded by the specially constructed *Chesapeake* in 1900. Like the *Bancroft*, the *Chesapeake* proved too small. She cruised midshipmen until 1907, when she was relegated to a school ship and her name changed to *Severn*, to allow the history of the first *Chesapeake* to drop into oblivion. Farragut's famous *Hartford* made the last sailing practice cruise in 1909, fifty-eight years after Tom Craven's first cruise in the *Preble*. Against the opposition of some die-hards the Navy Department decided that time could not be spared for cruises under sail. Probably all old-timers regretted the necessity for eliminating sailing cruises, but even the remote possibility of having to sail a captured prize into harbor could not justify the time consumed in teaching midshipmen to sail a full-rigged ship.

By 1904 the number of midshipmen had increased until it required a squadron of the North Atlantic Fleet to embark them, including the battleships *Indiana* and *Texas*, the monitors *Arkansas, Florida,* and *Nevada,* the *Hartford,* and seven destroyers. Since that time the increasing number of midshipmen has added to the difficulties of providing ships to cruise them. The Department tried distributing midshipmen among ships of the fleet and trusting to the fleet officers to train them in addition to carrying on their regular ship's duties. The plan failed; the demands of the fleet took precedence over training midshipmen, just as it had done in the Mediterranean Squadron in the 1830's. The Department now assigns to certain ships from the fleet the task of training midshipmen, which gives midshipmen precedence over fleet training. Midshipmen are sometimes transferred during a cruise from one type of ship to another in order to gain additional experience, but the bulk of the First and Third Class are trained on battleships, and the Second Class on destroyers.

Since the Civil War, midshipmen have received some instruction in marine engineering, and there has always been a steamer among the practice ships. During the era of a separate Engineering Corps, engineering instruction for midshipmen preparing for deck duties was elementary, but the cadet engineers specialized in engineering subjects dur-

ing the academic year and made practice cruises on the
sea-going tugs *Miles Standish, Mayflower,* or *Fortune.*
Their organization was derived from the one used in sailing ships for midshipmen. Engineer cadets were divided
into watches and stationed in the fire- and engine-rooms,
as midshipmen were stationed at guns and in the rigging. In
addition to standing watch and learning to fire a boiler and
run an engine by actual practise, cadet engineers were required to keep rough notes and sketch-books in which they
sketched free hand, and later drew to scale, the steam and
water pipes, the drainage system, the boilers, pumps, and
engines of their own ships. They were rotated in the fire-
and engine-rooms until they were at home in every part
of the engineering department. Their summer itinerary
took them first to the Washington Navy Yard to inspect
the gun foundry, next to the Norfolk Navy Yard, and
then along the coast as far as Boston Navy Yard, visiting
private shipbuilding plants, and the heavy industries such as
foundries, rolling mills, and machine shops. In 1875 forty
major shore establishments were visited. The system employed for engineers was in every respect modeled after the
practice cruises of Commander T. T. Craven.

In addition to practice ships, sail and steam, there have
been stationed at the Academy from time to time school
and gunnery ships. The most famous was the *Constitution,*
which arrived in August, 1860, and served as a mother ship
and instruction hall for the Fourth Classmen. Her presence
was a continual reminder of early naval history. The
Fourth Classmen quartered on her were brought up exactly as if she were at sea, and this practice was followed
when the *Constitution* was transferred to Newport.

The ship longest associated with the Naval Academy was
the 44-gun frigate *Santee.* Named for a noble river in South
Carolina, her keel was laid in Portsmouth, New Hampshire,

THE U. S. SLOOP-OF-WAR "PREBLE," FIRST NAVAL ACADEMY PRACTICE
SHIP

NAVAL ACADEMY PRACTICE SHIPS "SANTEE," "CONSTITUTION," AND
"JOHN ADAMS"

in 1820. She began life as a wayward sister, a "political ship" kept on the stocks to provide work for prospective voters during the last weeks before hotly contested national elections. She was not commissioned until June, 1861. After fifteen months' blockade duty in the Gulf of Mexico, she appeared at Newport in October, 1862, and joined the *Constitution* as a school ship for midshipmen. She sheltered, drilled, and disciplined fifty classes of midshipmen before laying down her heavy task. In April, 1912, her slowly opening seams gaped a little more widely and she settled lower and lower until her frames rested comfortably in the soft mud of the Severn. She died in her sleep.[3] Her brief war record could not compare with her famous sisters *Constitution* and *Constellation;* she managed to capture a couple of schooners attempting to run the blockade; she had been prostituted by political henchmen for forty years; yet accounts of the *Santee* fill pages in *Shakings, Fag Ends, Junk,* and the *Lucky Bag,*[4] for the humbler *Santee* enjoyed long and intimate relations with midshipmen. On her decks many learned to sleep in hammocks, not without risk, as told in *Junk,* 1889:

> You no sooner get to dozing
> And on Morpheus get a mash
> When some one cuts your foot-rope
> And down you come "Kersmash."

During the Civil War, midshipmen at Newport ate their breakfasts on her berth deck by smelly oil lamps, which faintly illuminated the mess tables, after their appetites had been sharpened by a brisk run over the mastheads in the crisp winter air.

[3] C. S. Alden, "The *Santee:* An Appreciation," *Naval Institute* (June, 1913).
[4] Of these early midshipman publications, only the *Lucky Bag* has survived.

Traditionally, the *Santee's* bedbugs were the Navy's most voracious, her rats the largest, and her cockroaches the most intelligent. Imprisoned midshipmen whiled away the time coaching the roaches to race; they even steeplechased over the lee scupper. In 1866 the *Santee* became Gunnery Ship *Santee*, and at her 24-pound guns midshipmen were trained at target practice.

Embryo poets were often inspired by the *Santee*. The desperate condition of one midshipman confined for smoking is poetically rendered:

> Must I give up the fragrant weed
> And of good comfort feel the need,
> Or pace the deck firm as a rock,
> Upon the ship down at the dock?
> *Santee.*

During Captain Ramsay's vigorous régime the *Santee* harbored its most distinguished prisoners. Almost an entire First Class was quartered aboard the "prison ship." Their affection is revealed in verse:

> When in trouble and disgrace
> Who protects the hardened case
> Who will, with parental care
> Shelter, shield and keep him there?
> The *Santee.*

Before being broken up for the copper on her bottom, the *Santee* inspired an ode among the talented class of 1881 which began:

> Oh, noble mass of wood, and guns, and ropes, and sails,
> Poetic remnant, left by well met gales.

The *Santee* had many proud moments. Admiral Porter showed his comrades-in-arms, Generals Grant and Sherman, around the famous old ship, explaining how she shel-

tered her web-footed warriors, and before June Week she
was holystoned and polished till she fairly shone for the
benefit of the Board of Examiners. Her 32-pounders were
cast loose and provided with real round shot with which
expert midshipmen pointers bombarded Greenberry Point
across the Severn River.

The Department has kept up the original practice of
routing new ships to the Academy, thus keeping midshipmen informed of the latest developments of naval archi-
tecture. After the Spanish-American War it sent the small
torpedo boat *Manley* to Annapolis, where it became better
known as the judge's boat for all crew races. The *Holland*,
our first modern submarine, after two visits in 1901 and
1902, became a regular school ship for the midshipmen.
To this was added the *Vesuvius*, with its dynamite-throw-
ing guns from which so much was expected during the
Spanish-American War. Midshipmen are still instructed
in the various types of ships; learning by seeing and doing
is the approved Annapolis method.

During the present emergency no capital ships, cruisers,
or destroyers are available. Midshipmen are cruised in sub-
chasers or other small craft.

Ordinarily the summer practice cruise commences at the
end of June Week. The midshipmen of the new Third
and First Class embark in a squadron of battleships for a
summer of practice cruise. Until the European War of
1939 it was customary to include three or four ports in
western Europe. During the cruise midshipmen of the
Third Class perform the duties usually done by seamen;
they scrub the decks, fire the boilers, operate the engines,
steer the ship, and familiarize themselves with life aboard
ship. Throughout the cruise they have practical instruction
in gunnery, navigation, seamanship, electrical and marine
engineering, and radio. The high point of the cruise is the

midshipman target practise, when they fire the 5-inch and the 12- or 14-inch guns.

The Second Class is divided into three sections. Each section spends one month aboard a destroyer cruising along the Atlantic coast. The midshipmen act as junior officers of the deck and stand watch in the engine- and fire-rooms. The two remaining months are spent at the Academy where Second Classmen are given practical instruction in aviation, engineering, navigation, and seamanship.

The midshipmen of the First Class cruise in the battle-ship squadron with the Third, but their duties are prac-tically those of junior commissioned officers. They alternate duty on deck and in the engine-room and do a day's work of navigation just as Commander Craven's midshipmen did on the cruise of the *Preble*.

The colorful tumult of June Week reaches its high point for the graduating class when they give three cheers for those they leave behind and sail midshipmen caps high in the air with the last note. The Senior Class is graduated! Long live the Senior Class! The next day they embark on their last midshipman cruise to get the finishing touches in seamanship, ordnance and navigation, and steam en-gineering; to stand their last midshipman watches and con-tribute a bit to the Academy by assisting in training the Third Classmen who accompany them. In rotation they spend one month doing navigation, another in deck duties, and the third in practical engineering.

Midshipmen who cruised with Commander Craven on the *Preble* would feel at home with the midshipmen of to-day on the battleship *Arkansas*. They would shoot the same stars at morning and evening twilights, measure the altitude of the sun as it neared the prime vertical, and follow it more and more assiduously as it neared the meridian at local apparent noon. Craven's midshipmen would prefer the modern sextant with its telescopic attachments and sharply etched vernier; they would be puzzled at first by the greatly enlarged Bowditch and by Dutton's new and extensive treatise on navigation with its many strange formulas. But they would recognize the elements of the astronomical triangle and quickly see that the formulas were only new ways of determining elements of that famous triangle as it patiently pursues its endless journeys through the heavens. The midshipmen of 1851 would need much instruction in Weems' aerial navigation; in return they could show the modern class how to work a "lunar" and obtain the longitude.

The 1851 midshipmen would welcome the patent logs which make it unnecessary to heave the "chip log" every hour to get the ship's speed, and would be much impressed with the fathometer which automatically sounds and records the ocean depths; it was an all-hands job to use the "deep sea (dipsy) lead" in the fifties. They would understand the principle of the gyroscopic compass and rejoice at its accuracy, for the magnetic compass required constant care. They would have difficultiy in concealing their amazement at the "dead reckoning" machine which continuously plots the ship's position on the chart. Craven's midshipmen might be astonished at the speed of destroyers and cruisers, but they would not be confused. Sailing ships required instantaneous mental reactions to constantly changing situations; sailors, then as now, always had their wits about them.

The midshipmen of 1851, accompanying those of to-day to the anti-destroyer batteries, would quickly get the idea of the training and elevating gear and would be enthusiastic over the efficient mechanism which handles the heaviest guns with ease. They knew the batteries of their time, from the 6- to the 42-pounders, and could fire anything from a carronade to a howitzer, afloat or ashore. The present-day midshipmen would have some difficulty in explaining, and his brother of 1851 would have more difficulty in understanding, the fire-control system used against hostile aircraft—that superhuman instrument which almost pulls the pointer onto a fast-moving airplane. Both classes would content themselves with knowing how to work it and leave to ordnance experts the explanation of how its compli-cated mechanism is actuated. In the main battery turrets, midshipmen of 1851 would soon understand the explana-tion of salvo firing and, with modest pride, would tell how they had been instructed by the veterans of 1812 to fire 32-pounders in salvo "on the down roll" which sent 22 round shot crashing through the sides of enemy frigates and sloops-of-war. Two hours would determine a naval engagement in those days.

Craven's midshipmen would be taken aback when they visited the engine-rooms and fire-rooms; they were familiar with the boilers and engines of the *John Hancock* and were prepared for improvements. Prophets were predict-ing that sails would give way to steam, but the oil-burning steam generators—formerly called boilers—and the smooth-running almost silent turbines in no way resembled the engineering plant which drove the *Hancock* through the water at seven to eight knots. Craven's midshipmen could show a modern class how to stow a locker and take care of their possessions; which gangway to use; the etiquette of the quarterdeck; how to lash and carry a hammock, to muster a watch, to keep a bright lookout and to see that the watch on the forecastle was alert, to belay or lead out a boat falls, to man and lower a life-boat. In fact, the mid-shipmen of the *Plymouth* could challenge their successors on the *Arkansas* to equal their 1858 record in dropping and recovering a life-buoy, hoisting and securing the boat, and resuming the course and speed.

The old and new classes would mingle indistinguishably around the galley in the morning watch and regale themselves with the morning coffee. Their sweaters, blouses, and reefers would differ, but their trousers would roll up in the same manner. The decks of the practice ships would be different, but the "holystones" would be the same. The same sand and canvas would be used on paint work; the First Classmen would keep the same fatherly eye on the Third Class to see that holystoning was properly done. The mates of the decks would find "clothes adrift on the berth decks"; the junior officer of the watch would have to report the same proportion of underclassmen "late to muster" or "inattentive on drill." There would be about the same amount of grumbling and skylarking at the mess tables. The middies of 1851 would be astonished at the modern menus and the gallons of milk consumed by their successors. Their captain sometimes had a nanny goat, which gave him some milk for his morning coffee, but no midshipman aspired to such luxury. There would be the same last-minute hustle to get navigation and seamanship books ready to turn in to the officer in charge; and worst of all, that dreary inevitable midshipman's journal, that has defied every modern improvement.

The classes of 1851 and the present would have much in common, for they are products of the same daily routine of drills and exercises. They would be drawn together by their interest in three fundamental professional subjects—navigation, seamanship, and gunnery; they are reared by and on the sea; they are blood brothers, descendants of the same breed of sailor-men who, in the seventeenth century, regarded their homes along the Atlantic coast as places to shelter their women and children while they went to sea.

From the Mexican War to the Civil War

☆

THE presence of the Naval Academy at Annapolis, its accessible harbor, and its proximity to the national capital soon made Annapolis Roads the official gateway to Washington. In the spring of 1852, midshipmen of the Royal Netherlands Navy on the frigate *Prince of Orange*, the forerunner of men-of-war from many navies, anchored in the Roads for an exchange of official and social visits. In the autumn the steam frigate *Mississippi*, flying the broad pennant of Commodore M. C. Perry, arrived. During his visit the commodore made final arrangements for his voyage to the Far East, and President Fillmore, Secretary Kennedy, and other distinguished officials came aboard to wish him success in his forthcoming effort to open Japan to western trade. The Academy officials took advantage of the *Mississippi's* visit to conduct the midshipmen over our first sea-going steam frigate.

It was not all work for the midshipmen of the fifties; they were given a holiday when a circus came to town, and before 1855 they had a bowling alley and a boat-house, which suggest bowling teams and boat crews. During 1846 a formal ball was given, which became an annual affair, often attended by the highest government officials. Informal dances, called "hops," were frequently given by midshipmen, dancing being one of the exercises taught at the Academy.

Dewey and Mahan have given different accounts of

Naval Academy life in the fifties. Dewey said it was a steady, hard grind, with no amusements except "stag" hops; Mahan describes many hops, with girls in plenty, and emphasizes the friendly relations between midshipmen and families of officers and professors, and the sociable, humanizing atmosphere of the Academy. Dewey was the first of his family to enter the naval service; he probably had few friends among the officers and professors and was certainly unaccustomed to discipline. Mahan, who had been raised in the stricter régime at West Point, did not find Annapolis irksome, and on account of his family he had numerous friends among the officers and professors at Annapolis. Dewey was obliged to study harder than Mahan, who was better prepared when he entered and learned easily. Undoubtedly Dewey found life at the Academy less pleasant than did Mahan, who was welcomed at most of the homes of the officers, easily stood second in his class, and spent much of his time reading novels and flirting with the Annapolis girls.

Dewey states in his autobiography that what his class knew they knew well. The system of daily recitations and relentless monthly and semi-annual examinations permitted "no subterfuge of mental agility" and no superficial familiarity with a variety of subjects to take the place of exact knowledge of a limited number of subjects. And although he found his four years at the Academy at times very bleak, as many other midshipmen have done, Dewey states flatly: "I think I may say that no four-year course in any institution gives its students more in mind and character than the school from which the officers of our navy are drawn." [1]

---

[1] After graduation Dewey served on the *Wabash*, flagship of Commodore La Vallette, who had distinguished himself at Lake Champlain under Commodore Thomas Macdonough. Subsequently he was execu-

Dewey stated in his autobiography that hazing was rife; Mahan is equally positive that it did not exist. Dewey wrote from memory many years afterwards, Mahan from letters he had written as a midshipman. Other evidence supports Mahan's statement. There was considerable class distinction, and Senior Classmen did not report violations of the regulations by their classmates, but hazing of underclassmen came in either at Newport or when Admiral Porter tried to change the Naval Academy into a military "college" in 1865-69.

In the autumn of 1848 the Superintendent delivered letters of reprimand to three midshipmen who participated in a duel within the grounds of the naval school, probably the last at the school. During the late 1850's personal difficulties between midshipmen began to be settled by pre-arranged fights with bare fists under an American version of the Queensberry rules. Later, gloves were worn. With or without gloves, the rules were simple. Opponents must be of approximately the same weight; if there was a substantial difference in size, a friend substituted for one of the belligerents. If the fight was between midshipmen of different classes, class officers arranged the preliminaries and provided a substitute when necessary. Contests usually took place just before reveille, and frequently the contestants knew little of boxing; they simply slugged, with little effort to ward off blows. After a contest both contestants needed a few stitches from a surgeon.

The favorite midshipman song of the 1850's had a line, "Take your tobacco lively, And pass the plug around," and Dewey writes that few midshipmen resisted the in-

---

tive officer on the *Mississippi* in Farragut's squadron. As a young officer Dewey served under two flag officers who had served under Truxtun and Preble. Many officers still on the active list served under Dewey. The naval succession is direct and unbroken.

A BIRD'S EYE VIEW OF ANNAPOLIS IN THE LATE 1850's

vitation to enjoy the famous "Navy plug." Dewey admits indulging as a midshipman, but later he gave it up. The custom was so prevalent that the Academy authorities offered extra privileges to midshipmen who abstained from chewing. The custom persisted nevertheless, and several years after the Civil War a superintendent enjoyed the famous Navy plug and would unblushingly help himself to a generous quid whenever the spirit moved him, heedless of the horror of more refined observers. After the Spanish-American War, many of the senior officers continued the habit at sea, and they nearly all displayed a phobia against cigarettes, which began to compete with pipes and cigars. One particular captain would sit aft, in an easy chair on the snowy quarter-deck of his monitor, descanting on the filthiness of cigarettes, pausing only when it was necessary to expectorate in the general direction of a highly polished spit-kid, the pride of the quarter-deck division, the captain's own. Much practise had made him extremely accurate, but in his indignant denunciation of the filthy cigarette habit he sometimes neglected to aim carefully, with disastrous results to the quarter-deck.

In 1856, the new steam frigate *Merrimac* visited Annapolis and was inspected by the midshipmen. President Pierce came down to attend the Naval Ball and visited the *Merrimac*. Pierce later returned to Annapolis Roads on the frigate *Wabash*, and was again entertained at the Academy. Midshipmen were also escorted on a tour of the *Wabash*. At this early date the Department began ordering new ships to the Academy so that midshipmen could see the latest developments in naval construction. On March 4, 1857, the first football made its appearance. Officers, instructors, and midshipmen kicked it around the parade ground; its instant appeal to all hands explains football's premier position in college athletics. In the following spring the class of 1858 organized the first midshipman literary society and named it for Lawrence.

During its first decade and a half, the Naval Academy graduated fifteen or more midshipmen annually. The number slowly increased to twenty-five in 1860. Officers at sea were skeptical of the new school but they welcomed the youngsters into the service, broke them in aboard ship, and asked many questions about the school. Flag Lieutenant Magaw of the Home Squadron expressed the misgivings of some officers to Midshipman Mahan in 1858; Magaw thought it was a mistake not to permit midshipmen to learn to drink liquor at the Academy, for when they went to sea and visited a foreign ship they would not be able to hold their own with foreigners. Magaw believed that too much time was given to French and Spanish—if he got into difficulty with a foreigner, he would send the despatch in the American language—and he feared midshipmen were not given enough seamanship. Magaw stated with pride that he could work alongside the ablest seaman on his ship, and do anything the sailor could do, and do it better. Such accomplishments can be carried to extremes, but our earliest officers earned their commissions by excelling their men in all branches of seamanship and gunnery. The obvious professional competence of officers soon gained the respect and eventually the ready obedience of their men.

Graduates of the Academy in the period prior to the Civil War proved their professional fitness, and when the problem of enlarging the Navy arose in 1861, the senior officers decided to promote the junior officers recently graduated and to graduate the midshipmen at the Academy early. Commodore Dupont was one of the officers responsible for the decision. The Board was convinced that midshipmen were better acquainted than merchant officers would be with the organization, battery, and equipment of a man-of-war and that because of their youth they possessed greater ability to assimilate the military characteristics of the naval profession. The little cherub aloft who watches over the American Navy established the Naval Academy at just the right moment. If it had been established earlier, the characteristics of the naval officers who formed it would not have been fixed and they would not have established a proper academy; if it had been later, the expanded Navy of the Civil War would have been filled with officers of the merchant marine lacking naval discipline and training, and the Navy would have passed through another difficult period of adjustment.

The eras 1798-1818 and 1852-1861 profoundly influenced our Navy. During the first period naval officers recruited from our merchant marine established our Navy on a sound foundation. They had a more accurate appreciation of the future of the nation and the Navy than contemporary statesmen. These former merchant officers realized that the Navy must be organized upon a different basis and, without abandoning their own seafaring virtues, discarded merchant ship discipline and customs. Similar wisdom and foresight were shown in the second period when senior officers, many of them scantily educated and self-taught, deliberately chose the educated graduates of Annapolis in preference to officers of the merchant marine. Older naval officers obtained their education the hard way, but they realized that it was better for the Navy to be officered by scientifically trained midshipmen. Senior officers were influenced in this decision by their experience with academy graduates, who convinced them that during their practice cruises midshipmen acquired the necessary sea habits without which no one can become an efficient seagoing naval officer.

In the late 1850's the bitter feeling between the North and the South made itself felt at the Naval Academy. Mahan reports that as early as 1857 midshipmen from the South were reconciled to disunion. He quotes a conversation with a midshipman from North Carolina who referred to Buchanan as the last President of the United States. After the election of Lincoln and the secession of South Carolina, the Naval Academy still went at its accustomed pace. On November 3, 1860, the first of the season's informal "hops" was held, and the officer of the day logged it "a tasty and elegant affair" which "passed off to the intense satisfaction of all concerned." Two weeks later there was a more brilliant ball on the *Constitution*, which had arrived the previous summer to quarter the Fourth Classmen, and leave was granted midshipmen to escort the ladies home from the "soiree." A large number of midshipmen were granted permission to attend the 1861 New Year's Ball on the *Constitution*. On January 4th officers and midshipmen joined the nation in a day of fasting and prayer proclaimed by President Buchanan; the next day the midshipmen on the *Constitution* gave a hop, which was well attended by the ladies. Mississippi seceded on January 9th, Florida on the 10th, and Alabama on the 11th. Many midshipmen from southern states had already resigned, but on January 14th all midshipmen from Alabama resigned in a body.

Benjamin reports very affecting scenes between classmates who suddenly realized that they might be opposing each other soon in battle. Midshipmen are usually reserved; their dislike of scenes is proverbial. There was probably much banter about being kind to any taken prisoner, and many quiet assurances of personal esteem and extra hard handshakes at parting. Friendships made at Annapolis generally survived the Civil War, and many classmates who had fought against each other renewed their friendships after peace. Most graduates who "went South" fared badly after the war. Some entered the navies of Central and South America.

Annapolis was southern in sentiment, and there was loose talk in the town of seizing the *Constitution* for the Confederate States Navy. Her crew had been reduced and many of her guns removed to increase the accommodations for midshipmen; she was secured to the dock and at low water was grounded in the oozy bottom of the Severn. She would have been difficult to take but easy to destroy if a field battery were placed on the bluff across the river. Commodore Blake determined to hold the *Constitution* at all costs and the Academy as long as possible. On April 14th Sumter surrendered; the next day the commodore informed Secretary Welles of his plan of action. Academic activities had been suspended; the midshipmen were armed and were garrisoning the Academy; the reduced crew on the *Constitution* was alert and her guns had been double shotted; an armed schooner patrolled the approaches to the harbor. If compelled to evacuate, the commodore proposed to load all ammunition and stores possible on the *Constitution*, destroy the remainder, embark the officers and midshipmen, and sail for Philadelphia.

On April 17th Virginia seceded, and Lieutenant William H. Parker, head of the Department of Navigation, left for Richmond where he established the Confederate Naval Academy. Commodore Blake had two stalwart assistants, Lieutenant C. R. P. Rodgers, the Commandant of Midshipmen, and Lieutenant George W. Rodgers, a nephew of Oliver Perry, in command of the *Constitution*.

On April 20th the Norfolk Navy Yard was evacuated by Union forces, and the commodore redoubled his vigilance. On the 21st the patrol schooner challenged a steamer coming down the bay, which proved to be the ferry steamer *Maryland* with part of a Massachusetts regiment aboard under General B. F. Butler. Commodore Blake accepted the general's offer to tow the *Constitution* into the Roads, which was done the same day. The remainder of her guns were mounted, her skeleton crew reinforced by some Massachusetts soldiers, and her berth shifted to cover the landing of additional troops.

Annapolis was strategically located for an Army base. The Superintendent recommended, and the Secretary approved, the transfer of the Academy to Newport. The *Constitution* sailed for Newport via New York, arriving on May 9th; the same day the steamer *Baltic* arrived from Annapolis, bringing books, furniture, laboratory gear, navigation instruments, and other educational impedimenta. Four days later, under the vigorous direction of Lieutenant C. R. P. Rodgers, academic work was resumed in the casemates of Fort Adams. In addition to carrying on their classes, midshipmen were stationed and drilled at the army guns, to assist in the defense of Newport. Commodore Blake remained at Annapolis to complete the transfer of the Academy grounds to the Army, but he had demonstrated that the Naval Academy was a mobile institution, prepared to go where it was needed by the Navy.

Before the *Constitution* sailed from Annapolis, ten midshipmen of the Senior Class were ordered to active duty. Soon after arrival at Newport the remainder of the class which entered in 1857 was ordered to sea; these were quickly followed by the classes which entered in 1858 and 1859, leaving at the school only the class that entered in 1860. To fill the vacancies, Congressmen were given two appointments. About two hundred midshipmen entered and were quartered on the *Constitution* which was moored at the dock at Goat Island. The casemates were inadequate for quarters for the staff and midshipmen, and a summer hotel, the Atlantic House, leased by the government, served as the Academy until the return to Annapolis.

During the Civil War, midshipmen educated at the Academy met their first test of war. An account of a few of those who distinguished themselves in the United States Navy and the Confederate States Navy is offered to show that their education ashore had not adversely affected their skill or courage.

William B. Cushing, Samuel W. Preston, and Benjamin H. Porter entered the Academy in 1857, 1858, and 1859 respectively. Their records alone would prove that the Naval Academy had not diluted the audacity that characterized early American midshipmen. Cushing and a classmate, William F. Stewart, operating in small armed boats, destroyed Confederate schooners in the Virginia creeks around Quantico during the spring and summer of 1861 almost under the bows of larger and heavier armed enemy ships. From that time Cushing displayed ingenuity, resourcefulness, and an ardent desire to participate in the most dangerous enterprises. He was as practical and resourceful as he was zealous and soon gained the confidence of his seniors. When he proposed a plan to torpedo the *Albemarle*, he was sent to the New York Navy Yard to superintend the construction of a launch and its apparatus for discharging a torpedo which he himself had designed. In sinking the *Albemarle*, Cushing not only displayed the indomitable determination to persist to the end on which the old Navy prided itself most, but also that very rare trait—the ability to think clearly in critical situations. When he discovered a protective "boom" of logs around the *Albemarle*, he was already under fire of the Confederate sentries, and some of the *Albemarle's* gun crews were ready to fire upon his unprotected launch. Circling in a wide arc until his boat was going full speed, he steered directly for the Confederate ship, partly hurdled the boom, and got his launch near enough to the overhang of the *Albemarle* for the spar topedo to reach her side. Not until the torpedo pressed against the side of the *Albemarle* did he pull the lanyard which detonated the percussion cap in the war head.

Commodore Dupont reports that Samuel W. Preston, his flag lieutenant, displayed throughout the day when Port Royal was captured "an undisturbed intelligence which proved very useful." This was the same rare trait that Cushing revealed and it was the distinguishing characteristic of John Churchill, first Duke of Marlborough, the finest soldier of his generation. Preston served on the *Louisiana* and helped to fit her up as an "infernal" modeled after Somer's *Intrepid*. The *Louisiana* was as unsuccessful as her predecessor.

In the capture of Roanoke Island, Midshipman Benjamin H. Porter commanded a battery of six naval howitzers that had been landed to support the Army corps of General Foster. The support of his howitzers had much to do with the success of the Army operation.

Cushing, Preston, and Porter led the Naval battalion into action at Fort Fisher. Preston was struck down on one side and Porter on the other; Cushing alone of that heroic trio survived, and he did not live to become a flag officer, dying as a commander. All three of these young graduates gave great promise, and the short career of Cushing indicated that he would have made a superb flag officer.

In sinking the *Albemarle*, Cushing avenged the death of his former commanding officer, the gallant Charles W. Flusser, date of 1847, who laid his gunboat *Miami* almost alongside the *Albemarle* in the hope that his guns could penetrate her armor, only to be killed by a fragment from one of his own projectiles which rebounded from the side of the enemy ship.

William T. Sampson, a classmate of Cushing, was second in command of the *Patapsco* when she was sunk off Charleston so suddenly that he barely had time to step from the top of the turret into the water. Dewey was executive of the *Mississippi* when she was stranded and burned off Port Hudson. The two victorious admirals in the Spanish-American War were trained in adversity.

Lieutenants Sproston, date of 1846, J. H. Russell, 1841, Francis B. Blake, 1853, and Midshipmen Steece, Moreau Forrest, and F. J. Higginson distinguished themselves in a boat expedition from the *Colorado*, sent to capture the privateer *Judith* at Pensacola, Florida. In the attack on Forts St. Phillip and Jackson in Farragut's capture of New Orleans, Midshipman Woodward earned the approbation of Captain Bailey, while Midshipman Stewart gallantly worked the gun on the topgallant forecastle. Lieutenant James O'Kane, severely wounded, would not go below until he had primed, sighted, and fired two ranging shots.

Samuel Dana Greene, graduated in 1859, was the second on the *Monitor* and in command after Worden was disabled in the final phase of one of the decisive battles of the war.

Lamson, Roland, and Robertson graduated in May, 1861, and in November commanded the pivot guns and spar-deck batteries of the flagship *Wabash* directly under the observation of Commodore Dupont, who reported that "they sustained the reputation and exhibited the benefits of the Naval Academy training ... only which could make such valuable officers of such young men."

Among the Naval Academy graduates who went South, the following are among the better known: William H. Parker, who had been head of the seamanship department of the Naval Academy, established the Confederate States Naval Academy and commanded the gunboat *Beaufort* during the Battle of Hampton Roads. Lieutenant-Commander J. W. Alexander, class of 1857, commanded the gunboat *Raleigh*. W. B. Hall, class of 1855, commanded the Confederate school ship *Patrick Henry*. A. F. Warley, 1840, commanded the *Albemarle*, which had successfully resisted all Union attacks and was a menace to Union ships until torpedoed by Cushing. J. M. Kell, 1841, was executive officer for Captain Raphael Semmes on the *Alabama*. J. I. Waddell, of the same date, almost duplicated Porter's cruise in the *Essex* in 1813; in the *Shenandoah* in the winter of 1864-65 he destroyed the American whaling industry in the Pacific. F. E. Shepard, 1849, commanded the C.S.S. *Mobile* in the Mississippi River. John T. Wood, 1847, commanded the *Tallahassee* on a nineteen-day raid in the summer of 1864 and captured or destroyed twenty-six vessels. Hunter Davidson, 1841, commanded the James River defense in front of Richmond; his electrically controlled mine field was a formidable barrier behind which Confederate vessels lay in 1864-65, threatening to cut Grant's line of communication. Farragut was sent from Washington to take command and performed his last active duty opposite Davidson in the James River.

This list is not intended to be comprehensive, only to indicate the part played by Naval Academy graduates in the United States Navy and the Confederate States Navy.

Over two hundred of the older naval officers went South, including Samuel Barron, Raphael Semmes, Matthew Fontaine Maury, Josiah Tatnall, T. A. C. Jones, and Franklin Buchanan. They filled the most important naval positions in the Confederate States Navy. Franklin Buchanan, the first Superintendent of the Academy, probably had the most distinguished record in the Confederate Navy. He commanded the *Merrimac* in the first battle in Hampton Roads when she sank the *Cumberland* and *Congress*. With his flag on the *Tennessee*, he was in command of the Confederate squadron which fought against Farragut's squadron in Mobile Bay.[2]

[2] The best descriptions of the Academy in the days before the Civil War are *History of The United States Naval Academy* by Edward Chauncey Marshall (1862); *Historical Sketch of the United States Naval Academy* by J. R. Soley (1876); *History of The Naval Academy* by Thomas G. Ford, Assistant Librarian before the Civil War, in manuscript in the Library at the Naval Academy. The flavor and atmosphere of the Academy are recorded in George Dewey, *An Autobiography* (1913); Samuel R. Franklin, *Memories of a Rear Admiral* (1898); A. T. Mahan, *From Sail To Steam* (1907); A. T. Mahan, *Letters of Alfred Thayer Mahan to Samuel A'Court Ashe* (1858-1859), edited by Rosa Pendleton Chiles. The account given by Park Benjamin, *The United States Naval Academy* (1900), is breezy and somewhat overdrawn.

CHAPTER 9

The Period of Naval Stagnation

IN September, 1865, after serving longer and under greater difficulties than any other Superintendent, Commodore George Blake was relieved by Rear Admiral David D. Porter, who came to the Academy with all the prestige of his victory at Fort Fisher. Admiral Porter had received the formal thanks of Congress on four occasions during the Civil War, and had influential friends in the executive and congressional branches of the Government who assisted him to carry out the many plans he had conceived for the development of the Academy. During the next four years he needed all his own energy and courage and the assistance of his friends, for he and his successors faced a different but scarcely less formidable situation than Commodore Blake. There was no agency in the Navy Department to make plans for peace and war, or even for demobilization and mobilization. The Union Navy was stronger than the Confederate States Navy, which commenced with no organization and few naval resources. Under the leadership of Secretary Welles and Assistant Secretary Gustavus Fox, a former naval officer and a capable executive, the Department took vigorous measures during the first year of war which enabled the Union Navy to meet its responsibilities by drawing freely upon northern industries and merchant marine.

The collapse of the Confederacy found the Navy with no plan for demobilization. Assistant Secretary Fox resigned and his office was quietly abandoned. The country lost all interest in the Navy, and Congress naturally wished to reduce naval expenditures. Some naval officers on their own initiative had studied naval warfare and could have explained to Congress the reasons for maintaining and training a navy in peace time; but there was no agency in the Department charged with this duty. No program of demobilization was submitted by the Navy to Congress. The ironclads and steam frigates were laid up, shore establishments were curtailed or abandoned, and the ships retained in commission were distributed on foreign stations to protect American trade. No particular group of naval officers was at fault for not providing a demobilization plan; the Navy had evolved from certain manifest necessities and had not created an agency to make long-range plans or to prepare a program to offer Congress. If a well-considered plan had been offered, it would have received little support. After four years of civil war, the American people were eager to return to peaceful pursuits. These conditions in the Navy and the nation influenced the history of the Academy between the Civil War and Spanish-American War. Congress should not be blamed for failing to educate and commission ensigns for a navy which did not have enough ships in commission to provide duty at sea for the officers already commissioned.

Doubling the number of appointees in 1862 steadily increased the number of graduates, although less than half (418) of those entering during the Civil War (858) succeeded in graduating. Among those dropped was a son of Admiral Porter. The act of July, 1866, fixing the Peace Establishment, provided for 857 line officers, almost twice the number of regular officers then in the Navy. Provision was made to retain 150 volunteer officers who had served at least two years and who could qualify by examination.

The remaining vacancies were filled by promotion from the lower grades. Some midshipmen became lieutenant-commanders within three years. With no thought of the future consequences, the line was filled with officers of practically the same age. The class of 1868, on the tail end of this wave of promotion, became lieutenants in 1872 and marked time in that grade for twenty-one years.

In 1867 Congress reduced the appointees to one for each district, but the number graduating was not reduced until 1871, and in 1870 the congestion was increased by reducing the lieutenant-commanders from 180 to 80, increasing the lieutenants from 180 to 280, and decreasing the number of masters and of ensigns from 160 to 100. The cumulative effect of the reduction fell upon midshipmen at the Academy, whose chances of future promotion became steadily worse. The engineer officers suffered as badly; practically all the volunteers were honorably discharged, and of 474 regular engineer officers in the Navy in January, 1865, 155 resigned within four years on account of the dismal prospect of promotion.

Admiral Porter was able to obtain appropriations to rehabilitate the Academy after its service as an army base and hospital and to construct new buildings, including a chapel, an armory, a midshipman's hospital, a building for the new department of steam engineering, marine barracks, and new quarters for midshipmen and officers; to purchase additional land and the residence of the Governor of Maryland, which lay almost inside the Academy grounds. All Porter's buildings and those which preceded them, except two small brick buildings used as guard houses near Gate Number Three, have been demolished to make way for the present buildings.

New Quarters deserves mention; it was an architectural eyesore but, compared with Old Quarters, it was commodious, well planned and well equipped. It was five stories high, with offices, reception rooms, recitation rooms, and the mess hall on the first floor. In one end of the basement were real porcelain bath tubs for midshipmen, and in the other the kitchen, pantry, and tailor shop. About thirty-two classes of the ninety-six that have graduated lived in these quarters. Rear Admirals J. M. Bowyer, the twentieth Superintendent, and Russell Willson, the thirty-first, both occupied rooms in New Quarters, along with about 1,800 other graduates.

Admiral Porter brought a distinguished group of officers, many of whom had served with him at sea, to replace the civilian instructors who had relieved officers needed for active service during the war.[1]

The admiral emphasized the military side of the organization; he submerged the guns crews, the distinctive unit of the Naval Academy, into four divisions, modeled after naval gun divisions. He changed the adjutant into the cadet lieutenant commander, and even altered the sea-going uniforms and caps of midshipmen into blue coats with stiff standing collars and stiffer caps that could not be kept on the head in a breeze. The new coats of cadet officers were covered with gold chevrons like those worn at West Point. He reorganized the midshipman band, designed a gorgeous uniform for the bandsmen, accentuated infantry and artillery drills, and held a dress parade every afternoon the

[1] Lieutenant-Commander Stephen B. Luce became Commandant of Midshipmen. Other heads of departments included Lieutenant-Commander R. L. Phythian, Navigation; F. M. Ramsay, Ordnance; R. L. Miller, English; Professor of Mathematics W. M. Willcox; and Chief Engineer William W. W. Wood, the new Department of Engineering. Among the other officers who served under Porter at the Academy were Lieutenant-Commanders George Dewey, Breese, Selfridge, Sicard, Greene of the *Monitor*, Farquhar, Fitch, O'Kane, and John G. Walker. Professor Lockwood, who had served with distinction as a division commander in the Army, returned in 1865; he was the only member of the original Academic Board to serve with Admiral Porter.

weather permitted. The admiral did not neglect seamanship drills; the midshipmen could march aboard the *Marion*
with all her sail bent, her rigging rove, top gallant and
royal yards across, and strip her to her tops, stow and
label all the gear within eighty minutes.

It was fortunate that the admiral introduced organized
athletics. Until the Civil War, the regular exercise obtained
in sailing drills was enough to keep the midshipmen agile
and hard as nails, but they were entering a period when
the increasing number of steamers deprived them of the
natural exercise of all seamen. The Superintendent equipped
a gymnasium in Fort Severn and endeavored to remove the
bleakness which he thought had existed at the Naval Academy. He encouraged midshipman "hops," and the afternoon dress parades were turned into garden parties by
the ladies of Annapolis and the academy, who attended
in large numbers. Admiral Porter was free in his criticism
of his predecessor, which drew the stinging retort from
Commodore Blake that he thought midshipmen were sent
to the Academy to have their heads educated, while Porter
apparently thought it was to have their heels trained. Admiral Porter did as he liked with the Academy and made
some mistakes, but his contributions for good exceeded the
harm he wrought. Porter gave the military and engineering
branches the consideration due them. He went to extremes
in uniforms and dress parades, but he corrected the previous overemphasis on sailoring.

Commodore M. C. Perry had established the engineering
corps in 1842 by hiring a certain number of chief and assistant engineers for each steam vessel commissioned in the
Navy. Lieutenant Ward had started an elementary course
in engineering for midshipmen in 1845. Perry's system
worked fairly well, and the engineering officers of the
Navy in 1860 were usually efficient. Many resigned and

some were dismissed when the Civil War broke out, and the increasing number of steam vessels added to the Navy made it necessary to increase the number of engineering officers without sufficient opportunity to ascertain their qualifications. In 1863 Secretary Welles reported that "many of our most efficient vessels have been disabled ... in consequence of the incapacity of the engineers." It should be emphasized, however, that on numerous occasions during the Civil War, engineer officers displayed skill, courage, and resourcefulness. Two third assistant engineers, William Stotsbury and C. L. Steever, accompanied Cushing when he sank the *Albemarle*. Secretary Welles also recommended that midshipmen be taught "steam engineering as applied to running the engines"; he expressly excluded "the art of designing and constructing" engines, asserting that his plan would give the Navy a homogeneous corps "of officers who will be masters of the motive power of their ships in the future, as they have been of seamanship in the past."

The senior line officers of the Navy bitterly resented what they considered excessive claims of engineers to Navy rank and title, but they did not obstruct the education and training of cadet engineers or acting assistant engineers. Their experience during the Civil War had convinced them that they could not depend upon engineers obtained from the merchant marine.

Admiral Porter, aware of the need for naval engineers, put all his energy behind the department of engineering, but in spite of its new building, equipped with models of engines and boilers, and the constant support of the Superintendent, the first attempt failed and the engineering department was abandoned in 1868 with only two graduates to show for all the outlay of energy and money.

The plan was modified, and eighteen acting third assistant engineers were appointed in 1866 and 1867; they lived in Annapolis and took a two years' course in engineering at the Academy. They had little intercourse with midshipmen. Practically all these engineers graduated, but over half resigned within five years. This second plan was abandoned.

In 1871 Chief Engineer King devised a new plan which immediately received the support of Admiral Worden, who had become Superintendent in 1869. Appointments as cadet engineers were offered to all young men of the United States between certain ages, subject to competitive examination. The Bureau of Steam Engineering advertised the examination throughout the country; it was known in engineering circles that the Academy was prepared to give an excellent course in marine engineering. Very soon, ambitious lads interested in marine engineering were eager to take the examinations. The Bureau of Steam Engineering and the authorities at the Academy gradually raised the entrance requirements and the scope of the course at Annapolis. In 1874 the course was lengthened from two to four years; in addition to the theoretical instruction each summer, cadet engineers took practice cruises (see Chapter 7), and in a few years it was generally recognized that the Navy had developed the best course of marine engineering in the nation. A demand for its graduates arose in universities which were beginning to organize marine-engineering departments, and Congress authorized special leave for graduates who could be spared from the Navy to serve at these universities. Three of these, Ira N. Hollis, H. W. Spangler, and Mortimer E. Cooley, had distinguished careers in the educational world. This nation-wide competition, opened to all American youths, regardless of anything but their native intelligence, previous training, and good character, produced some excellent engineers, among the most brilliant being W. F. Durand, class of 1880.

Although determined to improve the engineer corps, Admiral Porter, who, after Admiral Farragut's death, was senior line officer of the Navy, was equally determined to protect the prerogatives of the line (command or executive branch) officers from what line officers considered the continual encroachments of the "non-combatant or staff" corps. This Navy quarrel made a deplorable situation worse; a devoted band of brothers could not have removed the causes of naval stagnation and its bad effects on the Navy and the Naval Academy, but the family fight made matters worse.

In 1873 Congress extended the course for midshipmen from four to six years, which delayed the appointments of ensigns for two years, temporarily relieving the strain and automatically reducing the number of midshipmen at Annapolis, as vacancies were not filled until the end of the sixth year. No effort was made to relieve the situation by retiring additional officers in the upper grades and providing a slow flow of promotion. The whole brunt of the stagnation was imposed on the junior officers and midshipmen.

Admiral Porter was followed as Superintendent by four admirals in succession, all distinguished for their services in the Civil War: John L. Worden of the *Monitor*; C. R. P. Rodgers, chief of staff for Admiral Dupont; Foxhall Parker, a student of naval tactics; and George B. Balch, one of the finest seamen of the Navy. Admiral Rodgers was Superintendent when the cumulative effect of the stagnation in the Navy impinged hardest upon the Naval Academy. His own pride in the Navy, his belief in the Academy, his confidence in the quality of its graduates, and his own personal courage enabled him to maintain the morale of the Academy during its nadir. Admiral Rodgers insisted that the Secretary sustain the Academic Board and the Superintendent "in withdrawing from unworthy cadets, the privileges which the government has given them . . . to become officers of the Navy." The Superintendent did not win his fight at once, but within a year the Secretary announced that the Department would not interfere with the Academic Board except in extraordinary cases, and hoped the regulations would be enforced with strictness "which the Superintendent and Academic Board will be regarded as more competent than the Department to decide." This was a reaffirmation of Secretary Bancroft's promise to support Commander Buchanan, and in general it has been kept faithfully.

Admiral Rodgers served for a second time as Superintendent for a few months in 1881, just before Commander Francis M. Ramsay, the first graduate of the Academy, became Superintendent. Ramsay had been head of the Department of Ordnance under Porter and had not approved of many of the changes introduced at that time. He replaced Porter's military insignia with naval rating badges, which are still used. He systematized the practical instruction, placing it on a basis comparable with classroom instruction. He quartered midshipmen by divisions instead of classes, and made a determined effort to break up class distinctions which had previously been encouraged as a means of accustoming midshipmen to gradations in naval rank. Ramsay had distinguished himself during the Civil War. He was, according to Mahan, with whom Ramsay was continuously at odds, a gentleman though a difficult one, and was an outstanding officer of his generation.

In 1882 the situation had become so bad that Congress passed legislation which limited the number of graduates taken into the Navy, giving those not accepted an honorable discharge and one year's pay. In the abstract, the contract was not a bad one for midshipmen. Congress had provided four years' education and a two-year practice cruise at no expense to the graduate, who left the service better equipped to make a living than when he entered, but there was an implied obligation to provide a place in the naval establishment for graduates who had looked forward to a naval career. The classes in the eighties who suffered should place a large part of the blame upon the senior officers of the Navy, who knew exactly what would happen, for some of them had gone through just such a decline in the thirties and forties as a result of the War of 1812. The classes of the fifties and sixties were promoted excessively; those of the seventies and eighties marked time.

Ramsay's radical reforms would have engendered opposition if wisely and temperately introduced; he made no attempt to soften their impact on the naval cadets, who were already depressed by the prospect of slow promotion if they remained in the Navy, and a worse prospect of being dropped at the end of six years' service and having to seek a livelihood in civil life after anticipating a career in the Navy. The class of 1883 was the first to feel the rigors of Ramsay's many reforms. A series of breaches of discipline culminated in the nearest approach to organized insubordination in the history of the Academy. Almost the entire class of 1883 was eventually demoted and placed upon the *Santee*.

Acting hastily under a mistaken impression, Captain Ramsay marred the graduating exercises of the class of 1883. He had issued a last-minute order that there be no cheering when the diplomas were awarded. A group of midshipmen who had not learned of the order cheered the first graduate to receive his diploma. The captain immediately ordered those cheering to be placed under arrest and marched to the *Santee*, and curtailed the remainder of the exercises, to the great disappointment of the families and friends of the midshipmen. Captain Ramsay was extremely self-reliant: during his incumbency he never asked the Navy Department for advice or assistance; he made his own decisions and enforced them with the ample authority vested in the Superintendent.

When the morale of the Naval Academy was at its lowest point, in 1883, Stephen B. Luce, class of 1841, founded the Naval War College at Newport, Rhode Island, where commissioned officers could be sent to study the theory of naval warfare. For his inspiration, Luce was indebted to General Sherman, who, after the capture of Savannah, twitted him about the Navy's inability to capture Charleston, prophesying that the city would fall like "a ripe pear" when the Union Army cut its communications with the interior. The fulfilment of Sherman's prophecy convinced Luce that war conformed to certain laws, and he commenced the study of war, only to discover that whereas there were many books treating of war on land, scarcely any serious studies had been made of war at sea.

Luce, convinced that the proper study of naval officers is naval warfare, also believed that the change from sail to steam would permit the same certainty of movement of fleets at sea possible to armies ashore. Therefore, argued Luce, a study of the principles of land warfare would enable a naval student to deduce some analogous principles of warfare at sea and thus lift naval war from "the empirical stage to the dignity of a science." Admiral Porter gave Luce strong support, and, despite considerable opposition, Luce got the War College under way just as the class of 1881 was being legislated out of a Navy which did not possess one first-class modern man-of-war.

Luce summoned Commander A. T. Mahan to demon-

FIRST CLASS MIDSHIPMEN ON THE DECK OF THE U.S.S. "CONSTELLATION," 1885

strate his thesis, which Mahan did. Incidentally, Mahan discovered the causes and consequences of sea power, which overshadowed Luce's development of the science of naval warfare under steam. Luce, of 1841, and Mahan, of 1859, complemented each other: they had served together at sea and at the Academy during the Civil War; both had served as heads of departments at Annapolis; both were "Naval Academy" officers, and together they did more to systematize the study of naval warfare than generations of European naval officers had done. They were assisted by Admiral Porter, Rear Admiral John G. Walker, and Professor J. R. Soley, at one time head of the Department of English, who became Assistant Secretary of the Navy.

Admiral Luce was a naval pioneer: he founded the apprentice system of training enlisted "boys" for the Navy and was a charter member of the Naval Institute, which since 1873 has offered any one from civil life as well as any officer an opportunity to express his views on naval affairs. The Institute has printed more criticism of the Navy and naval practices than all the newspapers in the United States. In affording the Navy a chance for self-criticism, the Institute has reduced the tendency of the service to become "ingrowing."

Fortunately Ramsay was succeeded as Superintendent by Commander Sampson, who was as strict as Ramsay but with a better understanding of human nature; he gradually restored the morale of the midshipmen without lowering the discipline. The fundamental causes producing the unrest could not be eradicated by Sampson, but he lessened their effect on the naval cadets, and his efforts were helped by the coincident and gradual improvement of the conditions in the Navy, which soon made itself felt in the atmosphere of the Naval Academy. After two years as

Superintendent, Commander Sampson, who had had more experience with scientific education than had any of his predecessors, secured a modification of the amalgamation plan which provided the same course for the first three years for line and engineering cadets. During the fourth year the line cadets concentrated on seamanship, ordnance, and navigation, while the engineers concentrated on marine engineering.

Captain Robert L. Phythian, Captain Philip H. Cooper, and Rear Admiral F. V. McNair presided over the Academy during the nineties. They continued in general the policies established by Commander Sampson until the amalgamation of the line and engineer corps in 1899. After that, the course given at the Academy was the same for all midshipmen throughout the four years' course. These Superintendents maintained the standards of the Academy, and were spared some of the difficulties of their predecessors because there was a gradual increase in the Navy, which, with the six years' course and the reduction in appointments to the Academy, provided commissions for all who completed the course.

The abilities of a Superintendent are not indicated by the innovations he makes at the Academy. From Buchanan onward, the daily, weekly, monthly, and annual program of the Academy has been limited only by the physical and mental endurance of the officers, professors, and midshipmen. The course has evolved with the Navy itself and has been geared to the technical developments in the fleet. An enlargement of one course can be made only at the expense of another or by an extension of the four-year term. A Superintendent with many new ideas could upset the delicate balance and do incalculable harm unless he carefully considered the far-reaching consequences of any change.

Every Superintendent fixes the tone of the Academy and inspires the officers, professors, and midshipmen. Some Superintendents who have made fewest changes in the written rules or the courses have, by the example they set the personnel, had the largest influence on the midshipmen. The Navy Department has exercised extreme care in its choice of Superintendents, as the roster of their names reveals (see Appendix, page 235). Following the precedent set by Bancroft, the Secretaries support the Superintendents and Academic Boards in maintaining the discipline and scholarship of the Academy. The Navy Department will immediately detach from the Naval Academy any officer whose performance of duty is not satisfactory and whose conduct is not exemplary.

One ugly feature of Naval Academy discipline of early days persisted until comparatively recently; this was the custom of punishing a class, company, or even a whole battalion when the authorities could not catch the individual perpetrator of an offense. This unholy practice was applied even to such minor infractions as rolling a china slop-jar down the stairs in midshipman quarters after taps; an entire class of midshipmen would be turned out in the middle of the night and be made to stand at attention until some one confessed to the heinous (?) crime. If it were near the semi-annual examination, some prospective "bilger" would confess to an act he had not committed in order to get the battalion dismissed and become a ten-day hero. Pressure was frequently put upon individual midshipmen who had not taken part in hazing but who had inadvertently witnessed it, or upon midshipmen who had been hazed, to testify against the offenders under penalty of being punished for deliberate disobedience to orders. This naval inquisition made perjurers or tale-bearers of otherwise upright midshipmen. Old Navy discipline was usually rigorous but fair; in a few particulars, however, Academy authorities stubbornly persisted in disciplinary methods which encouraged dishonesty among midshipmen. These pernicious customs have been discarded.

C H A P T E R   1 0

The Naval Renaissance

☆

THE Spanish-American War hastened the graduation of the class of 1898, whose members were given their diplomas without ceremony in April. The midshipmen departed at once for the North Atlantic Squadron. A month later, at their own request, members of the class of 1899 were ordered to sea. In June, the classes of 1900 and 1901 were offered leave but pleaded to join the fleet, and 46 of the class of 1900 and 29 of the class of 1901 were ordered to duty afloat. About a dozen members of the class of 1902 entered in May, and one, Midshipman John M. O'Reilly, who had served in the class of 1900 for about four months, was allowed to join the fleet. Every class in the Academy was represented in Sampson's squadron. O'Reilly, a midshipman of great promise, died of typhoid fever while on leave in 1901.

The Spanish-American War was over so quickly that it had no immediate effect on the Academy. The spirit of the midshipmen of 1898 was high, but few of them were afforded an opportunity to distinguish themselves. Midshipman Joseph W. Powell, class of 1897, demonstrated that the naval spirit was still in the midshipmen. In a small launch he followed Hobson in the *Merrimac* to the entrance of Santiago Harbor and steamed back and forth under the Spanish batteries to pick up the crew of the *Merrimac* which was sunk in the channel. Powell cruised until after daylight, when his launch was driven off by the galling fire of the shore patrols. A little later Admiral Cervera, in his own barge, rescued Hobson and his seven companions from the catamaran to which they were clinging.[1]

During the Philippine Insurrection, passed midshipmen were executives and sometimes commanders of small gunboats which operated in the waters of the archipelago. Naval Cadet W. C. Wood, 1899, of the gunboat *Urdaneta*, mortally wounded, continued to control the fire of his small battery until he died. Passed Midshipman H. D. Cooke, 1903, severely wounded in the ankle during a fight ashore, had himself propped up under a tree and directed the movements of his men.

The policy adopted by Congress in the eighties of commissioning only enough officers to man the Navy on a peace footing resulted in an acute shortage of officers when additional ships were commissioned during and after the Spanish-American War. The class of 1899 returned in October, 1898, and graduated early in January, 1899, to meet the pressing demand for officers.

The Senior Classmen were too busy exchanging notes about the Spanish War to haze plebes when the Academy resumed, but before the month was out the Sophomore custom had broken out in its usual fury. Semmes Read, 1902, a relative of Raphael Semmes, at first refused to submit, and accepted the alternative of fighting. An understanding First Classman reminded Read that every upper classman had been hazed as a plebe, and that none of them had suffered any physical harm or had been degraded by their experience. He admitted that there would be a few bullies who might become offensive but that for the most part it was mere buffoonery and no upper classman would be permitted to strike or lay a hand upon a plebe. With this explanation, Read submitted. The submission of Read, high

[1] The catamaran is now at the Naval Academy.

spirited and powerful enough to take care of himself in a fight, explains the persistence of hazing at the Academy. New-comers accepted hazing as a custom of the institution which had not perceptibly harmed their predecessors and probably would not harm them.

In 1900 quadrennial appointments to the Academy were restored. Appointments by Senators were authorized in 1902, and the number of appointees was doubled in 1903. Congress, under the leadership of President Theodore Roosevelt, was enlarging the Navy. And by good luck, the buildings to house the midshipmen were almost in readiness, for the Spanish-American War began a period of naval expansion which required the prompt enlargement of the Naval Academy. In 1895 the Board of Visitors recommended new buildings at the Academy to replace those built by Admiral Porter. At his own expense Colonel R. M. Thompson, 1868, engaged Ernest Flagg to develop a comprehensive plan for rebuilding the entire Academy. Flagg's plan was approved by the Department, and in 1898 Congress made the initial appropriation of $500,000. Appropriations were continued annually until the scheme was completed. In 1904 the northeast wing of Bancroft Hall was finished in time to accommodate the Second Battalion of the rapidly growing Midshipmen Regiment. The shortage of naval officers continued long after 1899, and in February, 1916, the number of appointees was increased to three for each Senator, Representative, and Delegate in Congress. At Colonel Thompson's suggestion, Flagg's original plans provided for the enlargement of Bancroft Hall and the academic buildings; this enlargement has permitted the addition of wings and new halls as required.

After the establishment of the War College in 1883, the apex of the Navy's educational pyramid, the service waited until 1900 for the intermediate post-graduate schools. In

1899 the line and engineer courses at Annapolis were combined. Thoughtful officers realized that post-graduate instruction similar to that adopted for naval constructors was necessary for line officers specializing in engineering and ordnance. In 1906 post-graduate courses in marine and electrical engineering and ordnance were established in Washington; in 1909 they were enlarged and transferred to the Naval Academy and placed under the Superintendent. In 1912 the curriculum was increased to include naval construction, civil engineering, ordnance, and radio telegraphy. A regular Post-Graduate Department was established at Annapolis under the supervision of the Superintendent and independent of the Academic Board. Some officers attending the Post-Graduate School were later sent to universities and technical schools to take special courses which could not be given at Annapolis. In 1917 the post-graduate system was suspended for the duration of the war and officers were sent to active duty.

In October, 1916, there were 1,231 midshipmen at the Academy. In April, 1917, the number of appointments was increased to four and subsequently to five for each Senator and Member of the House of Representatives. The class of 1917 graduated in March, three months early, and the class of 1918 graduated in June, 1917, a year early. In April, 1918, the course was reduced to three years. The class of 1919 graduated in June, 1918. The Academy followed almost exactly the program of 1861-65. The three classes averaged a little less than 200 graduates each; within sixteen months the Naval Academy had provided approximately 600 new ensigns to the fleet.

With all these increases, it soon became evident that the Academy could not meet the demand for ensigns and junior lieutenants. The Navy Department enrolled as reserve ensigns and sent to the Academy young college graduates and undergraduates with the necessary educational foundation. Under the energetic leadership of Admiral Eberle and his commandant, Captain William H. Standley, the officers and instructors at the Academy gave an intensive three to six months' course in seamanship, ordnance, and navigation to these specially selected collegians. Four classes of reserve ensigns were graduated before the armistice, furnishing about 1,400 reserve ensigns to the fleet.

Similar schools were developed for specialists. One for reserve ensigns for engineering duty only was established at Stevens Institute, Hoboken, New Jersey; a course in gas engines was given to reserve officers at Columbia University; an aviation ground school was established at Massachusetts Institute of Technology; and a special school for training naval aërographers to predict wind and weather for naval aviators was started at Blue Hills Observatory. There was a submarine school at New London, and adjacent to it an "anti-submarine" school to teach tactics for overcoming the submarine. Reserve paymasters were trained at Catholic University and later at Princeton.

Reserve ensigns were trained either in engineering or in line duties, and were qualified in only one branch. In engineering the reserve ensign was not expected to cover all engineering subjects: if competent in marine, Diesel, electrical, radio, or ordnance engineering, a reserve officer was assigned to that duty only. This system required the detail office in the Bureau of Navigation to keep an index card showing the qualifications of the reserve officers, for they were not interchangeable.

While enrolling collegians in their search for officer material, the Navy did not forget the enlisted men or the merchant marine. Five hundred enlisted men were promoted to junior lieutenants and two hundred and fifty were made ensigns. The Navy had previously enrolled many merchant officers in the reserve and had given them some naval training before war started. When the Navy took charge of the transport service, a school for deck officers was established at Pelham Bay Park. The merchant officers were retained as nearly as possible on the ships where they were serving when taken over by the Navy. In a few cases it was possible to leave the reserve captain in command of his ship; ordinarily it was necessary to send a commanding officer and a small signal detachment. The captain of the merchant ship remained as first officer or executive and acted as a second captain for internal organization, while the naval commander, with his signal force and armed gun crews, took over the military duties.

Before the armistice, naval units were established in the Student Army Training Corps, where retired naval officers were detailed as instructors. One vigorous retired admiral, sent to one of our most famous ivy-league universities, was so aggressive that the president appealed to the Navy Department, reporting the admiral for commandeering the entire university.

Practically all the reserve ensigns at Annapolis applied for duty in the war zone. The Superintendent announced that the most proficient would get the first opportunities to serve in converted yachts, submarine chasers, destroyers, or battleships overseas. Others were sent to the United States Fleet operating in home waters to continue their training and instruction, and were sent abroad as vacancies occurred. By June, 1918, the average American destroyer operating against German submarines, escorting transports, or patrolling the sea lanes carried three Naval Academy officers—the captain, the executive, who was also navigator, and the chief engineer. The gunnery, watch, and divisional duties were entrusted to reserve officers, some of whom had never been to sea until they entered the Navy. Most of the submarine chasers were commanded by reserve officers, and they frequently earned the Navy Cross for their efficient performance of duty. The general performance of duty by graduates of the improvised courses at Annapolis suggested and eventually justified the founding of the Naval Reserve Officers' Training Corps.

The war weariness that engulfed the United States in 1919 did not spare the Navy. All volunteers and practically all reserves sought immediate discharge, but the Navy had to bring the Army back from Europe. The Academy felt the let-down, and Rear Admiral Scales, the Superintendent, confronted a difficult situation, with many midshipmen tendering their resignations. An outbreak of hazing made matters worse. Admiral Scales was succeeded by Rear Admiral H. B. Wilson, who came to the Academy from the position of Commander-in-Chief of the Fleet and who, like Admiral Porter, had decided ideas about the Academy and the way to handle midshipmen. Although one of the tautest officers in the Service, Admiral Wilson thought the Academy was too strict and commenced to extend more privileges to midshipmen, including the privilege of smoking. "Uncle Henry," as he was soon called by the Regiment, granted Christmas leave and eventually Easter leave. First Classmen were allowed to visit Washington and Baltimore, and, strangely enough, the heavens did not fall, as some of the more conservative feared.

Pool tables were installed, card playing was permitted, and a chess club formed which functioned in Recreation (Smoke) Hall. The organization and drills of the battalion were altered to conform to those of the Army, and the Army rifle was adopted. In the other direction the old stiff choking blouses with buttoned-up collars were discarded and the midshipmen's blouses altered to conform to those worn by naval officers. Khaki working clothes gave way to working whites, with improvement in the appearance of the Regiment.

The textbooks and equipment in ordnance were brought up to date, and the course was extended to include airplane bombing, aviation ordnance and gunnery, and mines. The fire-control system used in the latest battleships was installed in Dahlgren Hall, with the director system for broadside guns. It is difficult to overestimate the importance of keeping the equipment at the Academy up to date; midshipmen leaving the Academy are expected to take their places in the fire-control parties, in the turrets, or with the broadside batteries as soon as they graduate. Ensigns who have been in the fleet for two years are transferred from battleships to destroyers, submarines, or aviation. Their places must be taken by their successors from the Academy, and the members of the graduating class, arriving aboard ship in the midst of preparations for target practice, must quickly get acquainted with the fire-control system or battery to which they are assigned or they will disarrange the entire organization. Manifestly if they have been trained on the same apparatus used on the Flagship *Pennsylvania*, for instance, they will be familiar with it and drop into their places quickly, but if they were brought up on out-moded gear they will have to start from the beginning.

A course in flight tactics was added to the Seamanship Department and a course in aëronautical engineering to the Engineering Department. Second Class summer was given over to ground-school training in aviation, with at least ten hours' flying time for each midshipman. This was done before the regular aviation school at Pensacola had been enlarged, and it was intended to make midshipmen air-minded and prepare them for a more advanced course later. Every battleship and cruiser now has its own planes: the *Lexington,* the *Saratoga,* and the pioneer *Langley* kept aviation in the forefront of the fleet. The enlargement of Pensacola permitted more and more ensigns to take the course, and the elementary course at Annapolis was abandoned. The course provided preliminary instruction for midshipmen in the duties of second pilot, navigator, radio operator, and mechanic in the air, and in cognate subjects such as aviation history, aërology, aircraft communication, and aviation scouting. At the very time air enthusiasts were accusing the Navy of neglecting aviation, it was requiring its future officers to take the most comprehensive course in aviation given to any but professional fliers.

Aviation affected practically every department in the Academy; navigation introduced aërial navigation.[2] The Engineering Department taught the theory of flight from the manual prepared at Pensacola School; gave instruction in aircraft structure and rigging materials used in aviation, in overhaul and assembly of heavier-than-air craft, and in aircraft engines, including carburetion, lubrication, cooling, ignition, the most common faults and the proper remedies.

Postwar improvements at the Academy were not limited to academics. In order to foster a proper respect for rank without any of the evils of hazing, former privileges of upperclassmen enforced by hazing were established by regulation. These included reserving certain benches and walks for upperclassmen. Admiral Eberle and his commandant, Captain W. H. Standley, had formed midshipman committees to assist the authorities in the management of the Academy, and these were valuable assistants in the transfer from old ways to new customs. Midshipmen who

[2] Lieutenant Commander P. V. H. Weems, 1912, pioneered in developing the instruments, formulas, and tables necessary for flying over the ocean.

had been dropped from former classes were not allowed
to reënter until September; experience had shown they had
a bad influence on new-comers, teaching them many tricks
they did not need to know. Admiral H. B. Wilson was
much more moderate in his reforms than Admiral Porter
had been, but he gave more and more privileges to midshipmen.

Admiral L. M. Nulton succeeded Admiral Wilson. He re-
established the midshipman drum and fife corps and took
the Regiment of Midshipmen to Chicago to play the Army,
the first time the team had gone so far west. The welcome
the Middle West gave to the military cadets and midshipmen was worth all the trouble. Even the tie score was
proper on that occasion; the hosts to the cadets and midshipmen in the heart of the country did not wish either the
Army or the Navy to be defeated, and a tie game was the
only way such a result could happen.

Rear Admiral S. S. Robison, who also came from command of the fleet to the Naval Academy, brought with him
that cheerful and efficient way of getting things done without apparent use of disciplinary methods which marked his
sea-going career.[3] He was succeeded by Admiral Thomas
C. Hart, now Commander-in-Chief of the Asiatic Fleet,
noted for his high sense of duty and his inflexible discipline.
He was just what some of the stricter "ward room officers"
in the fleet thought the Academy needed. Admiral Hart
could not set the clock back, but he did restore some of
the old customs. The atmosphere at the Academy has
gradually become less bleak, but midshipmen can never be
permitted the free and easy customs of the college campus.

[3] Admiral Robison is now President of Admiral Farragut Academy,
a preparatory school in New Jersey, and he has developed a crew that
will take on all comers of its age.

The Hub of the Navy's Educational System

THE efficiency displayed by reserve officers trained at the Naval Academy in 1917 and 1918 convinced the Department that there was an abundant supply of junior reserve officer material in American colleges and universities. To prepare undergraduates for commissions as reserve ensigns, it would be necessary only to add a course in naval science and tactics, embracing navigation, ordnance, and seamanship, to the regular college courses. Instruction could be spread over the four collegiate years, and the average undergraduate could take the naval course without its interfering with his regular college work. Thus the Navy would obtain a college graduate qualified to be a reserve ensign of the line or executive branch. Similarly, collegians majoring in engineering subjects could take a course in marine engineering, supplementary to their regular engineering courses, which would qualify graduates as reserve ensigns for engineering duty. All reserve midshipmen would be given practical training on summer cruises, following the same routine used to train midshipmen from Annapolis.

In 1924 the Department began with units at Harvard, Yale, Northwestern University, Georgia Institute of Technology, the University of Washington, and the University of California. These became miniature naval academies, av-

127

eraging two hundred reserve midshipmen within the particular institute, in which regular naval officers and chief petty officers conducted courses in the theory of navigation, ordnance, and seamanship, and supervised the drills in gunnery, seamanship, and infantry. The Department depended upon the university to instruct the reserve midshipmen in other essential subjects such as mathematics, physics, English, and modern languages. It was necessary to vary the plan to meet special situations at different institutions, but the conditions were substantially the same at all units, and when reserve midshipmen from different universities cruised on the same battleship or destroyer, their professional attainments reached the same high level.

The following description applies particularly to Northwestern, a pioneer unit, but it is typical of Naval Reserve Officers' Training Units. The requirements and the compensation of reserve midshipmen are identical in all units.

Reserve midshipmen must be citizens of the United States not less than fourteen years old. They must meet practically the same physical standards as those required for entrance to Annapolis, pass examinations in professional subjects conducted by regular naval officers, and successfully complete their regular college course, to receive their naval diploma. Although all students are eligible, those well grounded in mathematics are preferred, as much of the naval course requires mathematics.

The course in Naval Science and Tactics is divided into the basic course for Freshmen and Sophomores and the advanced course for Juniors and Seniors. The basic course requires two recitations and one drill per week, for which the university grants the student two semester hours of credit. The successful completion of the basic course is a prerequisite for the advanced course, which requires four recitations and one drill each week, for which the university grants three semester hours of credit. A student passing the naval course, the university course, and a physical examination is tendered a commission as a reserve ensign in the United States Navy.

All reserve midshipmen in the Junior class are required to take the summer cruise; Sophomores and Freshmen are encouraged to take the cruise, and space is provided for fifty per cent of them. About one hundred reserve midshipmen from Northwestern are cruised annually on battleships or destroyers, accompanied by two of their regular naval officers and three chief petty officers who supervise their practical instruction and drills at sea. For drill on the campus, the Northwestern unit is organized as a battalion of infantry of three companies, with its own drum and bugle corps.

The reserve midshipmen are furnished uniforms, books, and equipment, and those in the advanced course are allowed the commuted value of one ration, about twenty-five cents a day, commencing with enrolment in the advanced course and continuing through the calendar year. Transportation to the ports of embarkation and subsistence while on the training cruise are paid by the Department.

The extra-curricular activities are similar to those at Annapolis. Northwestern has a drum and fife corps, a unit paper, the *Purple Salvo*, an annual Navy Ball, and the presentation of the battalion colors by a beautiful young lady, all in the Annapolis manner. The atmosphere of all reserve units is astonishingly like that at Annapolis, and when regular and reserve midshipmen are cruised on the same ships, they fraternize and quickly become "shipmates."

The results obtained at the six original units justified the expectations of the Department, which gradually increased the number. When it became necessary to provide officers for the two-ocean Navy, the Department added still more, and to-day there are Naval Reserve Officers' Training Corps units in twenty-seven colleges and universities, with an approximate enrolment of 3,500 students, which will reach 7,200 by 1944. This number is more than twice the present capacity of Annapolis, which is 3,100. By reducing the course, increasing the number of midshipmen at Annapolis, and adding the reserve units, the Bureau of Navigation has provided a steady and adequate supply of ensigns, regular and reserve, who will become available as the ships are completed.

In addition, the Bureau had to obtain on short notice approximately 5,000 junior officers to officer the additional ships put in commission to carry on the neutrality patrol and to meet the limited national emergency. In 1940 it turned to the campus. In August some 6,650 college men were enrolled as reserve seamen and embarked for a ten days' cruise on battleships. During this time they were given a thorough examination by regular officers to determine their preparation and aptitude for commissions as junior officers. About 5,400 passed the preliminary examination and were sent to Annapolis, Northwestern, or the U.S.S. *Prairie State* and were given intensive courses in seamanship, ordnance, navigation, and marine engineering similar to those given in 1917-18. By June, 1941, 1,773 of these students had graduated and over 1,500 were on active duty in the fleets. Two thousand eight hundred more were graduated from the same schools by July 1, 1941, and sent to sea. Commencing in September, 1941, 4,900 more reserve ensigns were enrolled, and from the experience tables it is safe to predict that the Navy will obtain 4,200 reserve ensigns ready for duty by August, 1942. Seven hundred of these commenced an intensive course in engineering at the Naval Academy in January, 1942, to qualify for engineering duty.

These large increments of approximately 9,200 reserve ensigns will meet the immediate needs of the Navy for peace, prolonged emergency, or war. The Naval Academy and the twenty-seven institutions with their N.R.O.T.C. units now in operation will furnish a continuous supply of junior officers available for replacements and to officer our two-ocean Navy.

Thus the Naval Academy has become the hub of an educational and training system that is capable of almost indefinite expansion. It is the model of twenty-seven miniature naval academies teaching the same professional subjects, using the same training methods ashore and afloat, enjoying the same extracurricular sports and amusements, imbibing the same naval ideas, and absorbing the spirit of the American Fleet.

Any one who studies the record of the Naval Academy will be impressed with its responsiveness to the needs of the Navy. It has adapted itself to the expansion of the American fleets as neatly as the bark to a growing tree. No institution could have responded so nearly automatically to the necessities of a nation's navy without being truly national in its composition and spirit. Since the early fifties, midshipmen have come from every Congressional district and, in the words of a Superintendent, Rear Admiral Russell Willson, "from every walk of life, where there are found sound bodies, good minds, ambition and character." At the Academy they find an atmosphere of fair play, characteristically American, in which their finer qualities develop. The alumni have demonstrated, in and out of the Navy, the past success of the Academy.[1]

The nation wants to be assured of the future. What of

[1] In the appendix there is an account of the Academy alumni which supports this statement.

Annapolis now? Can the Academy continue to furnish officers for the modern Navy, in which are integrated aviation and submarines? It is a Navy which in a few years will become a two-ocean Navy and is already committed to the defense of the Western Hemisphere and the American way of life. Will recent and future graduates rise above initial reverses as did Preble's officers? Will they be equal to all the responsibilities of modern naval and air war? Only of those who have laid aside their armor can the positive word be spoken. But no one who has looked closely into the faces of the regular and reserve midshipmen at the Academy to-day will doubt the future of our Navy.

The reasons for the author's confidence in Academy graduates, past, present, and future, will be given in the remaining chapters. They are based upon numerous recent visits to Annapolis, discussions of its problems with the Superintendent, officers and instructors, and conversations with and observations of regular and reserve midshipmen.

Chapter 12 describes the present buildings and grounds, illustrating the physical growth of the Academy, and gives an account of the present interior organization. Chapter 13 traces the development of the present curriculum and the establishment of the Department of Physical Training. Chapter 14 outlines the extracurricular activities, showing how they fit into the comprehensive scheme of training present-day midshipmen for the many tasks that await them in the fleets. Chapter 15 describes the methods of entering the Academy and some of the problems that immediately confront the plebes, with some hints that may help them through the Academy. These last four chapters are closely related and should be considered together, for academics, athletics, and extracurricular activities combine to form the daily life of the midshipmen. These chapters give prospective midshipmen a clear idea of life at the Academy and offer substantial reasons for believing that Annapolis will continue to furnish American quarter-decks with capable, high-spirited, and aggressive officers, equal to any demands that may be put upon them.

Buildings, Grounds, and Daily Routine

WHEN the Navy rebuilt the Academy early in the century, it located its main buildings as close to deep water as possible, faced them toward the sea, and reclaimed enough of Chesapeake Bay to make a drill ground for its midshipmen. Consequently, the best approach to the Academy is not through the gates but by water in a small boat coming in from Annapolis Roads. The dome of the Chapel will be sighted first, then an indistinguishable mass of low-lying buildings which gradually separate into Luce, Macdonough, Bancroft, and Dahlgren Halls. The housed-over hulks of the *Reina Mercedes*, a trophy of the Spanish War, and the *Cumberland*, whose predecessor was sunk by the *Merrimac* [1] in Hampton Roads, lie across the dock from each other, testifying to the varying fortunes of the United States Navy. Old graduates who land at the dock will see the ghost of the *Santee* and visions of the *Constitution* and *Constellation*. All visitors will see a modern destroyer, a squadron of seaplanes with their attending crash boats, submarine chasers, and power boats, which show that the Navy is training its midshipmen with modern equipment. And in Santee Basin and Dewey Basin the presence of the yacht *America*, several ketches, numerous half-raters, sailing launches, and regulation Navy cutters assure the initiated that the Navy

[1] Under command of Captain Buchanan, first Superintendent.

is teaching its future officers to sail a boat and pull an oar. The service has not lost its salty savor.

The Academy is well worth a visit. The grounds proper (usually called the "yard") contain 184 acres; the hospital grounds across Dorsey Creek, 22 acres; the rifle range across the Severn, 151 acres; and the dairy farm thirteen miles from Annapolis, 855 acres. The Academy is continually acquiring additional land and buildings. Recently it constructed a seaplane hangar, barracks for enlisted men, and a machine shop. It has enlarged the gymnasium building, has added two wings to the Administration Building, two new wings to Bancroft Hall, and a new recitation building, Ward Hall. These enlargements are still insufficient. The Academy seeks to acquire more land to increase the power plant, to improve the ferry slips, to add to the officer quarters, and, if appropriations are available, to build a new auditorium large enough to contain the Regiment. The existing auditorium can not seat the present Regiment.

The Academy, like the Navy, is growing. Alumni returning after a long absence will see few familiar objects except the monuments. The midshipmen of to-day will have the same difficulty when they return in 1960. The Severn will be there, and the Bay, but only a bold prophet would predict what buildings will survive. In this respect the Academy is like the fleet. Its material is ever changing; only its personnel maintains a continuity with the past. The Academy personnel should be on guard lest these enormous buildings, these ever-enlarging grounds, submerge the seagoing school in a mass of brick and granite.

The first building encountered after landing is Luce Hall, named for Stephen B. Luce, 1841, head of the Seamanship Department at Newport, afterwards Commandant of Midshipmen, and author of the first text-book on seamanship. Inside Luce Hall are the Seamanship and Navigation Department, a merger of two of the original departments, and Languages. On the third deck are practical models used for instruction in seamanship. The sail loft on the fourth deck has been transformed into an examination room (if Luce were alive, he would protest such profanation), though there remains a jack stay where midshipmen are taught knotting, splicing, and some of the bends and half hitches and where, in the spring and summer, plebes are taught signaling.

Alongside is Macdonough Hall, commemorating Macdonough of Lake Champlain. It shelters the gymnasium and the offices of the Department of Physical Training. It provides wrestling lofts, fencing lofts, boxing rooms, locker rooms, a swimming pool, squash courts, and the famous "misery hall," where "charley horses" and other athletic animals are violently treated by heartless surgeons. Connected with it is the natatorium, one hundred fifty feet long by sixty feet wide, one of the largest indoor pools, whose water is chemically treated and continuously changed. It was the scene of many near deaths from suffocation in the days of water polo, when the midshipmen had a submarine grudge fight every year with the old Seventh Regiment of New York. Midshipmen must qualify in swimming before their Uncle Sam will present them with a commission.

In front of Dahlgren Hall is a Water Battery where future battery officers get their first drills with naval guns. This sea-going battery is on reclaimed ground; the site of the first naval battery of 32-pounders, erected by Commander Buchanan, was well inshore of the present battery. Dahlgren Hall contains almost the latest model guns and appurtenances. The Ordnance Department continually adds to the collection in Dahlgren Hall. A new recitation building has been completed, named Ward Hall for Lieutenant

THE UNITED STATES NAVAL ACADEMY, 1942

James Harmon Ward, the first Head of Ordnance. Seamanship, navigation, ordnance, and languages, the four subjects on which the Academy cut its teeth, are housed in the four halls adjacent to Bancroft Hall. Before there was a Naval Academy, American midshipmen prided themselves most on being prime seamen and top flight artillerists; next in importance were navigation and then the French language.

Dahlgren Hall has witnessed many gala occasions. It is the scene of the midshipman dances where young ladies can be assured of the undivided attention of future admirals with trained feet. Naval Lotharios (called "Snakes" on the banks of the Severn) occasionally issue too many invitations for the same hop; when they receive duplicate or triplicate acceptances, they provide substitutes from unwilling but loyal Red Mikes who are more at home on their lady's feet than on their own. A wise young lady will make sure of her escort before appearing at one of the hops. Dahlgren Hall is the scene of graduation exercises when they are held indoors. This is a magnificent event, often but never adequately described.

Connecting Macdonough and Dahlgren Halls is Bancroft Hall, which, with its newest wings, can house, by squeezing a bit, 3,100 midshipmen. One of the largest buildings, even its massive walls can not shut out the atmosphere of the sea, for the Chesapeake is a bare hundred yards away, and Memorial Hall is filled with paintings of naval scenes and portraits and busts of naval officers.

Directly in front and framed by two wings of Bancroft Hall is Wilson (Smoke) Park, where informality reigns. Only midshipmen and fathers of midshipmen are permitted within its precincts. Here upperclassmen take their brief leisure and enjoy their smokes. Across Cooper Road from Wilson Park is Farragut Field, drill ground and athletic field for football, winter track, plebe baseball, battalion soccer, baseball, and lacrosse. On the southeast end is the foremast of the battleship *Maine*, sunk in Havana Harbor in 1898. Only a bronze plate marks the site of Fort Severn, as if the Navy were determined to eradicate any Army influence over its future officers. When midshipmen drill or play on Farragut Field, they are really romping on the former bottom of Chesapeake Bay, and those old salts who feared the worst when the school was established ashore can be comforted. Present-day midshipmen still get barnacles in their shoes as they tramp across Farragut Field.

On the south side is Thompson Stadium, which will seat 20,000 spectators and could last forever, for it was built of steel intended for battleships that were scrapped. It, too, is due to be scrapped, and a larger stadium will be built outside the Academy grounds. Robert (Bobby) Thompson, 1868, for whom the stadium was named, first achieved fame with a "fish horn" with which he assailed the ears of Admiral Porter. After resigning in 1871 he was one of the early members of the New York Athletic Club, rode a highwheel bicycle, and competed in the "Century" matches and the races to Coney Island. He kept himself physically fit, and encouraged the midshipmen to do the same. During the dark days of Academy athletics, Bobby, as his intimates called him, spared no effort to prove to the conservative authorities that physical education and exercise were necessary for midshipmen. He worked like a Trojan to promote every sport from fencing to football, without too much success until a classmate, Commander Richard Wainwright, became Superintendent. After that time classmates or close friends of Bobby were in authority, and he began to get results.

While enthusiastic about athletics, Colonel Thompson was interested in all phases of life at the Academy, and was usually present for June Week in his houseboat *Ever-*

glades, where he dispensed regal hospitality, never forgetting to invite some midshipmen and giving orders to his steward to see that they had a drop or two of the punch—when the officers were not around. Bobby is the only person who has two *Lucky Bags* dedicated to him, the second by the Class of 1902, who broke Academy precedent by acclamation. The Academy has always been blessed with loyal alumni, and in their forefront is Bobby Thompson, who, in top hat and fur-lined coat, always led the rooters in his box at the Army-Navy football game. The "topper" grew more battered each year, for he wore the same "lucky" lid to every game, and whenever Navy scored or broke up an Army attack, the silk hat would sail high in the air. On those terrible occasions when by some lucky fluke Army won, Bobby would be as broken-hearted as the captain of the team.

For all its marble corridors, it is easy to recognize the sea-going organization of Bancroft Hall. The Commandant of Midshipmen is Commanding Officer of U.S.S. *Bancroft Hall,* flagship of the Superintendent. He has an executive officer, also the regimental officer, who is assisted by four battalion officers and a first lieutenant, comparable in all respects to heads of departments afloat, and twenty company officers, little different from watch and division officers. The first lieutenant is the Grand Housekeeper and Glorified Janitor, just as he is aboard ship; the other heads of departments are commissioned chiefs of battalions. One officer is "Inspector of Uniforms"; he keeps a sharp eye on the uniforms of the midshipmen. Each of the four battalions consists of five companies and lives in its own part of the ship, that is, in its own wing of Bancroft Hall. The four battalions form the Regiment, exactly as the fleet regiment is formed when it is necessary to seize an enemy harbor and no soldiers are handy.

The Regiment is directly commanded by a midshipman commander, with a regimental staff of midshipmen headed by an adjutant. Each battalion is commanded by a midshipman lieutenant commander, with his battalion staff. Each company is commanded by a midshipman lieutenant, assisted by a midshipman lieutenant (junior grade) and a midshipman ensign, with midshipmen petty officers for each squad. The ranks of midshipmen officers and petty officers are indicated by naval stripes and badges; Captain Ramsay restored naval insignia to midshipmen, which entitles him to some forgiveness for the riots he caused at the Academy in the eighties.

The formations and the infantry, field-artillery, and great-gun drills are the same as in the fleet. Throughout the corridors is the atmosphere of order characteristic of every well-disciplined man-of-war. The midshipman officer of the day wears a navy sword which he may carry through life. His service dress uniform is cut exactly like an officer's. At a little distance a smart-looking First Classman could be mistaken for a snappy young ensign. And in Smoke Hall can be heard the same discussions over every subject under the sun as characterize the "steerages" and wardrooms of the fleets: the same heated statements, flat denials, offers to bet, and the final reference to the *World Almanac*, the *Navy Register*, Jane's *Fighting Ships*, the *Naval Institute* or *Reef Points*.

There are many trophies in Memorial Hall. Midshipmen could easily gain the impression that the Navy has always sailed from one victory to another. There is nothing to suggest to the Regiment that an American man-of-war carried women for a sultan's harem; that one of the first naval schools was held in an infidel prison; that the frigates *President, Essex,* and *Chesapeake,* and all our original sloops-of-war, were taken during the War of 1812; that perhaps half of our best-known officers of the Revolution and of 1812 were made prisoners of war. There is nothing to remind the 1940's that their progenitors suffered defeats before they gained victories. It might be well to have an Adversity Corner in Memorial Hall and display models of the ships that were lost, to remind the Regiment that their ancestors were reared in adversity and taught in the school of hard knocks.

When the Regiment forms for luncheon, the midshipmen quickly take their stations. With almost regal tread come the First Classmen; a consequential heir-apparent look is on the faces of the Second Class; an air of recently gained independence glows in the countenances of the Third Class; and the meek and lowly Plebes ask only to be overlooked. Appearances tell much to the trained eye, and in the faces of midshipmen of the 1940's there is more than a suggestion of the midshipmen of the 1840's who sailed around Cape Horn on the crack *Brandywine*, and roared out their lusty songs of the "Brandy" in their transformed army barracks at Annapolis. When the Regiment marches on to Franklin Field or into the Chapel, or swings by in any formation, it is plain that in spite of all the soldiering received, from grand old Professor Lockwood down to 1941, midshipmen still march like sailors; they retain more than a suggestion of the Old Navy sea-going roll.

The commissioned officers in the Executive Department act as guides, philosophers, and friends to the Regiment, counseling them on a wide variety of subjects from discipline and morale to the management of their personal finances. But in the daily routine, commissioned officers are extremely careful to operate the whole establishment through the midshipmen officers. The experience gained by midshipmen officers is so valuable that some superintendents have rotated midshipmen as officers to benefit as many as possible. One objection to this system is that the Regiment does not become so smart, because one set of midshipmen officers is scarcely broken in before it is displaced. A plebe should lay his plans to become a midshipman officer, if possible, without becoming a "greaser," [2] for the experience adds to his poise and enables him to carry on his duties after graduation with less diffidence. If fate makes him a "clean sleever," [3] he can overcome the initial handicap in a few months aboard ship, where he will have numerous opportunities to acquire leadership.

As the Regiment disappears into the longest mess hall in the world, to enjoy a substantial meal, it is a good opportunity to stroll down the terrace to Dewey Basin opening off the Severn. Here are sheds for navy cutters with their oars heavy as lead on the end of which every plebe must sweat before he becomes eligible to sail the knockabouts, half raters, and whale boats moored along Sands Road.

Farther down Stribling Road is the bronze replica of the figure-head of the ship of the line *Delaware*, [4] a likeness of the Indian chief Tecumseh. According to midshipman tradition, the original Tecumseh was their patron saint, who interceded for those in danger of failing in their examinations. The sacred powers of the original figure-head were bequeathed to the bronze successor by placing portions of the original wooden head in his metallic interior. The powers of Tecumseh have grown with the years, but he is still intercessor extraordinary for midshipmen, who appease him with votive offerings of pennies prior to every Army-Navy football game and beg that he will be the twelfth player on the football team. About half-way to the

[2] A sycophant.
[3] A First Classman who has not been appointed a midshipman officer or midshipman petty officer.
[4] The *Delaware* was a smart ship of the old Navy in which both Farragut and Buchanan served.

"TECUMSEH," BRONZE REPLICA OF THE FIGUREHEAD OF THE "DELAWARE"

Academic Building is the Mexican Monument to Midshipmen Hynson, Clemson, Pillsbury, and Shubrick, who lost their lives during the Mexican War.

Near Maryland Avenue is the Macedonian Monument, a replica of the figurehead of the only British frigate brought into harbor by an American man-of-war, taken by Stephen Decatur in the frigate *United States*. Four carronades taken from the captured frigate surround the base. But lest we forget and vaunt ourselves, the U.S.S. *President*, commanded by the same gallant Decatur, became H.M.S. *President*, and her successor is moored in the Thames not far from the Houses of Parliament.

Across Maryland Avenue is the group of academic buildings, their names testifying to their naval origin—Maury Hall for the first American oceanographer; Mahan Hall for the exponent of sea power; Sampson Hall for the victor of Santiago who, in the piping days of peace, became a first-order physicist. Sampson Hall has a large laboratory, for chemistry, physics, and electricity. Maury Hall mainly houses classrooms. Mahan Hall contains the auditorium and the library of approximately 85,000 volumes, principally literature, history, biography, navigation, the usual reference books, and the outstanding current fiction. The walls of Mahan Hall are lined with glass cases containing battle flags captured in our naval wars. Behind the academic group the Department of Engineering has three buildings named for former wartime engineers-in-chief of the Navy —Isherwood, Melville, and Griffin—that contain the classrooms, mechanical-drawing rooms, model rooms, shops, and laboratories, among them a blacksmith shop, a metals laboratory, and an internal-combustion-engine laboratory.

Engineer-in-Chief Melville was much more than a chief of bureau; he accompanied DeLong on the Arctic Expedition in 1881-82. Across Dorsey Creek in the Academy

ANNAPOLIS: GANGWAY TO THE QUARTERDECK

Cemetery, plainly visible, is the reproduction of the cairn that the undaunted Chief Engineer Melville raised over the bodies of Lieutenant George Washington DeLong, 1865, and his devoted companions in Eastern Siberia. No one knows the day of DeLong's death, but his note-book, which reveals the full horror and heroism of his last days, indicates that he died in October, 1881. That note-book was recovered by Melville and proves that DeLong never faltered, that he and his comrades displayed true Navy stoicism as hope for rescue grew ever more dim. Their inflexible resolve to endure to the end was matched by the indomitable perseverance of Melville who, as soon as he reached civilization, led a relief party to search for his commander. Not until he was assured with his own eyes that his chief was beyond human aid did Melville think of himself. The Navy takes a peculiar pride in DeLong and Melville; one from the Academy, one entering from civil life, both absorbed the Navy spirit. Let him who can decide the braver of the two.

Only Arlington contains more naval dead than the Academy Cemetery. Admiral C. R. P. Rodgers, who stood guard with Commodore George Blake when Maryland secessionists uttered their threats in 1861, who never lost faith in its future, still watches over the Academy from across the Creek. Edward Simpson, 1880, a gentleman unafraid; Joel P. R. Pringle, 1892, a brilliant, forceful wartime chief of staff; W. E. T. Neuman and Thomas Ward, 1903, killed in a turret of the *Missouri;* Theodore G. Ellyson, with something of Cushing's spirit of deviltry and courage, the Navy's Number One aviator, charter member of the pioneer band who flew planes glued together of sticks, paper, and linen cloth; Midshipmen Grigsby E. Thomas, and Sherman M. Nason, who gave their lives, as many of their naval forebears had done, in a vain attempt to save the life of another—these are only a few whose names on simple headstones evoke poignant memories. Not far from DeLong and Melville is another heroic pair that the Academy can claim for its very own—Charles W. Flusser, 1847, and William B. Cushing, 1861, who for a boyish prank was denied his diploma. They served together on the gunboat *Perry* in the Blackwater River and again in Albemarle Sound when Cushing took over the uncompleted task of his captain and sank the Confederate ram *Albemarle*.

McNair Road, named for the genial Frederick V. McNair, 1853, Superintendent during the Spanish-American War, winds along the bank of Dorsey Creek. Admiral McNair might have been the victor at Manila Bay if the war had occurred two years earlier when he commanded the Asiatic Fleet. His successor at the Academy, Commander Richard Wainwright, improved his opportunity off Santiago in the *Gloucester*, but Captain Willard H. Brownson, who followed Commander Wainwright after giving brilliant promise in Rio de Janeiro, was denied the opportunity of battle. Naval careers abound in "breaks." Admiral Brownson passed a harder test. As Chief of the Bureau of Navigation, after carrying out an order from the President, his Commander-in-Chief, which he considered illegal and detrimental to the service, he resigned his position. Punctiliously correct and subordinate to the end, he left an example of what a proper officer should do under conditions more perplexing than battle. Some of that Brownson spirit was communicated to the Academy during his three years as Superintendent.

Worden Field conjures up pictures of the *Monitor* and *Merrimac* as well as recollections of brilliant dress parades. Charming girls in gay spring frocks make the proper setting for a martial display of midshipmen in blue dress jackets and white trousers. The day when the colors are presented to the winning company is a proud moment for the company commander. It also proves that "only the brave deserve the fair." After crossing Dorsey Creek over a fine new bridge, it is easy to reach the well-equipped headquarters of the Navy crew, named, as it should be, for John Hubbard, 1866, who stroked the crew to victory in 1870 and justified David D. Porter's challenge to the world to race his midshipman crew. If tradition is true, Hubbard, afterwards a rear admiral, did much to introduce golf into the United States. Just beyond the boat house is Lawrence Field where the Navy's baseball diamond, varsity soccer field, and plebe lacrosse field are located. Adjacent is Halligan Hall, the post-graduate school named for John Halligan, chief of staff at Brest during the war and exposer of the Teapot Dome scandal; fearless John risked his career to protect the Navy's oil reserves. He also reorganized the post-graduate school after the war.

Returning via Bowyer, Rodgers, and Balch Roads, each named for a former Superintendent, one can reach the officers' Mess in time to "splice the main brace"[5] with an old shipmate and relax for lunch. The Officers Club is the same comfortable place it always has been; that it has been invaded by the ladies, God bless them, adds to its cheerful chatter.

Directly in front of the Club is the Tripoli Monument bearing the names Richard Somers, Henry Wadsworth, John Dorsey, James R. Caldwell, Joseph Israel, and James Decatur, officers of the golden age of the Navy whose examples have inspired subsequent generations. Like the officers it commemorates, the beautiful marble statue led an adventurous life. Designed and executed abroad, brought home on the *Constitution*, erected in the Washington Navy

[5] To have a drink.

Yard, mutilated by the British in 1814, placed on Capitol Hill with the bare statement, "This is the way Britain makes war," it remained a barrier to good relations between the English-speaking nations until it was restored and removed to Annapolis in 1860. Close by is the Naval Museum whose energetic curator, Captain H. A. Baldridge, 1902, will soon have an option on all the scattered relics of the Navy. At least a week is necessary to explore this treasure house, which "Friends of the Navy" are filling with priceless mementos.

In the same building is the Naval Institute, an extra-curricular undertaking by naval officers and civilians interested in the Navy and nautical matters. The Institute, founded for the "advancement of professional, literary, and scientific knowledge in the Navy" has not interpreted its mission narrowly; its associate members, mainly civilians interested in ships, the sea, and the service, are among its most valuable assets. They contribute regularly to the monthly magazine, the *Naval Institute Proceedings*, enter its annual competition for prize articles, and frequently win them. Any reformer convinced that the Navy is "going to the bow wows" can give vent to his indignation and his ideas; he can be sure that his Philippic will be read, and that if there be merit in it, other officers will take up the cudgels for his forlorn hope. Current service problems are discussed in the *Proceedings*, and while language must be temperate, opinions can be fearlessly expressed. Among the regular features are "Notes on International Affairs," "Professional Notes," and "The Secretary's Notes." A busy officer or one who on a long cruise misses the daily papers can catch up with the current world situation by reading these notes, and a regular peruser of the press will find that he has overlooked many interesting naval items when he reads them here. The bound volumes of the Institute are an excellent record of naval activities since 1873. Any writer on naval history would do well to consult its index in planning his program of research.

Directly in front of the Chapel toward the Severn is a plain marble shaft in honor of Captain William Herndon who went down with his ship, the S.S. *Central America*. Herndon's monument reminds the Regiment of the oldest tradition of the sea, the privilege of the captain to be the last to leave his ship. Captain T. A. M. Craven gave a courtly version of this honor with his "After you, pilot," on the *Tecumseh* at Mobile Bay in 1864, and Captain Herbert G. Sparrow, 1899, commanding the *Tacoma* in January, 1924, proved that the tradition was still binding. In the Chapel, the windows to Farragut, Porter, Sampson, and the one presented by the Class of 1927 assure the visitor that the Navy has done its part in the past, and that her sons in the future will seek to realize "her ideals of honor, courage, loyalty, and duty in the service of God and country." Members of 1927 were buckling on their swords when they placed that window in the Chapel, and until they lay them aside no one can say how well they have kept the faith. But this much is certain: graduates with the spirit of the class of 1927 inspire confidence in the future of our Navy. The Chapel has many beautiful moments: Dr. Alden, who has seen it under all circumstances, believes the Regiment receiving communion on Easter Morning stirs the heart strings a little more than the Sunday before graduation, when visiting parents and relatives gather with the regular congregation to sing the Navy hymn, "For Those In Peril on the Sea."

Every one interested in the Chapel must visit the tomb of Commodore John Paul Jones in the crypt. Just outside the Chapel are yew and lavender bushes from Burnham-Thorpe, the birthplace of England's Nelson. After the battle of Trafalgar, Napoleon said that John Paul Jones had not lived to fulfil his destiny. What a fight there would have been if John Paul Jones had lived to command the French and Spanish Fleets at Trafalgar—a battle of the centuries. Admiral Nelson and Commodore Jones would have thoroughly enjoyed the battle royal. What would Paul Jones think of America's two-ocean Navy? With all his pride in the greatest navy in the world, might he not fear that line officers were letting the naval constructors win wars before they started? That prospect would have troubled him. John Paul Jones did not ask for odds; he would have concentrated one fleet in the Pacific, defeated one enemy, returned to the Atlantic and given the same treatment to another. Poor old Paul is hopelessly out of date. He did not know that it is smarter to let the ship's carpenters win wars. He thought that "hard fighting," and a whole lot of it, was the proper way to defeat the enemy. He would not approve of shipbuilding companies pilfering a victory in time of peace.

It is better to leave these perplexing problems to the younger generation. The 1840's solved their problems, and what to do with a two-ocean navy can be safely left to the Regiments of to-day who, even at the Academy, learn what sea power means, are alive to the competition between airships and surface ships, and already have more than a clue to the solution—for one midshipman essayist plainly contemplates a union of air force and naval force to gain and exercise sea power. Mahan could do no better; he always included army garrisons at necessary bases and important harbors. Good surface sailors will have to make room in the fleet for sailors of the air. Early in the century they admitted the undersea sailors in submarines. After all, Pensacola, Corpus Christi, Jacksonville, and San Diego are only post-graduate schools of Annapolis. The 1840's had to shift from sail to steam; the 1940's can sail on the sea, under the sea, and over the sea, and Uncle Sam can come into his birthright, sea power. These modern youngsters are scientific in their terminology; they will probably call it ocean power.

With the cheerful thought that the future is safe in the capable hands of midshipmen of to-day, a visitor can return to Maryland Avenue and pass out the handsome gates presented by the class of 1907.

Visitors leave, but the Naval Academy goes on forever. The daily tasks of a midshipman make it imperative for him to utilize every minute to advantage. He commences at 6:15 with reveille. Thirty minutes are allowed for the morning shower, shaving, and dressing. Breakfast formation is at 6:45, when daily orders are read and midshipmen are inspected by midshipmen officers and commissioned officers, who note their general appearance and see that their shoes and uniforms are in immaculate condition. The Regiment is then marched to breakfast, where they sit twenty-one to a table in a huge mess hall, the only place indoors where the midshipmen can be assembled simultaneously. After breakfast, morning prayers are read by the chaplain. Midshipmen then return to their rooms, make up their beds, and do all those chores which are reputed to bring on "housemaid's knee."

At 7:45 half the Regiment marches to the first recitation while the other half begins the study hour. The academic day is divided into six periods of approximately one hour each—four in the forenoon, two in the afternoon. These periods are subdivided into one-hour periods—one for study, one for recitation.

Lunch formation is at 12:20. Midshipmen are again inspected and regimental orders are published. The fifth recitation period begins at 1:15. For some battalions this is followed by long afternoon drills, and for others by the sixth recitation period and short drills. All drills are completed by 4:35. Until 6:40 the midshipmen, except those on duty, engage in athletics or extra-curricular activities. How little the daily routine has changed since 1850 is indicated below:

	1850	To-day
Reveille	6:15 to 6:30	6:15
Breakfast roll call	6:45 to 7	6:45
	Chapel before breakfast	Prayers after breakfast
Recitations	8 to 1	7:45 to 12:05
	Dinner	Lunch
Midday meal	1 to 2	12:20 to 1
Recitations	2 to 4	1:15 to 3:15
		Drill
Drills and recreation	4 to sunset	3:30 to 4:35
		Recreation
		4:35 to 6:40
Parade, roll call, followed by		Dinner
supper	At sunset	6:40
Evening study	6:25 or 6:55	8 to 9:50
	to 9:30	
Taps	9:30 to 10	10

In 1845 the authorities were under the same necessity as those of 1850 and of to-day to utilize every minute of the day. The courses to-day are more advanced and more difficult, but the Fourth Classmen enter better prepared. The numbers of midshipmen have risen and fallen, but over the entire period they have increased. In 1845 there was an average of fifty to sixty midshipmen, of whom only seven were acting midshipmen; the remainder were preparing for final examinations. In 1851, when the present system was established, there were nine midshipmen preparing for their final examinations and seventy-five acting midshipmen. In

1857 there were 176 midshipmen. This number rose to 281 in 1860, when twenty-five midshipmen graduated, the largest class to that time. The percentage of graduates has always been small; from 1852 to 1864, according to Park Benjamin, one-third of the applicants for entrance could not pass the entrance examinations, and of the 1,209 who managed to enter, only 269 graduated. (According to the Alumni Association records, only 258 graduated.)

This table illustrates the increase of regular midshipmen at the Naval Academy:

	October, 1845	October, 1897	October, 1916	October, 1940	September, 1941
First Class	25	39	184	400	570
Second Class ..	8	55	208	583	626
Third Class		71	214	654	817
Fourth Class ..	7	94	625	965	1,105
Total	40	259	1,231	2,602	3,118
	(Approx.)				(About capacity)

The regular class of 1941, about four hundred, graduated early in February; the Academy then received over six hundred reserve ensigns and graduated 583 in May. The regular class of 1942, 565, graduated in December, 1941, six months ahead of schedule. Another class of seven hundred reserve ensigns for engineering duty only took their places in Bancroft Hall in January, 1942, for an intensive three months' course. When they graduate, the plebe class of 1946 will enter, to begin the new three-year course. The class of 1943, now 626 strong, will graduate in June, 1942, a year ahead of time. Between January, 1941, and June, 1942, the Academy will provide about 1,800 junior officers for the fleet, compared with the 600 it provided in a similar period in 1916-18, and with the 184 between 1861 and 1864. Thereafter all regular classes will graduate after three years until the demand for junior officers of the two-ocean Navy is met.

These changes in the program, and the adjustments necessary to accommodate two large classes of reserve ensigns without interrupting the education and training of the regular midshipmen, is a tribute to the flexibility of the Academy's organization and the devotion of the officers, professors, and instructors to their duties. It is comparable to the loyal efforts of Buchanan, Upshur, Ward, Marcy, Chauvenet, Lockwood, George Jones, and Girault in the transition period of 1845-49.

Reserve Ensign Graduation week was in May, 1941; the pomp, the ceremony, all the colorful accompaniments of graduation were in honor of the reserve midshipmen on completion of their course and entry into active service of the Navy. As these reserve ensigns marched down Stribling Row, they gave promise of being easily absorbed into the fleet. They were somewhat older in appearance than the regular midshipmen and marched more stiffly, with a determined look on their faces that boded well for Uncle Sam and ill for all his enemies.

The readiness with which the Academy authorities accommodated the reserve ensigns, and the welcome the regular midshipmen extended them, is the best possible proof that the Naval Academy has not been used by its alumni to fasten an unnecessary monopoly on commissions in the United States Navy.

CHAPTER 13

Academics and Athletics

☆

THE Board of Examiners recommended a naval school in 1845 in order that "none but the meritorious will find their way into the Navy." Bancroft established the school "to improve the character of the younger branch of the service." Buchanan dropped a midshipman whom he did not think would be an ornament to the service. Admiral D. F. Sellers stated in 1935 that "the Naval Academy ... was created and exists for the sole purpose of training officers to fight the United States fleets." Rear Admiral Wilson Brown, who succeeded Admiral Sellers, asserted that midshipmen must be prepared on graduation to be "capable mariners and useful junior officers ... in the fleets." His successor, Rear Admiral Russell Willson, in a message to the Regiment, said, "I like to think of you, gentlemen of the Regiment, ... as young naval officers." In addressing the graduating class of 1941, Admiral Willson reaffirmed the statement of Admiral Sellers that the Naval Academy exists "for one purpose only, ... to train officers to fight the fleets of the United States," adding grimly that there was an immediate possibility the class of 1941 might have "the quality" of their Academy training put to the test.[1]

To understand the Academy, it is necessary to remember the reason for its existence, and that it is only a part of the

[1] Rear Admiral J. R. Beardall recently succeeded Rear Admiral Willson.

educational system of the Navy. The Navy Department controls the courses at the Academy and fits them in to other educational and training programs for commissioned officers. The Academy is the foundation of the Navy's educational system, and its subordination to the Department adds to its importance by making it a national institution. It must prepare midshipmen to perform certain specific duties on shipboard, accustom them to naval discipline and to the seemingly endless drills necessary aboard a man-of-war, and give them an educational foundation for their higher duties. Midshipmen are not finished with books on graduation day; they have only commenced to study. Throughout their careers they must continue to learn, and to teach and train others.

After graduation, ensigns will be assisted by the senior officers on their ships as they were at the Academy, but to a lesser degree. They will be expected in large measure to improve themselves. The emphasis in the fleets will be on training, not on education. The ship's duties will take precedence over the development of officers, and a junior officer must find the time to study new naval developments without neglecting his routine duties.

To meet its obligation to provide junior officers for the American fleets, the Superintendent, his officers, and instructors strive to develop midshipmen with alert minds and sound bodies, loyal, disciplined, educated, fit to accept ever larger initiative in the execution of orders, ready and eager to prepare themselves for higher responsibilities. The Academy authorities encourage the natural high sense of honor in midshipmen and strive to develop in them a bold, enterprising spirit, an ardent desire to contribute to the glory of the Navy, and a willingness to sacrifice life itself for the nation.

As all midshipmen are preparing to become junior

officers in the Navy they must necessarily take the same course after entering the Academy. Their instruction is practical rather than theoretical, and they are well grounded in the theory of certain essential subjects. They are not expected to become experts in all technical subjects in four years, but midshipmen must obtain the elements of these subjects. They must also learn how to continue their studies unassisted, to "dig" for themselves, and to acquire the art of leadership, the foundation of which is the ability to inspire respect among the men whom they may some day command in battle; leadership can never be attained unless officers are manifestly competent to perform their own duties.

In 1818 the Board of Navy Commissioners established a high standard for midshipmen aspiring to be lieutenants. Each midshipman had to satisfy every member of the Board of Examiners that he was competent to be a proper lieutenant. In 1846 Secretary Bancroft ordered the Board of Examiners to be present when the Academic Board held the first examinations at Annapolis to insure that previous standards should be maintained. Thereafter the Board of Examiners visited Annapolis during June Week to satisfy themselves of the professional competence of the graduating class. By 1855 the system of relentless examinations had been firmly planted at Annapolis. Sixty members entered with Dewey in 1854; twenty-three dropped out the first year and only fifteen of the sixty graduated. During the Civil War the high standard was maintained at Newport. Over half the midshipmen who entered failed to graduate.

The academic courses at the Academy have been altered to keep pace with the changes in the naval profession, but the subjects taught, though enlarged and more advanced, have evolved naturally from those taught in 1851. There are now ten departments under the immediate supervision of the Superintendent: (1) Executive, (2) Seamanship and Navigation, (3) Ordnance and Gunnery, (4) Marine Engineering, (5) Mathematics, (6) Electrical Engineering, (7) English, History, and Government, (8) Languages, (9) Physical Training, and (10) Hygiene. The emphasis is still on mathematics, navigation, ordnance, seamanship, and engineering; the last now embraces all phases of engineering but is still treated from the point of view of motive power for naval ships. French, Spanish, Italian, German, and Portuguese are taught. Approximately 22 per cent of the academic work is devoted to professional subjects, 51 per cent to mathematics and the sciences, 27 per cent to other subjects.

When the Naval Academy was founded, the entrance examinations were purposely limited to elementary subjects —reading, writing, and arithmetic—to enable young Americans with native intelligence who had been denied educational advantages in their youth to enter. In 1863, the educational facilities in the nation had sufficiently improved to justify entrance examinations in reading, writing, spelling, arithmetic, geography, and English grammar. By 1883, algebra and United States history were added, and in 1899 plane geometry and world history. From the beginning the entrance examinations have been thorough and they grew more searching, not from malice, but to save a candidate who can not hope to graduate the time and expense involved in entering and failing.

Between 1900 and 1925 there was a steady advance in educational facilities throughout the country, with a corresponding increase in the entrance requirements of colleges. Candidates for the Naval Academy usually had finished some of the subjects given in examinations and during the first year at the Academy. In 1923-25 the entrance examinations were raised to embrace English, United States history, ancient history, algebra (through quadratics, including the progressions, and the binomial theorem), plane geometry, and physics (one year's work).[2]

The increasing number of prospective candidates from the colleges created another problem. The entrance examinations included subjects that candidates had completed; to prepare for an Annapolis examination it was necessary for them to drop their college course and review the subjects required for entrance. At the same time statistics showed that a year's work in college was excellent preparation for the Academy, better than three to six months' cramming at a preparatory school. Since the sole purpose of the entrance examinations is to test the abilities of the candidate to remain in the Academy, the academic authorities came to permit the entry *without* mental examination of a regularly enrolled student in good standing in a university, college, or technical school. This provision prevented the interruption of college work to prepare for an examination.[3]

Until 1923 the last month of each four-month term was utilized to review the recitations of the previous three months. At the end of review months the semi-annual and annual examinations were held. In 1923, review months were discontinued.

Examinations are now held at the end of each term or on the completion of a particular subject. The examinations are still severe and searching. The recitation system followed by examinations is the Academy's scholastic method to-day, as it was in 1846, but there is much more instruc-

[2] Commander A. H. Rooks, U.S.N., "Entrance Requirements. U. S. Naval Academy," U. S. *Naval Institute Proceedings* (October, 1935).

[3] Certain provisions must be met. See page 194.

THE "STEADY STUDY METHOD" ENABLES PLEBES TO PREPARE THEM-
SELVES FOR DAILY RECITATIONS

EXAMINATIONS ARE AS MUCH A PART OF THE ACADEMIC SYSTEM TO-DAY
AS THEY WERE IN 1846

tion given in the classroom than there was formerly. Instructors are encouraged to employ about half the period in explaining the difficult parts of the lesson, devoting the second half to recitations by the midshipmen. If a lesson is unusually formidable, an instructor is authorized to employ the whole period in explanation; in this case no marks can be awarded for the day. In the Navigation Department, which usually has three periods a week, this allows one entire period a week for instruction if it is considered necessary. The practice in departments varies, but they all provide classroom instruction.

Prior to the beginning of each academic year the heads of departments, with their senior assistants, outline the scope of the year's work to the instructors, go over the course in detail, and emphasize the salient features which must be imparted to the midshipmen and upon which they will be examined. The instructors then prepare themselves to carry out the program. Civilian instructors are all experts, many of long experience, but they have to continue their studies, for the courses are continually changing. The officer instructors come from the fleets, are acquainted with the technical subjects from a practical point of view, and have had much experience in instructing junior officers and petty officers aboard ship. Officers have been trained to impart information to others, but they are not always familiar with the textbooks and the latest developments in some of the subjects they are called upon to teach. They study harder the first year ashore than the midshipmen, for they must be prepared to answer all questions asked. Throughout the academic year, heads of departments visit the classrooms to make sure that midshipmen are being properly instructed.

The Academic Board, consisting of the Superintendent, the Commandant, and the heads of all departments, is the court of final resort in all academic matters. After each head of department has prepared his program of instruction and drills and has outlined the scope and content of his course, the Board meets to allot the time in the very tight scholastic schedule. Often there is a struggle between two departments for instruction and drill periods. When a decision is made, it is loyally accepted, and then the Board fits the various courses into one another to avoid duplications and to obtain the necessary overlap between cognate subjects. The Board must insure that the midshipmen are given a comprehensive education in the subjects they will need immediately after graduation. Throughout all the planning and discussion of the various courses, the Superintendent keeps the purpose of the Academy in front of the Board. The final decision between two departments is determined by the question, "Which course will do more toward preparing midshipmen for their duties in the fleets?"

The Academic Board is accused every year, by a few Congressmen whose nominees have failed, of being too severe; it is criticized by some collegiate authorities because its courses are too elementary and lack cultural and optional subjects. Generally speaking, the members of Congress most familiar with the Academy have supported the Board against attacks from both directions. The Board of Visitors always includes college or university presidents who know from experience the number of semester hours a student can work; they scrutinize the Academy curriculum carefully. Practically all of them agree that the Naval Academy does not waste time and that the course is well designed to meet the Academy's primary mission of preparing young Americans to become junior officers in the American fleets. That is the reason Congress makes appropriations for its support, and it is the only justification for the annual expenditure of taxpayers' money to educate a particular group of young men.

When the entrance requirements for mathematics were increased, it enabled the Academic Board to shorten the course in pure mathematics from three to two years. The time saved was distributed among the professional subjects —ordnance, navigation, seamanship, marine and electrical engineering. Practically all these subjects involve the constant employment of mathematics; no midshipman is under the delusion that he finishes this subject at the end of his second year.

German and Italian were added to the course in languages in 1930, and Portuguese some years later. Among the extracurricular activities are the Language Clubs, sponsored by the Language Department. Each club has a reading room provided with newspapers and periodicals in the language studied. Midshipmen especially proficient in any language are designated as "interpreters" by the Department. Americans are notoriously poor linguists, largely because English has become almost a universal language. The Office of Naval Intelligence provides special courses in Japanese, Russian, Chinese, and other languages to junior officers of the Navy and Marine Corps to prepare them for duty as naval attachés. An officer must be proficient in all the subjects taught at the Academy, but the command of one particular language is a valuable asset to a young officer, and it will help any midshipman to qualify as an "interpreter."

The career of the brilliant Michelson has been an inspiration to the Electrical Engineering Department which has probably changed more than any other department in its determined effort to keep up with the continual improvements in electricity. This department has attracted some of the finest naval minds. Admiral Sampson was identified with it throughout his life; Dr. N. M. ("Cit") Terry and Professor "Navy Paul" Dashiell, long identified with the "Skinny Department," taught class after class of midshipmen who did not entirely appreciate the advantages to a seafarer of chemistry and physics. Most midshipmen first knew "Navy Paul" on the football field, for he coached the team for years. "Navy Paul" Dashiell gave powerful support to Academy athletics before the advantages of systematic physical exercise were generally recognized, and he will be remembered for this contribution long after his demonstrations that hydrogen and oxygen make water are forgotten.

The English and history courses were much improved in 1923 when the entrance requirements were raised. Since that time the Department has given an advanced course in composition and a course in English literature culminating in current English and American authors. Naval history has been broadened to include a study of sea power among the leading naval nations, and its influence on history, thus making Mahan's thesis and the reasons for a navy plain to young officers at the commencement of their careers. On Friday evenings, lectures on current subjects and present-day history are given by recognized contemporary authorities.

Many of the instructors and professors, and frequently the heads of the English and History departments, have been civilians. When they decide to remain at the Academy, they know they can never aspire to be Superintendent; at most they can hope to become head of their own department. And they must subordinate that department to the general educational plan of the Academy, which is primarily a technical school with the specific purpose of training midshipmen to become junior officers of the Navy. Civilian heads of this department, from Chaplain George

Jones to Doctor C. S. Alden, and the great majority of the professors and instructors, have loyally contributed to the Naval Academy.[4] Instructors assist midshipmen in editing the *Log*, *Reef Points*, the *Trident*, and the *Lucky Bag*. They sponsor the after-dinner speeches of the First Class, and for years have served on the editorial staff of *The Naval Institute*. The Navy before the Naval Academy inspired the same loyal spirit among most of its instructors and chaplains; it is impossible to read the reports and accounts of Chaplains Hunter, Thompson, and Wines, and the manuscript history of the Academy by Professor Thomas G. Ford, and not realize their deep affection for the naval service. To-day the civilian staff of the English Department enters fully into the lives of midshipmen.

Between 1798 and 1845 the daily routine of exercise at the guns and sails, the necessary evolutions in an average day at sea, could be relied upon to develop every muscle in a midshipman's body and to produce continual mental alertness. The hand-to-hand combats that characterized much of the Navy's fighting of that early period demanded and developed physical fitness, keen mental reactions, and a fighting spirit. No American midshipman could hope to distinguish himself in the fighting tops, at the end of a yard-arm, at the battery, or in boarding or repelling boarders, unless he was alert mentally, physically well developed, and trained in the use of the cutlass, pike, and tomahawk as well as the pistol.

Before being warranted, midshipmen were examined physically to ascertain whether they could perform the arduous duties at sea. All our early leaders insisted that midshipmen be physically fit. Commodore Rodgers recommented in 1816 that midshipmen, who then entered at a

[4] Chaplain Jones was an indefatigable advocate of a Naval Academy.

tender age, be taught the sword exercise as soon as they possessed sufficient strength. When the naval school was established, Commander Buchanan urged that a sloop-of-war be stationed at Annapolis to provide recreation and exercise as well as sail drill.

After 1851 there was always a sloop-of-war either at Annapolis or at Newport. Seamanship, gunnery, pulling boats, and later infantry and field artillery drills were depended upon to keep midshipmen fit until Admiral David D. Porter organized athletics at the Academy in 1866. He encouraged boxing and occasionally engaged in a bout with a midshipman, at the risk of his aquiline nose. He organized baseball teams, which played match games every Saturday afternoon, and race-boat crews which became famous in 1869-70. In 1867 athletic carnivals were held at the Academy, including track and field competitions, baseball, rowing, and gymnastics.

Admiral Porter also evoked the spirit of competition in athletics. During a practice cruise up the Hudson, he encouraged the midshipmen to challenge the cadets at West Point to boat races and a baseball game, and suggested to the Superintendent of West Point a competitive infantry drill between the two battalions. Admiral Porter aroused a competitive spirit which reached its first climax in the early 1890's in the annual football game between the two academies.

Midshipman Vaulx Carter organized the Annapolis football team in 1881-83. The Navy won its first game against the Clifton Football Team of Baltimore, 8 to 0. It was not a propitious time to begin football: upperclassmen were hazing more than usual; Commander Ramsay was beginning his series of reforms; Congress combined the midshipmen and cadet engineers into an unwanted union and legislated graduates out of the service.

By 1887 the physical condition of the midshipmen attracted unfavorable comment from visiting alumni and, inspired by Colonel Robert M. Thompson, class of 1868, they formed a Navy Athletic Association. In 1890 the first football game with West Point was played. The fierce rivalry displayed in the next two games caused President Cleveland to prohibit the Army-Navy games, but they had aroused interest in athletics at both academies and raised the standard of service teams. Colonel Thompson quietly began to plan for their revival, and in 1899 the second series of Army-Navy games began.

The natural attraction of football and the spirited rivalry between the two academies was enough to give an impetus to all forms of organized athletics at Annapolis. Eventually support from the Naval Academy alumni, as well as the gate receipts from football contests, financed the other non-profit-making teams. Any naturally active midshipman could find outlet for his energies in athletics. Strong midshipmen were made stronger. All midshipmen improved physically from the regular hours, the plain, substantial food, the setting-up exercises, and the infantry, field artillery, gunnery, boat, and seamanship drills. Those who were undeveloped, and for that reason hesitated to try for a team, did not directly benefit from the athletic program.

Beginning in the eighteen sixties, Matthew Strohm for forty years gave all midshipmen a start in gymnastics, a lesson or two in swimming, and a smattering of boxing and wrestling. Commencing at the same time, Swordmaster Corbesier gave fencing, broad sword, and single-stick exercises to all midshipmen for over fifty years. Pulling an oar, seamanship, infantry and artillery drills, hauling on the ends of the halyards, and hoisting boats built up some of the muscles of all midshipmen, but too many graduated in flabby condition. The Academy became aware of the situation and initiated various measures to make physical exercise more general. In 1923 the Department of Physical Training was created and was given the task of encouraging every midshipman to come out for some team. Gentle pressure was put on sedentary scholars by prescribing cross-country hikes, led by long-legged, fast-walking officers.

To-day physical training at the Academy fits the graduate for a long period of healthful service in the Navy, and also qualifies him to superintend the organized athletics in the fleet and coach the teams of enlisted men. As a result of the system at the Academy, athletics in the fleet have been systematized, and the physique and morale of enlisted men have been improved by the organization of ship, division, squadron, and fleet teams modeled after the academy teams. Practically all enlisted men have had two years at high school; many are high-school graduates. They are accustomed to high-school athletics and drop into the Navy's athletic system without any trouble.

The physical requirements of midshipmen are now prescribed for entrance, and a minimum of physical development is required each year until graduation. Standards must be met in swimming, muscular strength, jumping, running, correct posture, boxing, wrestling, and dancing. Fourth Classmen are instructed in football, baseball, crew, track and field, basket-ball, lacrosse, fencing, gymnastics, water polo, tennis, soccer, handball, squash, and calisthenics. Each succeeding year in the Academy, midshipmen must show improvement in swimming, strength, gymnasium, and posture. Second Classmen are taught to officiate at athletic contests, and First Classmen are given a course in coaching athletic teams. The physical improvement among the mass of midshipmen has not lowered the competitive standard of the Academy teams. Football, crew, baseball, and fifteen other organized teams which represent the Academy in extramural contests have done better since athletics were made universal.

The athletic system is simple but comprehensive. Every midshipman, on entrance, is encouraged to come out for the plebe (freshman) team of his favorite sport. He can pick from among eighteen different sports, ranging from football, crew, baseball, lacrosse, soccer, track, and swimming to fencing and golf. If he qualifies, he automatically becomes a candidate for the Navy (varsity) team in his Third Class year. If he does not qualify for the plebe team, he can find a place in intramural sports. In nearly every Academy sport there is also a battalion team similar to a collegiate intramural team. Each of these battalion teams requires a second team to practise against. The battalion teams provide opportunities for over 90 per cent of the midshipmen. The purpose of battalion sports is to get every midshipman to try for a team.

Football is the king of sports in the autumn. There are Navy, plebe, and battalion teams. The Navy team has a heavy schedule, playing three or four major teams such as Princeton, Pennsylvania, Cornell, and Notre Dame annually. The big game is with Army, and the Regiment usually judges a team on the result of that game.

The Navy's soccer team has been very successful. Those who have played soccer claim that there is no sport like it to build "leg and lungs." Even a spectator can testify that there is plenty of running, fighting, and good solid exercise in soccer, and the gallery has enough to watch.

Basket-ball, invented as a "filler in," has made its own place at Annapolis as shown by the steadily increasing attendance in the galleries. The Navy has made its place among the top-ranking eastern teams and can be depended upon to have a scrappy squad. Another early fall indoor sport is wrestling, which is a certain body builder as a doubting Thomas can discover by feeling the torso of any seasoned wrestler. Wrestling demands stamina, skill, courage, and determination. The head coach gives up-to-the-minute instruction to the veterans; the assistant teaches the elementary technic to the plebes. Candidates for both teams commence training in the early autumn and continue until March.

The small-bore rifle team has the highest competitive standing of any Academy sport, winning all but two of its dual matches in five years, and the intercollegiate championship oftener than any other team. The plebe team is depended upon to get an intercollegiate championship. The Academy system of coaching can claim the credit, for 75 per cent of the candidates have had no previous experience. There is a well-lighted small-bore gallery, and the records show that the eyes of members of the team *improve*. The practice on the rifle range during plebe summer (the first summer at the Academy) is a natural preparation for the small-bore competition, which leads to its big brother, the outdoor rifle. If a plebe is doubtful about making a satisfactory mark in recitations, he can study during the afternoon and still come out for small-bore rifle.

The rifle team is the only Navy sport open to plebes because it does not enter intercollegiate contests. The team competes with the sharp-shooting Marines and crack National Guard teams. The contestants have to make an almost perfect score to gain a place on the team, and the methods of instruction and training have produced marvelous results. Members of the Academy rifle team are almost certain to be detailed to coach the rifle teams of the ships to which they are ordered.

Swimming is another "natural" sport for midshipmen. The gymnasium in Macdonough Hall has a tank for training

AFTER PRELIMINARY INSTRUCTION WITH RIFLES, MIDSHIPMEN BEGIN
THE MARKSMAN COURSE ON THE RIFLE RANGE

BROADSIDE DRILL IN THE GUN SHED OVERLOOKING THE BAY IS A PRE-
LIMINARY TO OPERATING THE TURRET GUNS ABOARD SHIP

beginners; in addition, the Academy has one of the largest natatoriums in the country, and the Athletic Association furnishes excellent coaches. Ten years ago the Academy team won the national championship, and is now seeking to regain it. Before water polo was dropped from inter-collegiate sports, the Academy teams were among the champions. The ability to swim is particularly important, for in time of peace the Navy loses more men by drowning than by any other single cause. Although many victims are strong swimmers who become overconfident, or who fall overboard in a strong tideway with clothes and heavy shoes on, others drown who could be saved if they could stay afloat a short time. The Navy makes systematic efforts to teach every enlisted man to swim. Ensigns who have been on the swimming team at Annapolis are in demand as coaches when they arrive in the fleet.

Fencing and sword exercises have been a necessary part of a naval officer's training since the days of Commodore John Paul Jones, who included instruction in the use of the sword in his program for three naval schools. Commodore John Rodgers and all other officers who recommended a naval academy prescribed instruction in the use of the sword as a matter of course. If a midshipman was not skilful with the sword or pistol in the era of dueling, he might not live to get his commission. To-day fencing is one of more popular sports at Annapolis. Navy teams have won high standing with the foil, the épee, and the saber. As few of the plebes ever handled any of the three weapons be-fore entering the Academy, their standing is a tribute to the coaching system as well as to their own speed, coördina-tion, and balance. In the last four years the Academy team has been beaten *once;* in the last ten the plebe team only *twice.* Each year there is a match with the Army, and the contestants frequently wager the Navy's blue bathrobes against the Army's gray ones. Decatur would have counter-signed the invitation of the captain of the 1942 team, Mid-shipman R. C. Gooding, to the plebes, which reads, "The sword is an officer's weapon—learn to use it."

Another "natural" for the Academy is the crew. The Navy, old and young, felt intense satisfaction when the crew won the Olympic championship in 1920. As early as 1867, Admiral Porter had a crew, which in 1869-70 was good enough to justify his challenge to the rowing world. Winston Churchill, 1894, developed the first eight-oared crew in 1893. The crew to-day races the best of the eastern teams in the sprint races and then competes at the Poughkeepsie Regatta with the crack crews of the country. It is generally conceded that pulling in a crew requires just a little more dogged determination than any other form of sport; that last back-breaking stretch requires the "2:00 A.M. courage," the ability to fight to the end without benefit of cheering stands, only the far-off cry of a launch full of rooters. No other sport develops quite the same team spirit as those "eight men and a boy" in a shell, pull-ing as one man.

The basket-ball season is scarcely over before the base-ball pioneers are commandeering Dahlgren Hall, erecting batting cages, and calling out the whole squad. Under the watchful eye of the coach, the indoor training proceeds until the Ides of March permit the squad to begin regular outdoor practice. Baseball competes with the crew, fencing, lacrosse, track and field, the outdoor rifle team, tennis, and cross country for candidates from the plebes. Plebes are advised to go out for their company baseball team during plebe summer, but unless a plebe has already played base-ball the chance of his making the team is small. The aver-age plebe has played some baseball before arriving at the Academy, and the team usually finds sufficient candidates who have grown up with baseball, but the Navy team is handicapped in its collegiate competitions by the other spring sports.

There is no game quite so kaleidoscopic as lacrosse, which requires everything from foot work to head work among its players, and is sufficiently rough to satisfy the most exacting audience. It is understatement to say that the game has few dull moments. The Academy has produced excellent teams and has stood well in intercollegiate contests. An assistant coach trains the plebe team.

When Admiral Porter organized athletics at the Academy, he equipped a gymnasium in Fort Severn. Since that time some apparatus has been available for midshipmen. To-day skilful coaches patiently teach the plebes to use the horizontal bar, side horse, parallel bars, rope, flying rings, and tumbling mat. If a plebe appears at the gym and shows interest in any of the apparatus, some of the coaching staff will explain its intricacies, and if the interest continues, the plebe will be carefully instructed until he masters them all. In doing this he will discover and develop previously unknown muscles, and get the intense satisfaction that comes from having complete control over a well-developed muscular system. Under the tutelage of trained coaches there is no danger that one group of muscles will be overdeveloped or that the gymnast will become "muscle bound." There is plenty of competition, and in the Navy there is always inspiration to do just a little better than the other team. Such spirit leads to broken records.

Tennis is an entirely different game from what it was twenty years ago, largely because of American players, beginning with Big Bill Tilden. "Navy Paul" Dashiell used to practise on the Academy courts with Bill Larned, when the champion prepared to defend his title. Spectators thought they had a swift service. To-day, tennis has greater initial velocity, and Academy tennis has improved relatively more than the average. There are now twenty-five to forty courts on the grounds; six all-weather courts make it practicable to play occasionally in February. The numerous well-kept courts permit some excellent exhibition matches by leading players that always stimulate the home talent. One great advantage of playing tennis at the Academy is the ease with which the practice can be continued after going to sea. Tennis is an almost universal sport. In almost every port the tennis player can find a court: he needs only a partner, his racket, and a half-dozen balls.

Golf was considered an old man's game until the younger generation adopted it and compelled the grounds committees to lengthen the holes. When real estate became too valuable, the Golf Association slowed down the ball, but stronger and younger players continue to make the "par" score for most courses. Like tennis, golf is a lifelong game.

The track team offers opportunities to every candidate if "you have what it takes"—the ability to think and the combat spirit. Candidates for track enjoy expert coaching, and during the intercollegiate meets they see the track athletes of the country in action.

Closely akin to track is cross country. Only the lonely heart knows how tough the going becomes before the final line is crossed. Except for a few enthusiastic fans, there will be only a bored glance by the spectators of another more appealing contest, many of whom wonder what the bother is about. But the runner who can take the punishment alone, keep plugging, and win an anonymous victory is preparing himself for the "silent service," the Navy. His goings and comings in the fleet during peace and war will be shrouded in secrecy; no one will applaud that perilous periscope watch kept over an enemy base, because no one will be allowed to know about it. The inner satisfaction is greater; that feeling of having contributed to the Academy encourages the larger willingness to contribute to the nation. Cross country is deservedly popular at Annapolis.

For many years the Navy had a boxing team, but now the manly art of self-defense is limited to battalion contests, where Navy officials can preside. Plebes are still instructed in the art.

The latest addition to Navy sports is squash. Eight new courts have been constructed, permitting larger participation, and the incoming plebes are promptly informed of the increased facilities and that the coach is at their service. Squash is an easy game to learn, but a hard game to play well, but it is another exercise that helps in later years to keep that Academy figure, for squash courts are available in many city clubs.

The Academy is determined that its athletic system shall not be limited to making strong midshipmen stronger. The battalion teams are organized to pass athletics around to all, particularly to those who hesitate to try for the Academy or plebe teams. The primary purpose of battalion sports is to get every man possible out for sports. Numerals are presented to each member of the winning team in all sports, and points are awarded that count toward the company swords and the battalion cups and shields. One battalion football player, during his Second Class year, made the Academy team and an All-American team, but he was exceptional. Battalion teams are coached by Academy officers, ex-letter-men in their respective sports. *Reef Points* sums up the requirements for battalion sports in a challenging sentence: "A little red blood and a desire to make something of your body and character are the only requirements—are you wanting of these?"

Athletics at the Naval Academy are designed to produce

more than vigorous young men, radiating health, whose long supple back muscles ripple under their blue blouses. Bodies may be perfect, but if the fighting spirit is not there these physical giants are no use to Uncle Sam. Competition in athletic contests tends to produce the combat spirit. A deuce tennis match, an extra-hole golf match, a relay race where an undaunted runner starting from behind manages somehow to pull even or draw ahead, a hotly contested lacrosse or soccer match, a grueling crew race where the fast-pumping heart almost breaks the blood vessels—all such contests develop the will to endure, the determination to conquer, the spirit of combat that are essential in a fleet.

A football game perhaps approaches a little nearer to battle than any other sport. It requires the team spirit essential in a turret's crew of a battleship, a submarine, a destroyer, and a fleet itself: the individual must play when every muscle aches, when tendons are strained, ribs broken, eyes gashed and partly closed. The game creates a satanic desire to put the opposing player out of the road that is identical with battle emotions; it provides a feeling of exultation when the opposing side begins to crumble, the proud assurance that grips the soul when it feels the opponent is dominated and that spurs the body to the last ounce of effort always necessary to defeat a strong, resolute enemy. Clear heads must be kept in the bruised bodies to seek the weak point of the enemy line and send a crashing attack through it or a forward pass over it; or, if the players are standing under the shadows of their own goal posts, to divine where the enemy attack will come and break it up.

One of the best battalion commanders in the Marine Corps during the last war said a good battalion did not commence fighting in earnest until it had lost one-third of its men; his particular battalion was a crack outfit, but military records show that there have been many inspired organizations who will fight to the last man. This ability to endure and to think clearly when the contest rages, when the battle goes badly, is what enabled Perry to shift flagships at Lake Erie, Macdonough to wind ship and re-open the battle with a fresh battery, and Paul Jones to realize that his ship might be destroyed but that he could not be defeated. Athletic contests develop a willingness among midshipmen to take punishment for the Academy. This same spirit will inspire them to give all they have for their country.

With this spirit of sacrifice goes an understandable desire for distinction, to be first aboard an enemy ship like Charles Morris, or as Cushing put it, "Where there is fighting there we will be, and where there is danger in the battle, *there will I be*, for I *will* gain a name in this war." A few individuals inherit the almost divine spirit of a Cushing, a Somers, a Decatur, but even warlike races such as Sparta and Ancient Rome found it necessary to inculcate and encourage this martial spirit. Not the least of the Academy's responsibilities is to preserve the wonderful blend of ambition and sacrifice that existed among American midshipmen before Annapolis was founded. Its athletic teams offer the Academy a suitable instrument to meet this obligation.

Extracurricular Activities

BUSY people always have the most leisure, and in spite of their crowded daily and weekly routine, midshipmen find time to enjoy a comprehensive group of extracurricular activities. There is the Naval Academy Christian Association, headed by the Chaplain, assisted by a Council of Midshipmen, and supported entirely by the Regiment. Its programs vary from week to week with singers, trumpeters, quartets; high-ranking Naval officers, hypnotists, and even magicians are among the speakers and entertainers presented by the association. Their meetings are held after supper every second Sunday in Recreation Hall. The association also provides popular and technical magazines and it coöperates with the Maryland Bible Society in presenting Bibles to each member of the First Class immediately prior to graduation. The Newman Club is similar to Newman Clubs in universities and colleges and offers midshipmen an opportunity to learn of the "Godlike side of their natures." Every midshipman of the Catholic faith is considered a member of the Newman Club. At their meetings such subjects as Christian living, marriage, modern economics, labor, social and political problems are discussed from the viewpoint of the Catholic Church. All midshipmen of whatever creed are welcomed into the Naval Academy Christian Association and the Newman Club.

Since physical training was given its present status, athletics are no longer extracurricular activities. But physical training, drills, and recreations are closely related. For example, a plebe commences to pull an oar and to have rifle practice as drills, but he will progress to the Boat Club, an extracurricular, and the rifle team, a sport. To qualify as a member of the Boat Club, a plebe must become an adept with an oar in a cutter at boat drill and pass a preliminary examination in handling small boats; he will then become a junior member. During the academic year, he must learn enough theoretical seamanship to become a senior member. For administration purposes, activities are designated as academic, physical training, or extracurricular, but similar activities under different administrators are neatly fitted together.

All the fine old sailor-men who created our Navy look down from aloft and smile approvingly upon the Naval Academy Boat Club, the center of all sailing activities of the midshipmen. The club is an extracurricular under the Executive Department. All midshipmen are eligible to join. Landlubbers are soon taught the rudiments of sailing, and good sailors are given a chance to become more proficient. Every midshipman must eventually qualify to handle all types of these smart-handling small boats and yachts. All officers of the club are elected. The commodore is a First Classman; in addition there are a vice commodore, a treasurer, and a ketch captain for each battalion.

The craft available for sailing are numerous and varied. There are twenty knock-abouts, ten half-raters, eight star-boats, and twelve whale-boats especially designed and rigged to train green midshipmen. In addition there are twelve ten-foot dinghies and twenty fourteen-foot international dinghies for the exclusive use of the sailing team and certain privileged members of the club. Besides these small craft, there are four ketches—converted fifty-foot motor launches provided with a deck cabin. They have been christened *Bullfrog, Crocodile, Turtle,* and *Alligator,* and each battalion is assigned a ketch. The four latest acquisitions of the Naval Academy Yacht Squadron, a big brother of the Boat Club, have been presented by friends of the Navy who are interested in keeping alive the fine art of sailing in these days of steam fleets. The mahogany hull of the ketch-rigged *Vamarie* is beautiful to look upon, but it is her staysail and wishbone rig which have enabled her to make an enviable record as a racer. Among her trophies is the Bermuda Race blue ribbon. The sixty-eight-foot cutter *Highland Light* is another winner with a transatlantic as well as a Bermuda Race record. The racing schooner *Freedom* is two masted, topsail-rigged, with wide beam and fast counter, well balanced and beautifully appointed. The sloop-rigged speedster *Spindrift,* a deep water sailer, can outpoint any yacht in the Bay and is the easiest of the Academy's racing team to sail.

Every Saturday and Sunday the big ones are sailed by officers with volunteer crews from the Regiment, and there are many applicants for the all-day sails. Biennial races are sailed off the Academy between the Boat Club and the Annapolis Yacht Club. The races continue for six weeks and are extremely popular with the underclassmen. Intercollegiate sailing is growing in popularity, and the Naval Academy, with its unusual facilities, is becoming the center of mid-Atlantic contests. The climax of the sailing season are the ocean races; in the summer of 1941, the Academy racing squadron entered in the New London to Hampton, Virginia, race and took two of the first three places. Midshipmen gladly give up their annual leave to serve aboard these racers. Sailing gives midshipmen the feel of the sea, that instinctive realization of the effect of wind and sea upon a ship which will stand them in good stead when they

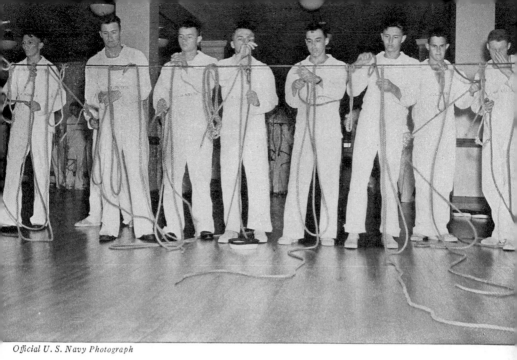

JACKSTAY DRILL—PRACTICE IN "KNOTTING AND SPLICING"

BOAT DRILL IS AN IMPORTANT PART OF THE PLEBE'S SUMMER
CURRICULUM

begin handling destroyers, submarines, cruisers, and finally battleships. Sailing is an inspiring sport, but it is also the basis of the naval profession. It is reassuring to know that the members of the Regiments of to-day turn out in ever increasing numbers for the sailing races; even a pessimistic old-timer will concede that the Academy has not gone to the bow-wows, when sailing is its most popular recreation.

The Academy has four publications. The *Lucky Bag*, the oldest, had brilliant ancestors in *Shakings, Junk,* and *Fag Ends,* which did not survive. The *Lucky Bag* is the year-book of the Regiment of Midshipmen, edited and published annually by the First Class. It reviews the activities and athletics of the Academy and contains a brief biography and pictorial record of each member of the graduating class. Each class elects the editor and business manager for its *Lucky Bag* toward the end of youngster year. Plebes and youngsters obtain valuable experience as assistants to the editorial and business staffs of the First or Second Class *Lucky Bag*. Membership on the staff means taking considerable responsibility, for the *Lucky Bag* is a $20,000 to $30,000 enterprise.

The *Log*, a weekly publication, cheers the Regiment every Friday afternoon with news, pictures, stories, and professional notes; its editors lampoon midshipmen freely and deal as broadly with officers and instructors as naval customs permit. It is issued by the joint efforts of a large staff. "Salty Sam" regularly purveys the latest from the scuttlebut, while "Old Navy Line" provides the weekly "rehash."

In January, 1941, the *Log* issued a Fleet Number, with an article on "The Influence of Sea Power in Present Mediterranean Conflict" by W. H. Esworthy and another on that burning question, "Sea Power versus Air Power" by W. R. R. Blett. In the June Week issue there were tributes

to the beautiful girls who blush unseen on "locker doors."
The arrangement of the pictures is a tribute to the editorial
staff of the *Log;* the pulchritude of the fair lady contestants
attests the good taste of the Regiment.

The editorial staff of the *Log* has won recognition from
its contemporary and bitter rivals, including the *Washington Boast;* but probably its sea-going editors—including
Salty Sam—are proudest of being chosen to decide the
"Queen and Court" for the University of Kansas City and
to select the two most beautiful girls in Georgia Teachers
College, Statesboro, Georgia. Their success in solving these
problems prove they possess two characteristics of the
naval profession—a discriminating eye for a beautiful girl,
and dauntless courage, in daring to choose among so much
loveliness.

All kinds of talents are needed on the staff of the *Log*—
writers, staff photographers, news sleuths, and solicitors for
the advertising department. All plebes with a flair for
newspaper work should cautiously consult upperclassmen
on the prospects for a job on the *Log.*

The Trident Assocation was organized to foster the pro-
duction of naval literature and to collect and preserve the
naval traditions now existing. It, too, needs a large assortment of talent. Two essays, "One Ton Per Acre" by John
G. Hill 2nd, 1942, on the Anglo-American trade of bases
for destroyers, and "Wings Over Corpus Christi" by Harry
H. Loeffler, 1944, describing the Navy's new aviation base
in Texas, exemplify the *Trident's* more serious articles.
Its art department deserves special mention; its cameras
bring out equally clearly the charm of an old hempen
hawser on a dock, or a spray of iris; and in the June Week
Number, 1941, is a superb series of "Ships In Color" reproduced from originals in the United States Naval Museum. All plebes interested in literature are welcome to

join the Association. The *Trident* calendars make beautiful presents; they are popular with the Regiment, and a smart plebe will get his order in early, for the stock is often exhausted. The Trident Society correlates the activities of all associations interested in art and literature, such as the *Log, Reef Points*, Quarterdeck Society, Art Club, Photographic Club, and the Christmas Card Committee.

Reef Points has a definite purpose: it exists to indoctrinate the new Fourth Classmen by giving them a brief account of the Naval Academy and the atmosphere surrounding it. It publishes an accurate description of the grounds, activities, and athletics, with pertinent facts about the Navy that will assist the plebe to get his bearings. It is comprehensive in its scope, supplying useful information about early naval history and continuing to descriptions of the sailing yachts at the Academy. The foreword of the 1941-42 *Reef Points* carries a challenging message to the new-comers: "Learn your navy so that you may know for yourself what our great organization has in store for you. ... Mold your way of living into one becoming to a midshipman ... which will enable you to become a fighting officer of the Navy and a service to your country."[1] The important part taken by *Reef Points* in the life of the Academy is indicated by a message it carries from a recent Superintendent, Rear Admiral Russell Willson, urging all midshipmen to accept "high and uncompromising standards of character and conduct. ... Remember that being of the Navy you are of an ancient and honorable profession ... a profession which during twenty-five centuries has often guided the course of history. ... You are fortunate young men. Be worthy of your good fortune."

Many of our early officers were noted for their pro-

---

[1] *Reef Points* and the *Log* have furnished the information on current athletics and extracurricular activities used in this book.

found religious faith. Macdonough dropped on his knees on the quarter-deck of the *Saratoga* to implore divine assistance before beginning the Battle of Lake Champlain. Farragut was a devout Christian, although his exclamation, "Damn the torpedoes" is most often quoted. Other names could be cited. In the old wardrooms religion was never discussed because around the same table were gathered members of different faiths. The Navy has never encouraged excessive psalm-singing. But every thinking officer knows that over the body is the mind, and over them both is the spirit or soul. In their own way, naval officers cultivate that spirit. At the Academy the Chaplain is supported by officers, some of whom do not attend services. *Reef Points* gives "The Prayer of a Midshipman" in which this sentiment, which might have been uttered by Macdonough or Farragut, occurs: "If I am inclined to doubt, steady my faith; if I am tempted, make me strong to resist; if I should miss the mark, give me courage to try again."

Reef Points is printed and ready for distribution to the plebes when they report in the spring of the year, and a wise plebe will immediately familiarize himself with its contents. If a new-comer follows closely its detailed instructions, he will avoid many pitfalls and enjoy a pleasanter first year in the Academy.

Reef Points contributes this valuable "Information for Plebes":

You will soon discover that you know very little about the service of which you have so lately become a part. Make it your duty to learn as much about it as possible. Academic subjects have manifest importance to you, but you may fail to realize the significance of another phase of your Academy life. You wonder, for instance, why you are denied privileges accorded to your seniors. You question the wisdom of being required to perform tasks for which there is no apparent reason.

Not only the Naval Academy but the entire Naval Service is based on a series of rates and traditions which must be strictly observed to maintain our recognized effectiveness and efficiency. A little thought will show you why you must be, at present, on the wrong side of nearly all the rates. As time passes, you will not only become more clearly aware of their value, but will find yourself continually falling heir to increased rights.

Privileges not had are all the more appreciated and enjoyed when you do get them. Remember that you will eventually acquire all of them. The highest ranking officers in the fleet were once in your position. The seemingly pointless tasks will teach you resourcefulness and cheerful obedience. We all learn it; never for a moment think that you are being subjected to anything which has not been included in the training of every naval officer. Above all, remember, "Be cheerful."

The following are guides to your "rates."

1. When you receive an order from a senior, say, "Aye, aye, sir," and promptly carry it out to the best of your ability. Never argue.

2. Be punctilious, as are all naval men, in the use of the word "Sir" in addressing seniors. Always include it in your conversation with officers and upperclassmen. In oral communication, refer to seniors as "Mister" if they are below the rank of commander. Commanders and above are addressed with their rank. Do not use "Mister" when referring to a classmate.

3. Maintain a correct posture, and take pride in your military appearance. If you do not, you will soon be reminded of it. When in uniform particularly, conduct yourself in such a manner as to bring credit upon it, whether you are in the Yard, in town, or on leave.

4. By all means go out for some sport during plebe year. If you turn out to be a zero athlete, there is listed in these pages a variety of non-athletic activities to occupy you. [*Caution, by author*—Not if it jeopardizes your 2.5.]

5. Keep track of what goes on around you. Subscribe to a daily paper for news of the outside world. Magazines will be found in Smoke Hall. At meals, plebes should know the menu,

the Officer of the Watch, the scheduled events of the day, the movies in Annapolis and at Mahan Hall, besides any questions previously asked them by upperclassmen.

6. Plebes are never allowed to drag, except to the Masqueraders, Musical Clubs, and Navy Relief Shows, and to the Concert Series performances. Whether dragging to the shows or not, you do not rate being on the floor at any of the official hops in the yard.

7. Double time to all formations, and clear of the terrace on return from classes. Do not leave your room before formation bell. Keep in the center of the corridors and to the outside of ladders at all times. Find out which are the youngster and second-class ladders in your battalion, and never use these.

8. Don't be afraid to ask questions of upperclassmen; request permission first. You will find them ready and glad to help you.

9. Youngster Cutoff, Lover's Lane, Smoke Park, and the first- and second-class benches on Stribling Walk are not yours during academic year. Keep off.

10. Do not loiter or talk in the corridors or at unauthorized times in the mess hall.

11. Keep in some complete uniform at all times until tattoo. It is not your rate to turn in before taps or to lie on your bed during the day.

12. Rings and fancy belts are taboo.

13. Learn all the songs and yells, word for word, to use at the football games this fall. Attend all varsity and plebe athletic contests, and stay clear of the first few rows at varsity events—they are reserved for the First Class.

14. Do not tolerate "gouging" among your classmates. Gougers should be reported without hesitation, but be sure you are right.

15. Remember that griping only makes matters seem worse. Show a smile; nothing can go further to make life livable.

16. Plebes rate attending N. A. C. A. always.

17. Be proud of your coming profession, that of a naval officer. Take pride in learning all you can about the past and present of this great organization. Maybe keeping a Navy scrap-book would help. Give it a try.

18. Work hard but don't get the reputation of being a "cutthroat."

19. Be a good sport. During an athletic contest the official may make a decision or an opposing player may do some act that appears unfair to you. No matter how it affects the Navy team do not boo.

20. When "carrying on" do so as quietly as possible. Be careful not to usurp upperclass rates.

21. Do not allow your behavior to subject a classmate to a reprimand or to the conduct report.

22. Keep careful note of the times and dates of your engagements and duties, such as tailor shop, parties, watch dates, etc.[2]

The admonitions to plebes evolved from long experience; the *Lucky Bag* of 1902 contained the following "Don'ts" for plebes, which are substantially repeated in *Reef Points:*

Don't

Labor under the impression you are an admiral; you are not.
Be familiar with upperclassmen.
Walk on Lover's Lane; the gravel might hurt your feet.
Cut corners.
Sit on First Class bench.
Swing your arms.
Wear your cap on the side of your head.
Purchase non-regulation clothes.
Go to hops.
Forget that everyone above you was once a plebe too.

The midshipmen have an association to develop the art of public speaking. It is known as the Quarterdeck Society, and there is considerable doubt whether some of the taciturn founders of the Navy would approve this organization which holds meetings twice a month on Thursday nights where they harangue each other in succession. In 1941 the Society entered the intercollegiate debates.

[2] To assist the plebe interpret this advice there is a glossary of Naval Academy slang on page 237.

The following is quoted from the *Log:* "The purpose of the Quarterdeck Society is to give midshipmen a chance to say what they want about anything, whenever and however they want to. There are no verbal holds barred. There is, of course, the danger of having to face an equally savage onslaught of language from another speaker, but seldom do arguments go beyond the word stage. In short, the Quarterdeck Society offers to all hands the opportunity of speaking their minds.... During the rest of our naval careers we will frequently, and unexpectedly, be called upon 'to say a few words.' Start now to eliminate any necessity of fumbling with an 'Unaccustomed as I am to public speaking.' "

The First Class have dinners, after which members are called upon "to say a few words"; these dinners are sponsored by the Department of English, History and Government and are not connected with the Quarterdeck Society, although they have the same objective.

The Navy has always been light-hearted and fond of music and the coming naval generations will not lack musical talent. There are four musical associations in the Regiment: the Orchestra, the Glee Club, the N.A. Ten, and the Mandolin Club. The N.A. Ten provides music for informal dances and occasionally for a First Class hop, but its real masterpiece is the Music Clubs Show which is an operetta-comedy. The Mandolin Club is open to any midshipman who can plunk a stringed instrument. Its instruments now embrace everything from violins to tenor guitars, and it is looking forward to a harp. The Mandolin Club is sometimes guilty of crooning, but the Glee Club is the place for those barber-shop tenors who love to sing "Home on the Range," "Dan Magrew," "Barnacle Bill the Sailor," and "Old Sailors Never Die."

There was a drum and fife corps at the Academy in the

eighties. For some reason it disappeared. When Rear Admiral Nulton, 1889, returned as Superintendent in 1925, he reëstablished it. It again became a "flourishing" organization, and when it played a Navy march at the Army-Navy game, gouty old legs limbered up and old-timers stepped out with a quick step. The "corps" were at the peak of form marching on Franklin Field. On account of the time lost from drills and recitations, it has been necessary to discontinue the corps. May it be revived in all its glory.

The Masqueraders produce one serious play each year by a ranking playwright. A few players manage to conceal their muscular, brawny arms and hairy chests, but generally they make a poor imitation of a sweet piece of femininity despite their praiseworthy efforts. They sometimes add amateur actresses to the cast. Male actors sometimes deceive the audience, and all hands thoroughly enjoy the show even when a deep-throated masculine voice chirps like some fair young miss just out of a convent.

Closely akin to the musical clubs is service on the Hop Committee and Reception Committee. Members of the Hop Committee have to be tactful Chesterfields. One of their diplomatic assignments is to prevent modernistic dancing offending the dignified precincts of Dahlgren Hall. The Hop Committee also invites a hostess for each hop, and one of its own members receives with her. The Reception Committee entertains visiting athletic teams during their stay at the Academy.

For one performer on the boards, many labor behind the scenes. Among those at the Naval Academy is the electrical gang that furnishes the electrical effects and displays for all midshipmen activities—in particular those for the Masqueraders. Its members are in charge of the score-boards of athletic games and produce colorful effects at Navy dances. There is also a movie gang which assists the regular attendants in operating the sound motion-picture equipment, and a property gang and stage gang who provide, prepare, and safeguard all the stage settings, costumes, and other paraphernalia necessary for the Masqueraders and the Musical Shows. The business gang must provide "best seats" for 1,300 midshipmen and numerous officers, instructors, and civilian friends.

The three upper classes have their class organizations, consisting of permanent class officers who are in charge of all class functions. These officers are a president, a vice-president, a secretary-treasurer, and one representative from each company. They are elected annually. The class ring committee consists of the class president, one member of the class from each company, and one from the class at large. This committee is selected during the Third Class year. Ordinarily the recommendations of the ring committee are accepted. During the early 1900's the class rings grew bigger and better each year until some members of one class rebelled at the size proposd by their committee. A bitter dispute was finally settled by having rings of two sizes, large and small. The class ring is the traditional symbol of honor, loyalty, and devotion to duty. It is generally worn for the first time on the first day of June Week of Second Class year. Some rings slip right off the midshipmen's fingers on to the fingers of their best girls before June Week is over.

Really heavy suitors sometimes present their girls with a miniature class ring. The *Log* insists that:

1. A girl who accepts a miniature has to marry the gentleman.
2. Your drag should not look at your ring before she slips it on your finger.
3. You should wear your ring with the class crest inboard (toward your thumb), until after you graduate. Then you turn it around.

4. Those elusive numerals "2.5" (the mark necessary to graduate) be included in the design of every ring.
5. The ring be baptized in water from the Seven Seas.

The Art Club encourages artistically inclined midshipmen. It makes illustrations, posters, and cover designs for the various publications. An amateur radio group maintains and operates station W3ADO; members have an excellent opportunity to qualify as Government-licensed operators.

On Friday nights during the football season the band plays the Navy songs in the Mess Hall. The cheerleaders are in charge. They direct all organized cheering and, assisted by the "pep" committee, develop the stunts and cheers for the Naval Academy teams, particularly for the football game between Annapolis and West Point. They are selected each year from the Second Class, who are given tryouts to prove their ability to lead the midshipmen in cheering. These cheer-leaders are at the top of their form at Franklin Field in Philadelphia, when they do their flip-flops and lead the midshipmen in their vocal support of the team. Among the most important functionaries are the goat keepers—two in number, who have charge of His Highness William the Goat prior to and during his pontifical presence at all important athletic events. The keepers are required to see that his honorable whiskers are properly combed and his horns burnished. In addition, each year they must devise a different and more imperial method of bringing him on the field, for His Highness gets more difficult to please as he grows older, and the goat keepers must not allow the Army mule to frighten the goat. It is rumored that to prevent such a humiliation, small portions of red pepper are kept at hand to make sure that the Honorable William the Goat shows the proper spirit.

William Chauvenet would approve the Mathematical

Department which—thanks to such professors as William H. Wilcox, date of 1841, W. W. ("Pop") Hendrickson, 1863, P. R. Alger, 1876, and the two Woolsey Johnsons, father and son—has constantly maintained the high standard he set in 1845; but he would glow with pride that the Naval Academy, which he did so much to found, had enough midshipmen interested in the philosophy of mathematics to create a Mathematics Club. The Board of Examiners who excluded calculus from the original curriculum would be startled to know that the basic qualification for membership is a knowledge of "integral calculus."

The Choir is an ancient institution, and when it sings the well-known hymn, "For Those in Peril on the Sea" on "Sob" Sunday, handkerchiefs come out in all directions, and hearty old admirals clear their throats with astonishing frequency. The Choir sometimes broadcasts on Navy Day, and it is a marble-hearted Alumnus who doesn't feel a tingling sensation when he hears that deep-sea hymn as plainly as if he were in the superintendent's pew in the Chapel.

The Chess Club is a new-comer at Annapolis, but the Navy followers of Paul Morphy are ardent fans. The Stamp Club makes a wide appeal, and collecting stamps is a hobby that a midshipman can enjoy throughout his service career. There is a Class Crest Committee and a Christmas Card Committee, for crests and Christmas greetings must be in the best Academy tradition.

All together, "extracurricular" offers outlets for practically every desire that ever surged in the breast of man. Lastly there is the Academy Library where the midshipman who enjoys an occasional hour with a good book can find almost anything an inquiring naval mind desires. Again the warning signal must be hoisted. There is a tempting display of the latest books on the world situation and the best of the recent fiction; great self-control is necessary lest the book lover acquire valuable information not about the subjects in which he will be examined.

Rear Admiral Russell Willson, recent Superintendent, adopted a policy of treating midshipmen as young officers. He modified the prohibition against upperclassmen riding in automobiles; he changed the time of chapel to 9:30 A.M., so that there would be time for midshipmen to get recreation after chapel; and he excused one of the four battalions in rotation from attendance. Midshipmen now attend chapel three out of four Sundays. Admiral Willson gave the Regiment more opportunity for recreation and for participating more fully in the extracurricular activities.

How to Enter and Graduate

THERE are five ways of obtaining appointments to the Naval Academy. Five appointees in the Academy are allowed each Senator, Representative, Delegate in Congress, and the Vice-President. These appointees form the bulk of the midshipmen, and the surest way for the average American lad to get an appointment is through his Senator or Representative, who awards appointments either outright or after a competitive examination. The President is allowed five appointees for the District of Columbia, who are usually chosen after competitive examinations, and twenty-five appointees from the nation at large, usually selected after competitive examination, open only to sons of officers and men of the regular Army and Navy. One hundred appointees annually are authorized from the enlisted men of the Navy, one hundred from the enlisted men of the Navy and Marine Corps Reserve, and twenty from the honor graduates of "honor schools"—the president of each institution with a Naval R.O.T.C. Unit can nominate three students to enter the competitive examination for these twenty appointments. The Department provides special instruction for enlisted men, regular and reserve, seeking to enter the Academy. In 1941 there were about four hundred and fifty former enlisted men, regular and reserve, in the Regiment, and there were eighty-seven of them in the class of 1942, which graduated in December, 1941. The system now in effect makes it possible for any enlisted man who can pass the required examinations to enter the Academy and prepare himself to become an admiral.

The Governor of the Panama Canal Zone is allowed one appointee from the American civilian employees of the Zone. Puerto Rico is allowed five appointees, and the Philippines four, but Filipinos are not eligible for commissions in the Navy. Twenty appointees from South American republics are authorized to attend the Academy.

As many as three alternates may be nominated with the principal candidate and all may take the same entrance examination; if the principal fails, the first, second, or third alternate may be admitted, provided he passes and those ahead of him fail. Some Congressmen name four candidates without preference, and the one with the highest mark enters. If one is unable to secure a principal appointment, alternate appointments should be accepted. Many officers in the Navy to-day entered on an alternate appointment. All appointees, except those from foreign countries, must be citizens of the United States; they must be not less than seventeen years of age nor more than twenty-one years of age on April 1st of the calendar year in which they enter the Academy. They must be unmarried, and must never have been married. These are basic requirements, but Congress may change them at any time. A prospective candidate should write the Bureau of Navigation, Navy Department, Washington, D. C., for the circular giving the latest "Regulations Governing the Admission of Candidates into the United States Naval Academy as Midshipmen, and Sample Examination Papers."

The following is based upon the circular of June, 1940. All candidates must pass a physical and mental examination before entering. They must be physically sound, well formed, and of robust constitution. There are many specific defects that automatically disqualify a candidate, and none of these will be waived. There are numerous cities in the United States where a preliminary physical examination will be given prospective candidates by Naval surgeons, which vary in number from two in Delaware to thirty-one in Texas. An appointee should go at once to the nearest station for examination, for if he is physically defective he should not waste time and money attempting to enter the Academy; some minor defects may be removed by operation, but any major defect is an insuperable barrier.

Having satisfied himself that he can pass the physical examination, the candidate should next consider whether he is eligible to enter upon a certificate, a certificate with substantiating examinations in English and mathematics, or by examination in the six subjects: English, United States history, physics, chemistry, algebra, and plane and solid geometry. The Examining Board facilitates the entrance of physically qualified appointees and welcomes those who can reasonably be expected to complete the four years' course. The Board will accept without examination a candidate that is or has been a regularly enrolled student in good standing in a university, college, or technical school accredited by the Academy, provided: (1) The entrance requirements of the course pursued in college include the fifteen secondary school units—or that, failing this, extra college credits are presented in these subjects. (2) At the time of entrance, the candidate shall have satisfactorily completed a year's work in the university, college, or technical school, with a minimum of twenty-four semester-hours' credit in English, natural science, social science, or languages, at least six of which shall be in college English, or history, and six in college mathematics.

If the college certificate shows low or barely passing

YOUNGSTERS MEASURING THE ALTITUDE OF THE SUN WITH SEXTANTS

SIGNAL DRILL

SECOND CLASSMEN OPERATING GEN-
ERATORS IN MARINE ENGINEERING
LABORATORY

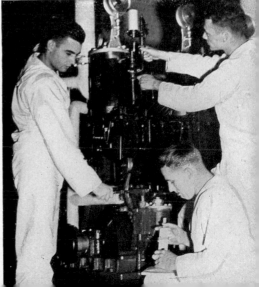

grades, or if the candidate has been out of college a year, he must qualify by mental examination.

A candidate presenting a certificate showing he has graduated from an accredited secondary school with marks above the school's minimum for passing will be accepted if he can pass substantiating examinations in mathematics through quadratics and beyond, including the binomial theorem, and arithmetic and geometric progressions, and one unit of plane geometry; and in English if the candidate has had three or more years of English composition and literature. The majority of candidates enter after presenting a certificate and taking the substantiating examinations.

All candidates from purely competitive sources, such as Presidential appointees, etc., must take mental examinations, as follows:

Time	Subject
FIRST DAY	
30 minutes...	Fill out declaration sheet (9:30 to 10 A.M.)
2 hours.....	1. United States History (10 A.M. to 12 M.)
2 hours.....	2. Physics (2 to 4 P.M.)
SECOND DAY	
3 hours.....	3. Algebra (9 A.M. to 12 M.)
2 hours.....	4. English (1 to 3 P.M.)
THIRD DAY	
3 hours.....	5. Plane and Solid Geometry (9 A.M. to 12 M.)
2 hours.....	6. Chemistry (1 to 3 P.M.)

Whether proposing to enter by the certificate, the certificate plus substantiating examinations, or by straight examinations, a candidate should write the Academic Board, stating his qualifications and the credits he can offer. The Board will advise him carefully, even giving him an informal opinion on the prospects of acceptance of his certificate. A candidate should regard the Board as his counselor who will explain in detail how to enter, or will warn him if his previous preparation or educational record indicates he can not meet the requirements.

The examinations are not tricky but they are thorough and searching and must be finished expeditiously; two hours each are allowed for history, physics, English, and chemistry; three hours each for algebra and geometry. Some candidates unaccustomed to time limits on examinations have failed, although with some experience in this form of examination, they could probably have entered. Any candidate should train himself to answer sample questions in the time limit prescribed. The fact that year after year five hundred to one thousand young Americans enter the Naval Academy is proof that it can be done without a herculean effort. No ambitious young American should be appalled at the prospect of the examination, but should apply himself diligently to the subjects required; he must know them thoroughly and must be able to express himself clearly enough to convince the Academic Board that he is well prepared in the required subjects.

After passing his mental and physical examinations and making a deposit of $100, to which the United States adds $250, to cover his immediate purchases from the Midshipmen's Store, the successful candidate with a group of his new classmates will be assembled to be sworn into the Navy. This impressive ceremony usually takes place in Memorial Hall in front of Perry's flag, "Don't Give Up the Ship," and surrounded by portraits, busts, mementos and almost sacred naval relics which remind the aspirants that if they live up to the best of their predecessors their memories will be cherished by their successors and they will be welcomed in the naval Valhalla. American youths are not given to heroics, and probably most of them are not as impressed as the officer who administers the oath, who realizes better than the candidates that they are taking a very solemn obligation, to uphold the Constitution and to defend it from all enemies whomsoever. Later, when a midshipman has had more time to reflect, he will recognize that at that particular moment he laid aside some of his privileges as an American citizen and accepted the obligations of an officer in the United States Navy. He also acquired privileges: he can not be punished except in accordance with the laws and customs of the Navy, and he will be treated with the respect accorded an officer and gentleman. He is no longer a young civilian, but a midshipman in the Navy, and hereafter he must remember that his conduct reflects upon the Navy as well as upon himself.

One of the early decisions is the choice of a room-mate. Some late comers have to take each other on faith, but those hasty combinations are likely to be as lasting as some of the violent friendships made during preparatory school days. With many similar interests, unless midshipmen are absolutely incompatible, they can live two, three, or even four in a room with little friction and frequently with increasing pleasure as the days go by. Friendships made at Annapolis usually endure; room-mates and cronies at the Academy grow old together in the service, and those going into civil life, though separated from those in the Navy for years, immediately resume their intimacy with them when their paths cross.

Other problems press upon the plebe: he has a credit established at the Midshipmen's Store, and he must obtain a hundred odd things, to begin housekeeping and equip himself with his Navy clothes. Every article from his undershirt and socks to his snappy blue uniform is regulation. He obtains most of them the first day—except for the blue uniform, which is made to measure—from that store which carries everything the well-dressed midshipman wears and needs.

A Second Classman will assist in the first shopping expedition. First the plebe gets two enormous clothes bags, into which he drops most of the odds and ends; he must have at least ten suits of whites, four white hats, two pairs of shoes, four pairs of leggings, and one suit of rain clothes. He is furnished a stencil and ink, and the first task after obtaining his outfit is to mark the whites with black ink, and the rain clothes with white paint. A Second Classman will give him some much needed coaching. For shirts, collars, underclothes, and pajamas there are stencils for indelible ink markings, and minute directions in just what spot the mark must be placed. At the end of three days all possessions must be marked. A plebe who is not deft will daub as much indelible ink on himself as on his new clothes. If clothes are not properly marked, they will not be promptly returned from the laundry. Unmarked clothes are separated from the others, and when they eventually find their way back to the owner they bring demerits for clothes improperly marked.

The plebe must try on his garments to see how closely the storekeeper estimated his sizes; some are probably too large, some too small; but he can get consolation by looking at his classmates, for they have fared the same. He next struggles to stow these clothes in the shelves in his locker. There is ample room for everything if he follows instructions carefully and keeps everything folded properly, for the cubic space in those lockers has been accurately calculated. Only toward the end of the week, when the clothes bag begins to bulge with soiled clothes, should he have any trouble in closing the locker door. If the plebe has never made a bed, he enjoys a unique experience; he must quickly learn to spread the sheets in the right position with the middle seam along the middle of the bed, and have the ends at the head and foot come out even. Those midshipmen with deft hands and the natural gifts that later in life constitute the handy man around the house learn quicker than others.

A plebe becoming a good housemaid avoids a dozen small reports such as bed not properly made, floor not neatly swept, and many unwanted demerits. If the extra shoes, neatly polished, are not in the customary place under the end of the bed, he will have to explain why. But he would never have been able to pass those entrance examinations if he had not been able to learn to do things, and in a surprisingly short time the room is straightened out and the locker stowed according to the regulation plan, and he is beginning to remember on what shelf his ties, neckerchiefs, and handkerchiefs are placed.

Before he has solved his domestic problems he is struggling with infantry and boat drill; and unless he is exceptionally big and strong he finds those oars in the navy cutters long and heavy. When he first tosses his regulation oar and tries to hold it in a fore and aft line with the others and at the exact height, he usually has trouble, particularly if he came from the interior and obtained his ideas of oars from those used in rowboats at summer camps. "Tossing" is tough, but keeping stroke is almost impossible during the first few drills, for when by some miracle Midshipman Smith gets the cadence he is certain to be out of stroke with his neighbor, Midshipman Jones, who involves them both in a tragic union and they catch an unwanted "crab." But everybody is doing it, except perhaps some college oarsman or some Navy junior whose father taught him to pull, and those tired muscles rest up overnight and in a few days the oars begin to look more like tooth-picks.

More plebes have had infantry than boat drill. Even the

first day they manage not to do too badly, and in a few days they emerge from the recruit school including the proper posture at attention, the correct salute, and the marchings when they learn to keep step and turn on a moving or fixed pivot—all elementary but essential. After the school of the squad and recruit, they are given rifles and promoted to the school of the company where they learn the manual of arms and company movements. No exercise yet invented has the immediate disciplinary effect of infantry drill; nothing else so quickly accustoms a young civilian with the habit of asking "Why?" to obey first and ask the reason afterwards. As midshipmen are educated and trained, tasks are not as specific or as simple as the manual of arms and orders not as detailed as for shouldering arms. They are given more initiative, but they must learn to obey with alacrity and loyalty before they can be extended any discretion.

After they have been given preliminary instruction with their rifles, the midshipmen march to the rifle range and begin the marksman course. American gunboats are still called upon to supply landing parties to protect American citizens abroad, and the company officers are ensigns and lieutenants. Midshipmen learn how to shoot a rifle in order to train the seamen in the landing force. It is generally true that a marksman or sharpshooter with a rifle makes an excellent gun-pointer at one of the big guns, and, in selecting gun-pointers in ships' batteries, men who have shown their skill with a rifle are given preference. From the moment he enters the Academy a midshipman is trained for his future duties as a junior officer of the Navy: he is taught to pull an oar, march, execute the manual of arms, and fire a rifle. All these things he must in turn teach the sailors.

Midshipmen enter in the summer, after June Week. A candidate should report as soon as possible after passing the examinations. Every day in the Academy before the academic work begins in October accustoms him to the régime and will assist him with academics later. Annapolis is warm in the summer, but the climate is pleasant, the trees and lawns are green, the sea breezes from the Severn and the Chesapeake are refreshing, and the white uniforms are cool and comfortable. The appetite is enormous, the fare is substantial and generally inviting. Those iron bedsteads have comfortable inner-spring mattresses, and slumber comes unsought in those first weeks at the Academy, in spite of the poisonous vaccines the surgeon has injected in the pulsing veins.

In addition to the drills and exercises, the plebes have a lecture and reading course under the Department of English during the summer, and in September they commence their academic work in order to familiarize themselves with the Academy methods of recitation and study. No marks are assigned for September except in mathematics. The whole period between entrance and the beginning of the academic year, usually the first Monday in October, is utilized to prepare the Fourth Classmen to stay in the Academy. They have been brought to a fine condition of health, and have been gradually accustomed to naval discipline and the routine of the Academy life. Uncle Sam wants to keep as many as can qualify, but he can't afford to keep any one who does not meet his standards. The Academy authorities will do all they can to see that this Fourth Class graduates as large a proportion as possible of its members.

In October, Fourth Classmen begin the real test. A few simply can't meet the mental requirements. Some do not get accustomed to the place. Others spend too much time trying for a freshman team or devote too much energy to extracurricular activity. They may skylark too much, or perhaps they can not settle down to the system of regular study and daily recitations. Others stand well in some subjects but neglect or can not manage others. There are no optional courses, and all midshipmen must complete successfully all the prescribed courses. This is too much for some who are accustomed to optional courses at high school or college.

The first essential for a Fourth Classman is to pass the term examinations and stay in the Academy. The average plebe can do this comfortably if he secures around a 3.0 in his daily marks. Unless he is unusually brilliant, a Fourth Classman should apply himself diligently for the first year and strive mightily for at least a 3.0. The best approach is the steady study method; application during the three daylight and the two evening hours set apart for study should enable any plebe to prepare himself for the daily recitations. It is astonishing how much can be absorbed by a solid hour's application; the habit of study can be acquired, and information gained regularly and continuously is enduring and useful. The midshipman should stow his information away in an orderly manner so that it can be easily drawn upon; his mind should be neatly and completely furnished like his locker. If he studies regularly twelve hours a week, he can master algebra, geometry, trigonometry, and need have no fears of differential calculus. He can devote that remaining hour at night to whichever gives the most trouble—modern languages, English, or chemistry, or he can split it and still have a solid hour before each recitation. The proper use of time becomes a fixed habit and not only will help a plebe at the Academy but will enable him to undertake more difficult tasks after graduation.

There is a knack to examinations; midshipmen learn to scan an examination paper closely and note the questions and parts of questions which can be answered rapidly and with assurance; they answer those first. Then they answer the remaining in reverse order of their length and difficulty. The following is an extreme case but it has happened to beginners: the first question was a puzzler on which a plebe expended over half the period allotted; the succeeding four questions could have been readily answered, insuring about 80 per cent or a 3.2. Selection of the order of answering is perfectly legitimate, for each examination question has the same standing and importance.

In justice to himself, his family, and finally to the Government, the plebe should make sure he survives the first term, and to that end he should subordinate every outside activity. He can get ample recreation in the hours reserved for drills and recreation. He will have some welcome breaks in the steady routine. Many of his recreation hours will be spent at "pep" meeting where he learns the Navy songs and cheers preparatory to the Army-Navy game at Philadelphia. These will not interfere with his studies. He may also get a trip to Baltimore or Princeton to witness one of the off-campus football games. On crisp fall afternoons he will have ample opportunity to develop his lungs and a quarter-deck voice for giving orders in a tone that will fairly lift his men along. Christmas is joyous even for plebes, and if the Navy has been defeated by the Army (which heaven forbid!), the gloom that descends on the Severn and lasts through early December will begin to lift as the Regiment contemplates the revenge it will get the following November.

Many little unpleasant things will happen to the plebe before the violets bloom in the spring: he will be reported for minor infractions which he had no intention of committing; he may confront difficult problems of loyalty to an imaginary boyish code which he will have to fight out for himself. He should talk over problems with his company commander, who will give him big-brotherly advice, and if they are very important ask to see the commissioned officer. He may have to take the blame for something he was not entirely responsible for; exact justice is not on this earth, even in the Naval Academy.

With his determination to stay in the Academy, the plebe should resolve to conform at once to naval customs, to be amenable to the regulations, to accommodate his habits and customs to the Academy routine. He should familiarize himself with naval nomenclature and use the correct nautical terminology, and should avoid like poison the word "gadget"; it limits the vocabulary. Orders must be given to sailor-men in language they understand. A sailor's vocabulary will help the plebe think like a sailor. He should always give the cheerful "Aye, aye, Sir!" to a senior instead of the familiar "All Right" or that vulgar newcomer, "O.K." While conforming to customs and discipline of the Navy, the plebe should not attempt to engratiate himself with officers, instructors, or, above all, upperclassmen. There is an ugly word, "greasing," applied to such practice. Officers, instructors, and upperclassmen are used to such wiles, and are not to be taken in except by modern Talleyrands who do such a smooth job of "slushing" that only their disgusted classmates are aware of it. The plebe must not be "against the Government," for he is already a part of Uncle Sam's armed forces and must obey loyally, not perfunctorily. The natural instinct of a red-blooded American lad will suggest the mean between "greasing" and being a non-conformist. A midshipman will make no mistake in regarding himself as an embryo officer from the moment he enters and will not go wrong when he acts as an officer would in a difficult situation.

It isn't always the dull midshipmen who graduate at the bottom of the class; reading novels during study hours is one of the best ways ever developed at the Academy to lose numbers: just a peek after recitation to see how the heroine escaped, who killed the fifth columnist, or how many redskins bit the dust has often resulted in the consumption of an hour in reading which should have been devoted to a less interesting chemistry or math lesson. Give up the favorite authors for at least a couple of years and secure that diploma; there will be plenty of time for fiction later.

Others stand at the bottom of the class because of devotion to extracurricular activities which invariably cost numbers; others from bravado, to see how near they can come to bilging; and, finally, there are some at or near the bottom who are slow to develop mentally, but who are determined to become naval officers; by sheer grit they fight their way through and frequently become outstanding officers.

There are many brave souls among those who can't quite make the grade, who have worked harder than many who passed, who yearned for a naval career, but had to resign. The course at the Academy is the best system yet devised for testing the fitness of young Americans to become officers in the Navy; but every class loses two or three midshipmen who would have made better officers than some who remained. The ability to learn the theory of the professional subjects can not guarantee the possession of the intangible qualifications which are necessary for a naval officer; nor does the failure to get through Annapolis invariably imply their absence.

After the first term the plebe has a good measure of the resistance he has to overcome; he can relax a little, but he should, first, last and all the time, keep a safe margin above the essential 2.5 which he has to have to graduate. In the spring he should look about him for the sport and extracurricular activity which will give him the most pleasure, for he need not become a "grind." The great majority of midshipmen who pass the first term with a fair margin can graduate, so far as recitations and examinations are concerned, and can take a large part in the life of the Academy *provided they systematically study during study hours and make graduation their primary concern.* The course is formidable, and it is difficult to say which year is the hardest, or which subjects the toughest, but the knowledge that other Americans have completed the course will sustain the courage of a doubtful midshipman.

Only the utilization of every precious minute of the sixteen waking hours will enable midshipmen to take part in the extracurricular activities without detriment to their academic work. Time passes rapidly; before plebes realize it they have become Third Classmen, have rushed Lover's Lane, have embarked on their first practice cruise, and have discovered that the lockers on the *Arkansas* are about half the size of the ones in Bancroft Hall which they considered too small. Disturbed conditions in Europe sometimes compel the Department to cruise midshipmen along the Atlantic coast; but wherever they cruise, they scrub the decks, fire the boilers, steer the ship, and operate the engines; and they are given practical instruction in gunnery, navigation, seamanship, electrical engineering, marine engineering, and radio. On the cruise they will also be given occasional lectures to help them through the maze of professional subjects. Not even the "savoir" of the class can absorb all the professional information that is fairly hurled at them during that three months' cruise, but a remarkable amount sticks, for many of their recitations and

MIDSHIPMEN BOARDING MOTOR LAUNCHES TO EMBARK IN BATTLESHIPS
FOR THE SUMMER CRUISE

drills during the academic year have been preparatory to just such a heavy program.

September comes; and rushing to pack up for leave, the average Third Classman will manage to forget two or three essential items—but not the souvenirs purchased for his friends at home. That first breath-taking leave passes like a dream—and he is back at Annapolis.

With the Army-Navy game, the Thanksgiving Hop, the first editions of the *Log*, and Christmas, the first half-year goes very rapidly. The Third Class strive for a 2.8 to 3.2 in calculus, mechanics, physics, mechanisms, languages, and naval history, for they know the second term is going to be tough. It includes turbines, reciprocating engines, auxiliary machinery, and boilers. Marine engineering has four hours a week, but mathematics is still king, although reduced from six to five hours. Electrical engineering now takes three and one half hours a week instead of two. It is harder to study in the spring when the bees are droning outside the window and the chatter of the lawn-mower turns into a soporific rhythm. Preparing for that last afternoon recitation requires extra will power in April and May. A little margin collected during the fall and winter may help a lot in the spring. Toward the end of the academic year, the *Lucky Bag* Committee begins work, and perhaps the Ring Committee, and nine out of ten of the Third Class will probably be trying to make one of the athletic teams; there is plenty to do. Time flies. The calendar can not be trusted; it reports another June Week, which passes too quickly, like its predecessor.

One-third of the Second Class starts on a month's cruise on destroyers. They are the senior midshipmen aboard and are treated as junior officers. The atmosphere in destroyers is not as formal as in the old "battlewagon *Arky.*" After paying their respects to Neptune all over again, the mid-shipmen get accustomed to the unexpectedly rapid motions as their destroyer rises just in time to escape taking the whole Atlantic Ocean aboard; she sidesteps so many green combers that she is forgiven when she fairly wallows her forecastle into one, as if wanting to show how deep she can dive before rising to free herself and resume the side-stepping game. In any decent weather she will do her thirty-five to forty knots, and make the sedate twelve knots of "battlewagons" seem like going backwards. After grad-uation and a year at sea, midshipmen are eligible for a watch and division on a destroyer. Many future destroyer officers are recruited on these Second Class cruises. Back to Annapolis, and the second section of the class takes to the destroyers while the first and third sections keep on with the practical instruction in aviation, engineering, navi-gation, and seamanship.

Second Classmen have considerable dignity. They are not as important as First Classmen but are gentlemen of some consequence. They have a tough year in academics, with thermodynamics, electricity, hydrographic surveying, interior ballistics, and navigation—not a subject except lan-guages and English that does not require a higher or lower form of mathematics, and English includes modern thought, which is not easy. In addition, they are more active in extracurriculars and athletics. In the spring the lawn-mowers commence their sweet refrain, and spring fever is again epidemic, but ordnance offers a menu of torpedoes and mines, steam insists upon teaching all there is to know about heat transfer, and English gives American foreign policy.

June Week comes again, and the First Class goes aboard the old *Ark* feeling like "plank owners." They know their way about her. They bring up the Third Class as they were brought up, act as junior officers of the deck, carry out the daily routine, inspect to see that boats are called away on time and the decks swept down. With an occasional suggestion from the commissioned officer of the deck, a First Classman makes all necessary preparations and gets the *Ark* under way. With the stadimeter he measures her distance from the flagship as she takes station. The regular officer of the deck has to be convinced that the First Classman can measure the distance correctly; now and again he takes the stadimeter for a check, but during the second hour the ship steadies down and it is rarely necessary to change the revolutions. Then the First Classman is told to keep the *Arkansas* in station. There are two or three extra heart-beats, but he manages an "Aye, aye, Sir!" and taking a few revolutions off or putting on a few, finds he can keep her in position. Just when he thinks he has the situation in hand she suddenly gains on the flagship. That is a bad moment, but the officer of the deck restores the situation, explains to the captain, who looks up on the bridge, that it was a sudden sheer on the part of the flagship. The First Classman recovers his composure, is again given the stadimeter, and commences hanging on five hundred yards from the flagship. Doing a day's work in navigation, standing watch on deck and in the engine-room, keeping order on the forecastle, and acting as mate of the gun and berth deck, he gets the final preparations for his duties as ensign.

First Class year at the Academy is a formative period in an officer's career. First Classmen are treated as junior officers by the officers and instructors. To the lowly plebes, they loom larger than the Superintendent. First Classmen are encouraged to direct the activities of the Academy. "Extracurricular" demands more and more time, but they have all found their approximate places in their class standing, and none of them grudge a few numbers to produce a better *Lucky Bag, Trident,* or *Log.*

The course becomes more and more professional. There is evident reason for studying seamanship, navigation, fire control, and exterior ballistics. First Classmen must also learn about internal-combustion engines and alternating currents, though some of them may have made up their minds to be line officers and nothing else. They must concentrate on gunnery instructions, naval regulations, fleet operations, tactics, signals, and official correspondence, and make sure of the "2.5" in everything. As the weeks go by, First Classmen give orders with more poise, feel more at home in front of battalions, companies, and sections. And they begin to understand why navy regulations are necessary. Unconsciously, they are changing from midshipmen into officers.

The long-anticipated graduation day brings a variety of emotions, but most graduates are too eager to take their places in the fleets to have much regret at leaving Annapolis. The fleets have been the goal of four years of hard work. Also, there are far-off ports that many of them look forward to seeing. And there is the satisfaction of having successfully completed a difficult undertaking. They have met the Navy's requirements for a commission. Whatever the future holds, they have not been found wanting in those basic qualities of an officer and gentleman. The past four years are secure.

The graduating address, the cheerful crowd, the cap-throwing, the cheers for those left behind, impinge on already surcharged minds. A day or two later comes the full realization that they are now Uncle Sam's commissioned officers, with added responsibilities which they can not divest themselves of, afloat or ashore. Wherever they go, whatever they do, they must live up to the traditions of the Navy—those high standards of conduct which were formed in four naval wars by officers of our Navy who never had the benefit of the Naval Academy.

UPON graduation the midshipman receives his diploma, the degree of bachelor of science, and his commission as ensign in the Navy. If he remains in the Navy, he enters a seven-year probationary period during which his commission may be revoked for misconduct or inefficiency. His first two years at sea are usually spent on a battleship, where he serves in rotation as assistant navigator, junior officer in a turret, anti-destroyer or anti-aircraft battery, in the fire-control division, and in the engine-rooms carrying on as he did on his First Classman cruise. He must learn all parts of his ship, from the fire-control tower to the double bottoms, and, like his predecessors who fought with Truxtun and Preble, he turns his hand to every odd job, gets responsibility early in life, and matures rapidly, for he must develop initiative and sound judgment to meet his continually increasing responsibilities.

At the end of two years' commissioned service he is eligible for either an aviation course at Pensacola or submarine training at New London. Sometimes he is ordered to watch and division duty on cruisers and destroyers even before this. Junior officers are usually glad to go to smaller ships where they are assigned more responsible duties. Aviation and submarine duty appeal to young officers. Submarine officers attain command at an earlier age than those on any other type of ship. Commands are eagerly sought, for early experience as a captain is the best preparation for higher responsibilities.

Three years after graduation an ensign is promoted to lieutenant, junior grade, and four years later he becomes eligible for shore duty. Between the fifth and tenth year after graduation an officer is expected to attend his first post-graduate school. The lieutenant takes either the school of the line course, which prepares him for more responsible duties in the executive branch of the Navy, or one of the technical courses such as ordnance engineering, radio engineering, internal-combustion engines, and so forth. He then returns to sea, and between the tenth and twentieth year, during another tour ashore, is expected to attend the junior course at the War College and obtain a thorough course in tactics and the minor operations of war, with some instruction in the technic of staff work. After another cruise and during another shore detail he will be given the senior course at the War College to prepare for flag duty and ultimate command of an American Fleet, the goal of every ambitious officer.

In any serious survey of Annapolis as an educational institution it is necessary to consider its course in relation to the Navy's post-graduate schools for which the Academy is the basic academy or college. The purpose of the Naval Academy is not to prepare a midshipman to command the Fleet or to introduce him to all the cultural subjects that add much to life; the Academy exists to prepare a graduate to be an efficient ensign, ready to do certain important and specific duties as a junior officer on one of the ships of the fleets and with sufficient instruction and training to continue his own education. That is why a midshipman is trained to "dig it out" himself. There are no "spoon-fed" courses, no skilful coaches to make learning easy. Officers are available for extra instruction of midshipmen in danger of "bilging," but the American midshipman is taught to teach himself. He will find time and books in the libraries that will enable him to supply any cultural deficiency by reading—but not much time, for the daily schedule in the fleet is as heavy as at the Naval Academy. His daily duties will add to his professional knowledge, and in order that he may keep abreast of new developments or refresh himself by study of subjects which his daily duties did not embrace, during his first decade of service he is given a year at a post-graduate school for his own professional development. By the time he takes this course he has selected the particular professional subject for which he has a natural inclination, and he is given an opportunity to specialize in that subject, but he must also keep abreast of all professional subjects.

Each year a few Naval Academy graduates are transferred to the Civil Engineering and the Supply Corps; before being commissioned in their new branch they take special courses prescribed by their bureau chief. Also a few staff officers of high rank are sent to the Naval War College. The Bureau of Medicine and Surgery is responsible for the post-graduate work of the naval surgeons. The Marine Corps maintains its own post-graduate school system, mainly centered at Quantico, Virginia. In addition it sends senior officers to Naval and Army post-graduate schools. Many Naval Academy graduates enter the Marine Corps; usually they are sent directly from Annapolis to Quantico, where they are given one year's basic instruction in the school of the Marines.

This is the comprehensive scheme of the Bureau of Navigation to educate officers of the Navy from the time they leave the Naval Academy until a few hardy survivors in each class hoist their Admirals' flags. No naval generation is ever permitted to carry through such a long-range plan; war or national emergencies invariably interrupt some features of the program. Yet, war itself is the most valuable school for naval officers; the experience it affords more than compensates an officer for an interruption in his education. As for the Naval Academy, it was created during the Mexican War, and carried on at Newport during the

REGULAR AND RESERVE ENSIGNS DISTINGUISHED THEMSELVES ON SISTER SHIPS TO THIS DESTROYER AT PEARL HARBOR

Civil War. It laid out its new buildings with the purpose of expanding its plant in the Spanish-American War, and during the war of 1917-18 it uncovered an almost inexhaustible supply of junior officers in American colleges and universities. During past wars and the present conflict the Naval Academy has demonstrated its ability to train an ever-increasing number of junior officers for the United States Navy; that is the reason it was founded and maintained.

To appreciate the Naval Academy of to-day as an educational institution one should regard it as the basic academy where the fundamentals of the naval profession are taught to young Americans between eighteen and twenty-four, who are trained at sea while they are instructed ashore. Beyond the theoretical and practical training is the continuous effort to instil into naturally high-minded youths the naval code of honor and duty. The Navy wants no intellectual sharks, no smart sea lawyers who can argue their way through the service. It wants the keenest minds, the finest bodies, but most of all it wants that indefinable thing called spirit. Poise is expected of even junior officers; they got it from responsibility in the old Navy. Character they must bring with them, and unselfishness, and the desire to make their contribution to the Navy and the nation. Finally they need the most delicate sense of honor, that willingness to swear to their own hurt which inspired Oliver Hazard Perry to testify against himself when court-martialed in the Mediterranean. That illustrates the indefinable Navy spirit. On these foundations the Navy can train its officers not in four years but during their careers in the service.

In addition to supplying the officers needed in the permanent Navy, during national emergencies or war the naval personnel must immediately expand. Reserve officers, mainly ensigns and junior lieutenants, are needed to officer the additional ships. No country can afford to maintain in the regular navy all the officers it will need in wartime. In its early history the Navy turned with confidence to our sea-going ships in the merchant marine for its officers; to-day ships of war are entirely different from merchant ships. The Navy now looks to the colleges of the nation as the principal source of reserve officers. College men with trained minds and a basic education can familiarize themselves with the professional subjects. Collegians are young, and it is in the junior ranks that the most reserve officers are needed. On demobilization these young reserve officers can return with the least disturbance to their civilian careers. No system can make reserve officers average as well as regular officers with the small amount of time that they can afford to devote to naval training; and they can rarely be prepared to be senior officers or for command rank, but they do make competent junior officers and it is in those ranks that the greatest need will arise.

During the present war the Navy is offering reserve-officer graduates of the R.O.T.C. units appointments in the regular Navy "in such numbers as the President may deem necessary provided that they are less than twenty-six years of age, and have served one year of continuous active service on board ships of the Navy and shall before appointment establish their moral, physical, mental, and professional qualities in accordance with such rules and regulations as the Secretary of the Navy may prescribe."

Similar provision is also made to appoint Naval and Marine Corps reserve aviators into the regular Navy and the Marine Corps. They are eligible if they have completed "not less than eighteen months of continuous active service next following the completion of their duty as aviation cadets undergoing training." Like other candidates for commissions in the Navy and Marine Corps, aviation reserve officers must establish their moral, physical, mental, and professional qualities in accordance with the rules and regulations prescribed by the Secretary of the Navy.

The Naval Academy has become the instrument which has enabled the Bureau of Navigation to solve the problem of supplying commissioned personnel to the American Navy. The Naval Academy has reproduced itself in twenty-seven colleges and universities, and is prepared to instruct reserve midshipmen in professional subjects and imbue these future reserve officers with its own standard of duty. In wartime the regular and reserve officers, mobilizing to grapple with an enemy, merge into one homogeneous body inspired by the ideals which have come down from John Paul Jones, John Barry, Thomas Truxtun, Edward Preble, and John Rodgers.

☆ **A P P E N D I X 1** ☆

The Academy and Its Alumni

IN MAY, 1940, a board of visitors to the Academy, consisting of three Senators, three Congressmen, and six presidents of universities, colleges, and technical institutes, concluded its report with an expression of its "deep feeling of admiration for the fine work being done in every branch of activity, for the morale of midshipmen and officers, and for the spirit of devotion to the Service which is so marked." The board believed that "Every citizen should have a feeling of pride in this great national institution." Every member of the board signed this report. One member, a Congressman noted for his sincere interest in the Navy and convinced that the United States has "the finest Navy in the world and by far the finest corps of commissioned officers of any navy," recommended that the Academy be turned into a "technical training school." He would require midshipmen to complete their "academic education" before they entered the Academy. He believed that midshipmen enter too young to have absorbed "the civilian point of view of our great democracy." Without knowing it, he was offering the essential reason for midshipmen entering the Navy early, for they must absorb the point of view of the Navy in their formative years.

The report of the board is gratifying, but the Naval Academy must be judged by the records of its alumni, not by its good intentions, its efficient organization, its well-equipped buildings, and its attractive grounds. The records of some of its alumni will be offered, commencing with those who left the Navy after graduation.

During the naval stagnation between 1868 and 1898, Academy graduates were encouraged to resign. In 1882, graduates about to complete the six years' course were legislated out of the Navy. But even under normal conditions a few graduates resign each year. Some leave for physical reasons, usually defective eyesight; others become restless at the repetitious drills and slow promotion; others do not find naval life congenial and are not happy at sea. Some resign because of peculiar talents which can not be developed advantageously in the Navy.

Among the first to go and the most successful in private life were Robert M. Thompson, 1868, and Edward J. Berwind, 1869. A. A. Michelson, 1873, who measured the velocity of light, could not find an adequate outlet for his natural genius in the service. He was the Academy's greatest contribution to the scientific world. William H. Stayton, 1881, after serving in the Judge Advocate General's office, resigned and became a leading admiralty lawyer.[1] During his presidency of the Alumni Association, Captain "Bill" endeared himself to old and young graduates alike.

After a successful business career, J. W. Weeks, 1881, served in the House and the Senate and as Secretary of War. Curtis D. Wilbur, 1888, became Secretary of the Navy. O. E. Weller, 1881, served in the Senate from Maryland, and R. B. Howell, 1885, from Nebraska. J. B. Robinson, 1868, Richmond P. Hobson, 1889, and E. V. M. Isaacs, 1915, served in the House. V. S. Houston, 1897, and S. W. King, 1910, served as delegates from Hawaii; L. C. Stark, 1908, as governor of Missouri. After serving as Chief of Naval Operations, Admiral W. D. Leahy,

[1] Captain Stayton married Annie H. Henderson, a lineal descendant of Commodore Truxtun. During the World War one of their three sons volunteered for the Army, one for the Navy, and one for the Marine Corps. In addition to being represented in the regular service by Captain T. T. Craven, U.S.N. and other descendants, Commodore Truxtun was represented by three volunteers.

Captain "Bill's" successor as President of the Alumni Association was E. J. Sadler, 1899, who successfully prospected for oil in all parts of the world, and also improved the processes of distillation. Sadler strengthened the position of the United States in the international struggle for oil and thus assisted its oil-burning Navy.

1897, was appointed Governor of Puerto Rico and later Ambassador to the Vichy government in France.

The Academy has produced a number of presidents of universities or technical institutions—C. H. Stockton, 1865; Ira N. Hollis, 1878; G. H. Rock, 1889; Ralph Earle, 1896; W. T. Cluverius, 1896, and the following distinguished deans: M. E. Cooley, 1878; H. W. Spangler, 1878; W. F. Durand, 1880; Jerome Hunsacker, 1908. Winston Churchill, 1894, is the Academy's best-known novelist. Cyrus T. Brady, 1883 and E. L. Beach, 1888, wrote popular juvenile books. Admiral William L. Rodgers, 1878, Dudley W. Knox, 1896, Fitzhugh Green, 1909 and Holloway Frost, 1910, have well-deserved reputations as naval historians. Thanks to the U. S. Naval Institute, there are numerous Academy graduates with sufficient literary skill to develop a professional thesis in a style that any reader can understand.

A large group of graduates entered the ship-building and allied industries and contributed directly to creating the heavy industries in the United States without which a modern fleet can not be constructed. The research of W. L. R. Emmett, 1881, in electrical engineering made possible the engineering plants of the *Lexington* and *Saratoga*. F. T. Bowles, 1879, Lewis Nixon, 1882, Lawrence Spear, 1890, H. G. Smith, 1891, H. L. Ferguson, 1892, Gregory Davidson, 1892, W. G. Groesbeck, 1895, R. H. Robinson, 1896, J. W. Powell, 1897, Roger Williams, 1901, and R. E. Gillmor, 1907, have been associated with the construction of every type of ship and all naval equipment, including battleships, aircraft carriers, cruisers, destroyers, and submarines.

Graduates contributed largely to the creation of the Naval Militia. Among the pioneers in this movement were J. W. Miller, 1867; M. K. Eyre, 1880; J. W. Weeks, R. P. Forshew, Gilbert Wilkes, W. H. Stayton, Macdonough Craven, E. H. Harrison, and E. M. Harmon of 1881; W. B. Duncan, 1882; S. D. Greene, Jr. and J. H. Barnard, 1883; C. C. Poe, 1885; George Breed, 1886; Irving Blount, 1891; E. T. Fitzgerald,

1896. Later graduates continued the same interest in the organization of Naval Reserve divisions. The Navy Department knows from experience that the services of any graduate of the Academy in civil life are at its disposal.

After being chiefs of bureaus, Rear Admiral H. I. Cone, 1894, and L. C. Palmer, 1896, became heads of the Shipping Board, and E. S. Land, 1902, became Chairman of the Maritime Commission. Edward McCauley, Jr., 1896, and H. L. Vickery, 1915, are also members of the Commission. George Wolfe, 1913, is president of a private shipping company. Other alumni have served with the Merchant Marine and have helped to maintain a close liaison with the Navy.

Graduates generally do well in industrial establishments, and Mr. Beach, the manager of the personnel of the Dupont Company of Delaware, wrote that Academy graduates "present a better front to the employer than the graduates of any other institution. They are poised, confident, assured and courteous; they have an attitude of definite purpose which is a prized asset to a man in any walk of life." Year after year, Mr. Beach had interviewed Academy graduates who, for various reasons, were leaving the service. He stated: "The naval authorities take men from the Kansas plains, the fishing ports of New England, the ranches of Texas, who represent all shades of economic security, and yet when the job is complete each young man lives up to the ideal of the Naval Academy in producing men of whom it can be said that they are officers and gentlemen."

It is evident that a good number of Academy graduates have succeeded in civil life. Some have not done well, which is not surprising, for the training at the Academy is designed to prepare midshipmen for service as junior officers in the Navy. But if every individual graduate leaving the Navy had gone to the top of his chosen profession, it would not justify the existence of the Academy. Has it produced and maintained a homogeneous, proficient corps of officers, capable of creating, maintaining, and fighting American fleets? Has it produced leaders receptive to new ideas and fit to command fleets during war? Unless these questions can be answered affirmatively, the Academy, at least in part, has failed.

In the middle eighties, Academy graduates who had taken the full four-year course, began to take charge of the Navy. Since that time, every important position in the Navy Department, the shore establishments, and the Fleet has been in the hands of graduates of the Naval Academy, except in the staff bureaus such as Medicine and Surgery, and Supplies and Accounts. No other school in the world has had such complete control of a navy.[2] The Academy has had a practical monopoly on line officers in the Navy and the naval constructors,[3] and has supplied many officers to the Marine Corps. These officers, except in the matter of appropriations, have had practical command of the entire Navy establishment.

Richard Gatewood and F. T. Bowles, Cadet Engineers, class of 1879, entered the Construction Corps after taking a postgraduate course in Scotland. J. L. Schock, J. J. Woodward, J. H. Linnard, all of 1881, and Lewis Nixon, 1882, followed. Since that date, graduates of the Academy have supplied practically all naval constructors, who have been in charge of the design and construction of the hulls of men-of-war. Similarly, graduates who have subsequently specialized in gunnery and engineering have been responsible for the design of armor, armament, and engines. In a progressive art like ship-building there is always serious difference of opinion. The designs of our ships have been severely criticized, sometimes justly, and most often by line officers who are called upon to fight the ships. Undoubtedly many errors have been made, but on the whole American ships will compare favorably with all contemporary foreign ships. The design of the original *In-*

[2] In the absence of a naval general staff, it is possible for chiefs of material bureaus to obstruct Departmental action. But if the Chief of Naval Operations is supported by the Secretary of the Navy, obstructionists can be compelled to coöperate or resign.

[3] The constructors were recently amalgamated with the line officers.

diana class of battleships with four 13-inch guns and eight
8-inch guns was superior to any of its period.

Chief Constructor D. W. Taylor, 1885, was a pioneer in
the development of "model tanks" in which resistance of
various models to propulsion through the water could be
tested. Admiral Taylor's experiments did much to develop the
art of ship-building, and his model tanks suggested the development of wind tunnels in use by the Navy, Army, and
civil designers of aircraft. Jerome C. Hunsaker, 1908, is a leading aircraft designer. Similarly, C. W. Dyson, 1883, devoted
much of his life to the design of ship propellers, and designers
in the Bureau of Engineering have continually improved the
main and auxiliary engines and boilers. Like the constructors,
they have made errors, but progress can be achieved only by
trial and error.

W. N. Jeffers, 1840, the fourth midshipman to graduate
from Annapolis, was the first graduate to become Chief of
Ordnance, serving from 1873 to 1881. Among many able successors were W. T. Sampson, 1861, W. M. Folger, 1864,
Joseph Strauss, 1885, N. C. Twining, 1889, and Ralph Earle,
1896. Obviously the success of the Bureau of Ordnance will
depend in large measure upon the efficiency of heavy industry,
particularly steel-making. In the early eighties, the steel industry in the United States was unequal to the task, and only
gradually did it develop to the point where steel for guns and
shells was equal to the demands of ordnance designers. John
F. Meigs, 1867, served in the Navy until 1891, mainly in developing ordnance, and then resigned to enter a steel company to improve the steel necessary for naval ordnance. In
designing breech mechanisms, telescopic sights, range-finders,
and fire-control gear, Academy graduates, including B. A.
Fiske, 1874, R. B. Dashiell, 1881, F. F. Fletcher, 1885, F. C.
Martin, 1902, G. S. Schuyler, 1906, and W. H. P. Blandy, 1913,
took leading parts.

Continual improvement in guns, projectiles, and sights increased the practicable battle ranges, and W. S. Sims, 1880,

led in improving gunnery methods afloat. President Theodore Roosevelt took a personal interest in the target practice, and with his support Sims revolutionized the gunnery methods and standards of the Navy. Sims was assisted by all the battery officers and many of the senior officers including C. P. Plunkett, 1884, Ridley McLean, 1894, L. C. Palmer, 1896, and T. T. Craven, 1896. Simultaneously the designs of torpedoes and mines were improved, and during the World War, the mine field stretching from Scotland to Norway, laid by Rear Admiral Joseph Strauss, a former Chief of Ordnance, was a material contribution to the defeat of the submarine.

No graduates of the Academy entered the Marine Corps prior to 1883, when nine graduates, including W. H. Stayton, C. A. Doyen, Lincoln Karmany, and George Barnett, who was its commandant during the World War, entered the Corps. The Marine Corps had already established its own high tradition and code of conduct, somewhat different from that of the line, but just as lofty and severe. Academy graduates have generally done well in the Marines, and J. A. Lejeune, 1888, was an outstanding commander of an Army division on the Western Front. Had the war continued, he would have been entrusted with larger formations.

What of the Navy High Command? During the Spanish-American War, the Navy, which was not organized for war, did not face a formidable enemy. The naval strategy of the West Indies and the Caribbean had been studied at the Naval War College under Rear Admiral Luce and Captain Mahan. There was general competence among the commissioned personnel, and some preparation, including extra target practice which had been made possible through the personal intervention of Assistant Secretary Theodore Roosevelt. Luckily, Assistant Secretary Roosevelt and Captain A. T. Mahan were friends, and they were in close touch during the year preceding the Spanish-American War. Before he left to command the Rough Riders, Secretary Roosevelt had been made Chairman of the Naval Strategy Board, which consisted of himself,

Rear Admiral Sicard, class of 1855, A. S. Crowninshield, 1863, and later A. T. Mahan, 1859. This Board, under Secretary Long, directed the naval operations of the war. Practically all the alumni who had gone into civil life volunteered, and many of them were called into service during this short war. In Manila Bay, Admiral Dewey, and off Santiago, Admiral Sampson, showed that Academy graduates were still equal to the responsibilities of naval high command.

Subsequent to the Spanish-American War, in both the Filipino and the Boxer insurrections, naval commanders showed their ability to meet new and unexpected situations. Rear Admiral Bowman H. McCalla displayed rare resolution in the relief of Peking. His determination to proceed to the aid of the beleaguered garrison had much to do with the success of the operation. Among Sampson's captains at Santiago were F. E. Chadwick, 1864, who after his retirement wrote the only comprehensive history of that war; C. E. Clark, 1863, who brought the *Oregon* from the Pacific; R. D. (Bob) Evans, 1863, who subsequently commanded the Atlantic Fleet on the first leg of its cruise around the world; and H. C. Taylor, 1863, who, next to Luce and Mahan, had most to do with the preservation of the War College. As Chief of Bureau of Navigation, Taylor did his utmost to establish a naval general staff, and did much to achieve Mahan's plan of concentrating all the battleships in one fleet, the Atlantic.[4]

Before the Atlantic Fleet reached California, Rear Admiral Evans was detached on account of illness. Rear Admiral C. M. Thomas, 1865, who became Commander-in-Chief, died suddenly at Del Monte, and Rear Admiral C. S. Sperry, 1866, who succeeded Admiral Thomas, took command and completed the world cruise on schedule. When the fleet reached Hampton Roads in February, 1909, it was in better material condition than when it left; its personnel was better prepared for

[4] The United States Navy was the first modern navy to realize the advantage of concentration. President Theodore Roosevelt approved the recommendation of Mahan and Taylor.

battle. The fleet lacked cruisers, but in battleships and destroyers it was second only to Great Britain.

During the First World War, Admiral W. S. Benson, 1877, Chief of Naval Operations, directed the activities of the Navy. Admiral H. T. Mayo, 1876, was Commander-in-Chief of the Atlantic Fleet; Admiral W. S. Sims, 1880, was Commander of the Naval Forces in Europe. Admiral A. M. Knight, 1873, was Commander-in-Chief of the United States Asiatic Fleet. All these officers had important and exacting duties which they ably performed. The three flag officers who saw the most active duty were Hugh Rodman, 1880, commanding the 6th Battle Squadron (American battleships) in the Grand Fleet; Joseph Strauss, 1885, who laid and recovered the gigantic mine field in the North Sea; and C. P. Plunkett, 1884, who commanded the 14-inch naval railway battery in France, its long range enabling Pershing to attack the German main line of railway communications at Montmedy in October, 1918. These three entirely different tasks required resolution, judgment, and versatility. Admirals Rodman, Strauss, and Plunkett met every test. Admirals Wilson at Brest, Niblack at Gibraltar, Mark Bristol in the Adriatic and at Constantinople, and N. A. McCully in Russia and the Black Sea proved their professional fitness by directing the forces operating in their areas. The performances of flag officers, from Admiral Benson down, showed that in spite of their long stagnation in the lower ranks, they had not lost their professional competence.

Among Rodman's captains in the North Sea were included C. F. Hughes, 1888, H. A. Wiley, 1888, and L. R. de Steiguer, 1889, all of whom subsequently commanded fleets. They brought to the fleets all the experience gained in the North Sea.

The younger officers saw more active duty; the destroyers were commanded by the classes of 1898 through 1912. There was a uniformly high standard of performance of duty from the time Commander J. K. Taussig, 1899, reported "Ready now" to Admiral Bayly at Queenstown, until the armistice.

Lieutenant Commander H. R. Stark (now Admiral Stark, Chief of Naval Operations) brought a division of small coal-burning destroyers from Manila to Gibraltar. This operation, involving extreme logistical difficulties, was scarcely known outside naval circles.[5]

American submarine commanders in the war zone met the severest test of any officer personnel. Engaged in stalking German U-boats, they were often attacked by their own forces. They proved their skill and courage from the moment they entered the war zone.

A naval aviation unit was established at Dunkirk a few miles from the German lines. Its members patrolled the English Channel in their slow planes, despite the immediate proximity of German fighters. Other aviation units were established in England and France under direction of Admirals Hutch Cone and T. T. Craven and Captain David Hanrahan.

During the First World War, officers ashore at navy yards and in the Department worked ceaselessly to provide the ships and stores. Their names are rarely known except to some curious naval student who reads them in the roster of various offices, or scans their portraits in the offices where they worked. Two officers must be mentioned, Admiral E. W. Eberle and Captain William H. Standley, Superintendent and Commandant at the Naval Academy, who trained the reserve ensigns at Annapolis and who proved the practicability of the Naval R.O.T.C. system.

Since the First World War, the commissioned personnel has faced a different situation. There was the customary hasty demobilization which navy morale enabled the service to surmount. Then followed an era when Americans convinced themselves there would be no more war. The Navy Department could not prevent the Navy's being reduced, but senior naval officers proved their loyalty to the nation by protesting

[5] Naval Academy officers serving in destroyers received a welcome reinforcement from the reserve ensigns and junior lieutenants; many of the reserves also commanded sub-chasers.

cuts in appropriations, by pointing to the growth of the Japanese Navy and Japan's disregard of American rights in the Far East, and by opposing provisions of the Naval Limitations Treaty, although they knew such opposition meant the disfavor of the administration. Officers unselfishly sacrificed their professional careers in defense of the service.

Reducing the Navy and neglecting the fortifications in the Far East increased the difficulties of the Commander-in-Chief of the Asiatic Fleet in protecting American interests in face of Japanese encroachments. Tension rose to a temporary climax from 1937 to 1940, when Admiral Harry E. Yarnell was Commander-in-Chief, becoming acute when the American gunboat *Panay* was bombed in daylight during high visibility. Admiral Yarnell refused to withdraw American gunboats from the Yangtse River, with the brief statement that his ships were there to protect the lives and property of Americans in peril. The career of Admiral Yarnell proves that the Academy still produces that best of all combinations, a commander-in-chief of sound judgment and resolute courage.

Have naval officers been receptive to the submarine and airplane? Commander H. H. Caldwell, 1891, commanded our first modern submarine in 1902, followed closely by Lieutenant-Commander C. P. Nelson, 1898. Other early entrants in the service included D. C. Bingham, 1902, Ralph Koch, 1903, and C. W. Nimitz, W. L. Friedell, Kenneth Whiting, and T. G. Ellyson, all of 1905. Both Whiting and Ellyson subsequently pioneered in aviation. C. R. Hyatt, 1907, A. S. Carpender, 1908, G. A. Rood, 1911, C. A. Lockwood, 1912, and Sherwood Picking, 1911, were among the early submarine commanders, along with Arnold Marcus, 1913, who gave his life in a vain endeavor to rescue one of his men during an explosion aboard *A-7* at Manila Bay. Picking was especially selected to command the *V-1*, the first American 3,000-ton submarine. By 1916 the submarine service had reached the stage where it was made a separate unit under Rear Admiral A. W. Grant.

Officers and men in the submarines perform their duties with the knowledge that a mistake on the part of one individual will submerge their craft beyond the depths for which its hull is designed, probably with fatal results. Kenneth Whiting had himself fired from a torpedo tube to test the practicability of escape from a sunken submarine. His experiment was carried on by others. C. B. Momsen, 1920, invented the "lung," and A. R. McCann, 1917, invented and developed the "rescue chamber." The submarine service has developed an auxiliary service of deep-sea divers whose personnel have the same high courage of submarine crews. The salvage of the *Squalus* off Portsmouth, New Hampshire under the direction of Rear Admiral C. W. Cole, 1899, was possible only after years of patient experiment and training had developed both the rescue apparatus and the personnel. Unfortunate as the accidents to our submarines have been, they afford proof of the continued discipline, resourcefulness, and determined courage of the present-day Navy personnel.

A long list of naval aviators, headed by Admiral W. A. Moffett, class of 1891, T. G. Ellyson, 1905, John Rodgers, 1901, and Zachary Landsdowne, 1909, have given their lives to develop naval aviation. A longer list of naval aviators carries on under Rear Admiral J. H. Towers, 1906, pioneer aviator and now Chief of the Bureau of Aeronautics. Among Towers' predecessors was Admiral E. J. King, now Commander-in-Chief of the United States Fleet and a qualified naval aviator. Naval aviators are flying faster and higher, and their planes are carrying greater loads. They are subjecting the new weapon to the same control they exercised over old weapons, fitting the new arm into the Fleet and also preparing it for independent missions far from the support of the Fleet.[6]

[6] Academy graduates have called in large numbers of aviation cadets from civil life who, like the reserve ensigns, are trained with the Navy and have been indoctrinated with naval methods and spirit. They soon earn their places in naval aviation and are indistinguishable from their air-mates from Annapolis, except that they are not available for general duty with the Fleet.

Under the progressive leadership of Rear Admiral W. A. Moffett, the Bureau of Aeronautics developed the aircraft carriers and perfected the catapults which made it practicable to launch planes from surface men-of-war. Simultaneously the Navy's flying boats were improved until they were capable of operating independently and at a great distance from the main body of the fleet; this naval arm is prepared for distant scouting, to attack with torpedoes, or to serve as long-range bombers. Rear Admiral A. W. Johnson, 1899, was a pioneer in the flying boats. At the limitation conference in London, Admiral Moffett had great difficulty in preventing disarmament enthusiasts from scrapping American aircraft carriers; Moffett's leadership preserved for the Navy one arm, aviation, in which it had definitely established its superiority. He sponsored the first flight across the Atlantic, successfully accomplished by A. C. Read, 1906, and a flight over the North Pole, eventually accomplished by one of his aides, Rear Admiral R. E. (Dickie) Byrd, 1912. Moffett spurred his aviators to greater feats: he shared their dangers and, like many other naval aviators, gave his life to develop this new naval arm.

The development of naval aviation necessitated more accurate predictions of the weather. The Navy Department continued the work began at Blue Hills Observatory during the war, by giving specially selected junior officers a two-year course in aërology. Graduates of this school serve in major aviation units of the fleets, and on the staffs of fleet commanders. Aërology is in its infancy. Naval aërologists maintain liaison with the scientists in the Weather Bureau and at technical schools and universities. The combined efforts of these scientific groups have added to the safety of flying over land and sea.

The record proves that the Navy has integrated submarines and aircraft into the fleets. Moreover, the adaptation of new weapons to the needs of the fleets has not been made at the expense of the efficiency of battleships, cruisers, and destroyers. Officers on battleships increased the accuracy and rate of fire of their turrets and anti-destroyer batteries, developed anti-aircraft batteries, and, using their own aircraft to spot, extended the range of their guns to greater distances. Destroyer officers developed anti-submarine tactics and added anti-aircraft guns to their batteries. Cruiser officers solved the problems of battleships and destroyers and prepared themselves to link the battle line and the destroyers. The High Command modified all former tactical concepts to allow for the new weapons, and maintained a judicious attitude between the extremists who would entrust the safety of the country to an untried weapon and the conservatives who would put entire faith in the old.

The only conclusive test that can be applied to the personnel of any navy is the test of battle against a well-trained enemy of about the same strength. It is impossible to say just how well the American Navy would emerge from such a contest. This can be said: American officers, from commanders-in-chief to the latest ensigns who have joined, have spared themselves no labor. The same endless drills that commenced in the first American squadron in the Mediterranean continue to this day in the fleets. There is only one danger, and that is somewhat remote: that the personnel will become overtrained and stale.

In addition to providing leaders, the Naval Academy must continue to produce junior officers capable of taking their places in ever larger and more complex fleets. Can it meet these increased requirements? The following evidence can be submitted by the writer. As a midshipman, he knew the classes of 1899 through 1905; he knew the classes of 1909, 1910, and 1911 as an instructor at the Academy; and he knew the class of 1922 as executive officer on board the *Wyoming* and the classes of 1933 and 1934 as captain on the *Mississippi*. From this experience he is convinced that the classes of 1909, 1910, and 1911 were better prepared on leaving the Academy for their duties in the Fleet than was his own class of 1902; that 1922 was better prepared than 1909, 1910, and 1911; and that

1933 and 1934 were better prepared than 1922. He believes the Academy accomplished this improvement because during the past forty years it has been more and more closely linked with the fleets. Its Superintendents and all its officers came from the fleets; they realize what the midshipmen need to know to become efficient junior officers. At the Academy the officers are assisted by a loyal and efficient group of civilian instructors. The continuous improvement in the preparations of midshipmen for their duties afloat is not a happy accident; it has resulted from the determination of the officers and instructors at the Academy to develop efficient junior officers for the fleets. It is their exclusiveness of purpose, their dedication of the Academy to the fleets, which have made this gratifying result possible.

In estimating the success of the Academy in meeting its responsibilities to the nation, the careers of some of its more distinguished graduates have been submitted in evidence. Another writer unquestionably would offer a different and perhaps a more representative list. Those submitted are sufficient to support the author's conviction that the Academy has not failed the Navy or the nation. It was difficult to close the list. Names of other splendid officers crowded the memory and justly demanded inclusion. Only limitations of space excluded them. The feeling of regret that exact justice could not be done to all graduates is tempered with pride that Academy alumni average high, and with confidence that the Navy could depend, for the present at least, on the general competence that has prevailed among its fleets ever since the Caribbean and Mediterranean squadrons were organized by Truxtun and Preble.

The host of capable officers who daily perform their allotted tasks, who can be depended upon for their utmost exertions in fair weather and foul, make the feats of Farragut, Porter, Sampson, and Dewey possible. These unknown sons of the Academy are her greatest glory.

In a measure, all that can be asked of the Academy is to

provide a uniformly excellent corps of officers. But it could do still more. Every regular establishment tends to become a machine; even though the highest models are used, all our officers should not be fitted into the same mold. Leave enough flexibility in the Academy organization to let the unusual through; authorize the Superintendent to pass an exceptional midshipman, who can't quite obtain the sacred 2.5 or meet all the requirements. Remember that the Academy dropped Cushing for academic deficiencies and for spilling a pail of water on an instructor, and "bilged" John Rodgers out of the class of 1901. The Naval Academy need not fire another Cushing or Rodgers to assure a steady supply of highly competent junior officers to the Fleet.

In 1845 the Naval School was endowed with the heritage of the Old Navy. It could not live on ancient glories alone. It has been continually enriched by successive generations of high-spirited American youths who enter the Academy, the cradle of the Navy, with the resolve that they will equal or excel the splendid records of their predecessors. The Academy does much for its sons, but it has received more from them. The Academy can give professional instruction; it can inspire aspiring sons to merge their own fame in the greater glory of the Navy. But all the trophies in Memorial Hall will not evoke a single noble impulse in an unresponsive youth. The Academy can not put heart into the mean or the ignoble. Fortunately for the nation, its battleships, cruisers, destroyers, submarines, aircraft, and tiny mosquito fleets to-day attract the same high-spirited, adventurous type of young Americans as those who went to sea with John Paul Jones, Thomas Truxtun, and Edward Preble. May they ever continue to do so!

A P P E N D I X   2

Superintendents of the Naval Academy

☆

		Date of Accession
1.	Franklin Buchanan	September 3, 1845
2.	George P. Upshur	March 15, 1847
3.	C. K. Stribling	July 1, 1850
4.	L. M. Goldsborough	November 1, 1853
5.	George S. Blake	September 15, 1857
6.	David D. Porter	September 9, 1865
7.	John L. Worden	December 1, 1869
8.	C. R. P. Rodgers	September 22, 1874
9.	Foxhall A. Parker	July 1, 1878
10.	George B. Balch	August 2, 1879
11.	C. R. P. Rodgers (second term)	June 13, 1881
12.	F. M. Ramsay	November 14, 1881
13.	W. T. Sampson	September 9, 1886
14.	R. L. Phythian	June 30, 1890
15.	P. H. Cooper	November 15, 1894
16.	F. V. McNair	July 15, 1898
17.	Richard Wainwright	March 15, 1900
18.	Willard H. Brownson	November 6, 1902
19.	J. H. Sands	July 1, 1905
20.	C. J. Badger	July 15, 1907
21.	J. M. Bowyer	June 10, 1909
22.	J. H. Gibbons	May 15, 1911
23.	W. F. Fullam	February 7, 1914
24.	E. W. Eberle	September 20, 1915
25.	A. H. Scales	February 12, 1919
26.	H. B. Wilson	July 5, 1921
27.	L. M. Nulton	February 23, 1925

Date of Accession

28.	S. S. Robison	June 16, 1928
29.	T. C. Hart	May 1, 1931
30.	D. F. Sellers	June 18, 1934
31.	Wilson Brown	February 1, 1938
32.	Russell Willson	February 1, 1941
33.	J. R. Beardall	January, 1942

Usually, Superintendents are relieved by their successors at Annapolis. The date of accession of a new Superintendent is the date of departure of his predecessor. In some instances there has been a short interregnum. Rear Admiral F. A. Parker died as Superintendent. Rear Admiral C. R. P. Rodgers served twice; his second term lasted only a few months.

Current Naval Academy Slang

☆

Terms marked with an asterisk were in vogue as early as 1898. Authority: "Reef Points."

AGGIE. A member of the first battalion.
ANCHOR. Lowest, last in a group.*
ANCHOR MAN. There, but for the grace of God, walks a civilian.*
ASIAT. A fourth battalioneer.
ASSUME THE ANGLE. A working hypothesis.

BALTIMORE BEEFSTEAK. Calves' liver, so to speak.
BATT. Battalion.
BATTLEWAGON. Battleship, the backbone of the Fleet.
BEAR A HAND. Sea-going term for "shake a leg." *
BELAY THAT. As you were.*
BILGE. To be assigned to the U.S.S. *Outside;* flunk.*
BILL. The goat.*
BLACK "N." Mythical award for service aboard the *Reina.*
BLIND DRAG. Femme accepted sight unseen.
BLOU. Blouse.
BONE. To study.*
BRACE. A military posture.*
BREEZE, SHOOT THE. To refight the Civil War, etc.; purpose of a bull session.
BRICK. 1. The girl friend with the thick glasses (formerly "gold-brick"). 2. To saddle one with such a drag.
BULKHEAD. 1. Wall. 2. To gripe loudly, hoping one's superiors will overhear.*
BULL. English and history; the latter part of "sketch and describe."
BURLAP. *See* SACK.
BUSH. *See* TREE.

BUST. 1. To sound, as "formation's busted." 2. To fail. 3. To err.*

BUTT. Part of a day, used in calculating time.*

BUZZARD. The rating badge of a P. O.*

CAN. A destroyer (tin can).

CANTEEN. The midshipman's soda fountain.

CADET. *See* Webster.

CAULK OFF. Sleep, especially in the daytime.*

CHARLIE NOBLE. The galley smokestack.*

CIT. That happy-looking chap in clothes of his own choice; a civilian.*

COLLISION MAT. Pancakes à la Bancroft Hall.

COM. The commandant of midshipmen.

CRAB. A girl who lives in Annapolis.

CRABTOWN. Annapolis, a fishing village on the banks of the Naval Academy.*

CRACK. To open, as to "crack a port."

CRUISE. 1. Summer practice cruise. 2. Time served on the *Reina.*

DAGO. Any foreign language.

DEMO. Demerit; a black mark on the conduct record.

DRAG. 1. To escort. 2. Young lady escorted.

EXEC. Executive officer.*

EXTRA DUTY. Disciplinary infantry drill for victims of the pap; less serious than the *Reina.**

EYES IN THE BOAT. Head and eyes to the front.*

FEMME. Any young lady.*

FIN OUT. Straighten your fingers.*

FIRST CLASS ALLEY. Between the mess tables and the mess-hall bulkheads.

FIRST LUFF. The first lieutenant.*

FLYING SQUADRON. The last ten men in after the hop. They run all the way across town and get in late anyway.

FOG BOUND. In a daze.

FOO FOO. Perfume, or its equivalent.

FRAP. To get on the conduct report.*
FRENCH OUT. To take unauthorized liberty.*
FURLOUGH. That time when *tempus* really *fugits;* vacation.

GADGET. A whatayacallit; that which has no better name.
GOAT HERDER. Inmate of the third battalion.
GONK. The cranium.
GOUGE. 1. Solution to a prob, as written up for profs. 2. To cheat.*
GRAVY TRAIN. The friend in need, who lives in town and feeds the midshipmen.
GREASE. Pull or influence.*
GREASOIR. One who oils the wheels of his own progress.*
GREASY. His impression on his seniors is foremost in his mind.*
GREASE MARK. Mark in "Aptitude for the Service."
GRIPE. To groan and growl.
GUNDECK. To feign intoxication.
GYRENE. One of the *Semper Fidelis* boys; a Marine.*

HAM 'N' EGGERS. The lacrosse team.
HAPPY HOMER. A midshipman of the second battalion.
HELL CATS. The Drum and Bugle Corps.
HOLIDAY. A poor job; interstices in a paint job.*
HOLY JOE. The Head of Department of Faith and Morals; the Chaplain.*
HONEY BARGE. For refuse only.
HOP. The knee-cracking Annapolis brand of dance.*

JAMOKE, JAVA, JOE. Coffee plus boiler compound.
JIMMYLEGS. A yard watchman.*
JOE GISH. Midshipman John Doe.
JUICE. Electrical engineering.*

KAYDET. Our brothers-in-arms, the West Pointers.*
KIYI. A small scrubbing-brush.
KNOCK OFF. Stop whatever you are doing.*

LADDER. Stairway.*
LOST BATTALION. U.S.S. *Cumberland*, home of the Mess Attendants.

MAN OVERBOARD. Your spoon in your cup.

MISERY HALL. Overhaul spot for damaged athletes.

MISS SPRINGFIELD. The midshipman's drag at an infantry drill —his rifle.

MONKEY JACKET. Full dress blou.*

MONTHLY INSULT. The very small part of $65 on which we can get our hands.

NAV. Navigation.*

NON REG. Not regulation.*

NUMBER JUMPER. The cutthroat who writes five minutes after the word to knock off.

O.A.O. The One and Only. Sometimes "off and on."

OVERHEAD. The ceiling.

PAP. Daily conduct report.*

PIN PUSHERS. The fencing team.

PIPE DOWN. Keep quiet! *

PLEBE. That insignificant being, the Fourth Classman.*

PODUNK. The home town.*

POGEY BAIT. Candy.

POLLYWOG. One who has not crossed the Line (Latitude 0°).*

PORT. Window.*

P-POOR. Pretty poor; expressing scorn.

P-RADE. We're in 'em all, but we never see one; dress parade.*

P-WORK. Saturday inquisition; practical exercise.*

RADIATOR CLUB. Those whose recreation is sedentary; the non-athletes.

RATE. 1. A privilege by virtue of rank. 2. To give an opinion of merit.*

RATEY. One who uses the rates of others.*

RED-EYE. The great disguise, ketchup.

RED MIKE. A dyed-in-the-wool misogynist.

REINA. U.S.S. *Reina Mercedes*, station ship.

R.H.I.P. Rank Hath Its Privileges.*

RIVER. An exam.*

ROBBERS' ROW. The double row of Maryland Avenue merchants who covet our scanty stipend.

SACK. Official responsibility, as in snipe hunting.

SANDBLOWER. A member of the fourth platoon; a shorty.

SAT. Passing, 2.5 or better.*

SAVOIR. One who is academically brilliant.*

SAVVY. Mental condition of a savoir.*

SCOFFER. Inordinately rapid eater.

SCUTTLEBUTT. 1. Drinking fountain. 2. A rumor of doubtful origin.*

SEA GULL. Various types of bird served in the mess hall as "chicken."

SECURE. Knock off work.*

SEP LEAVE. A month of leave after the cruise.*

SHELLBACK. Opposite of POLLYWOG.*

SHIVERIN' LIZ. Jello. IN A SNOWSTORM, with whipped cream.

SHOVE OFF. Leave, depart, get thee hence.*

SICK-BAY. Place where we explain our ailments to hard-hearted doctors.*

SKAG. A cigarette.

SKINNY. Chemistry and physics.*

SKIVVIES. Underclothes.

SLEEP. All night, used with BUTT in counting days.

SLIP STICK. The magic rule on which you can find everything but money and leave-papers; a slide rule.

SLUM. Mess cook's holiday; stew or its equivalent.*

SMOKING LAMP. Now used figuratively. When out, smoking is forbidden.*

SNAKE. Opposite of RED MIKE.

SPANISH ATHLETE. Member of the Radiator Club.

SPOON. Upper classmen who drop all intimations of seniority with a lower classman. Originates with a handshake.*

SPUDS. Baked, mashed, fried, boiled, and parboiled.*

STAR. A sign of intellectuality; savvy.*

STEAM. Marine engineering.*

STEP OUT. Bear a hand.*

ST. JOHNNY. Inmate of St. John's College, Annapolis.*

STRIPER. Midshipman officer.*

SUPE. Superintendent.*

SWABO. Zero.*

TEA FIGHT. Annapolis tea dance, which must be seen to be appreciated.*

TECUMSEH. The God of Two Point Five, whose statue is in front of Bancroft Hall.

TIN CAN. A destroyer.

TREE. List of unsats, posted every week, month, and term.*

TROU. Trousers.

UNSAT. Not passing.*

VELVET. Anything over 2.5.

WHIFF. A period of time less than six hours.

WIFE. One who shares your money, toothpaste, shaving-cream, etc.; roommate.*

YARD ENGINE. A girl who lives in the yard.

YOUNGSTER. A Third Classman.*

ZIP. Zero.

Now You Know That

*Answers to questions often asked by upperclassmen.
Authority: "Reef Points."*

THE ALMA MATER of the Naval Academy is "Navy Blue and Gold." It is sung standing with bared head, and cap held over the heart.

The medley known as "NO MORE RIVERS" is composed of five well-known airs. The first is "Life on the Bounding Main," then the Naval Academy's own song, "No More Rivers," followed by "The Girl I Left Behind Me," "The Mermaid"—a famous old sea song—and "Auld Lang Syne."

Two royal graduates of the Academy were the grandson of King Louis Philippe of France and a cousin of the King of Portugal.

SOB SUNDAY is the name given to the last Sunday prior to graduation. On that day there is a special service held in the chapel for the members of the First Class and their relatives and friends.

Superstition has it that you will bilge out if you drop your rifle at infantry drill.

You will find much information in the dictionary, *Boat Book, Ship and Gunnery Drills*, Knight's *Seamanship*, and Soule's *Naval Terms*. Don't hesitate to refer to them often.

There are more than one thousand auxiliary motors in the U.S.S. *Lexington* and *Saratoga*.

SAMUEL BARRON was a midshipman at the age of two years. He was appointed from Virginia.

To get a rat out of the lee scupper, bring the ship about.

The width of the Panama Canal determines the maximum width of a naval vessel.

Caliber is the diameter in inches of the bore of a gun, measured between the tops of the lands.

The only red, white, and blue buoy in the world is off Fort McHenry in Baltimore Harbor, and commemorates the spot where Francis Scott Key wrote "The Star Spangled Banner."

The UNITED STATES NAVY carried 1,720,360 soldiers to the front in the World War without losing a man.

Some of the ropes in the Navy are: man, hand, foot, grab, bolt, and jaw. It is lubberly to call any line a rope.

The masts of a seven-masted ship are: the fore, main, mizzen, jigger, kicker, spanker, and pusher.

BATTLE LIGHTS are blue lights fitted about the ship at necessary points. They are for use in time of battle and are invisible at fifty feet.

A DEAD LIGHT is a round glass port in a deck to admit light below.

The LUCKY BAG aboard ship is the repository for misplaced belongings.

A raked mast or stack is a mast or stack slanting aft.

ROPE YARN SUNDAY is the Wednesday afternoon recreation period.

A STADIMETER is an instrument used on the bridge to find the distance between ships.

The United States Navy has had only four fleet actions, but in every one it captured and destroyed every enemy ship.

No United States man-of-war has ever mutinied or been in the hands of mutineers.

The VULGAR ESTABLISHMENT of Annapolis is the length of time between the transit of the full moon and the next high tide. It amounts to four hours and forty-two minutes.

VEERING of the wind is its change in direction with the sun, that is, from East through South to West, etc.

BACKING of the wind is its change in direction opposite to the sun, that is, from West through South to East, etc.

To HAUL TO WINDWARD (also called "hauling her wind") is to bring a vessel to the wind when sailing free.

HAUL. A change of wind in the direction of the hands of a clock.

HAULED UP. Changing course closer to the wind.

Ship with ready duty flies ROGER from the foremast.

Dutton's navigation, 85
Dyson, C. W., 224

Earle, Ralph, 221, 224
Eberle, E. W., 121, 228
 Superintendent, 121, 125, 235
Ellyson, Theodore G., 144, 229, 230
Emmett, W. L. R., 221
Engineering corps, 106, 107
Enterprise, 20
Essex, 13, 15, 25, 29, 100, 140
Esworthy, W. H., 179
Evans, Captain, 32
Evans, R. D., 226
Everglades, 138-139
Eyre, M. K., 221
Experiment, 19

Fag Ends, 81, 179
Fanning, Midshipman, 8, 10, 36
Farquhar, Lieutenant-Commander, 105n.
Farragut, David G., 27, 28, 90n., 99, 100, 101, 109, 142n., 148, 182, 233
Farragut, W. A. C., 27n.
Felch, Cheever, 32
Feltus, Midshipman, 29
Fencing, 169
Ferguson, H. L., 221
Filipino insurrection, Navy in, 118, 226
Fillmore, President, 88
Fiske, B. A., 224
Fitch, Lieutenant-Commander, 105n.
Fitzgerald, E. T., 221
Flagg, Ernest, 119
Fletcher, E. F., 224
Florida, 79
Flusser, Charles W., 98, 145
Folger, W. M., 224

Football, 91, 164, 165, 167
Ford, Thomas G., 101n., 163
Forrest, Moreau, 99
Forshew, R. P., 221
Fort Severn, 50, 51, 53, 57
Fortune, 80
Fox, Gustavus, 102
Franklin, 28
Freedom, 178
Friedell, W. L., 229
Frigates, first six in U. S. Navy, 11-13
Frolic, 28
Frost, Holloway, 221
Fullam, W. F., 235

Gamble, John M., 29
Gamble, Robert, 21
Ganges, 13
Gatewood, Richard, 223
General Greene, 14
Georgia Institute of Technology, Navy training at, 127
Gibbon, James, 21
Gibbons, J. H., 235
Gillmor, R. E., 221
Girault, 153
Gloucester, 145
Goldsborough, L. M., 235
Golf, 172
Gooding, R. C., 170
Gordon, Captain, 25
Graham, Secretary, 68
Grant, A. W., 229
Grant, General, 82
Green, Fitzhugh, 221
Green, Lieutenant, 71
Greene, Samuel Dana, 99, 105n.
Greene, S. D., Jr., 221
Gregory, Midshipman, 28
Griffin, Engineer-in-Chief, 143
Groesbeck, W. G., 221

(1)